Heaven's will,

...ies down still;

...t on the pine,

...ing to decline,

all in all —

of spring in fall.

Vikram Seth

六
十
而
玩

A BIRTHDAY BOOK FOR BROTHER STONE

石兄頌壽集

柳存仁敬署

A Birthday Book for
Brother Stone

for David Hawkes, at Eighty

Edited by

Rachel May and John Minford

The Chinese University Press

Hong Kong Translation Society

A Birthday Book for Brother Stone:
for David Hawkes, at Eighty
Edited by Rachel May and John Minford

© **The Chinese University of Hong Kong,** 2003

ISBN 962–996–111–3

THE CHINESE UNIVERSITY PRESS
The Chinese University of Hong Kong
SHA TIN, N.T., HONG KONG
Fax: +852 2603 6692
    +852 2603 7355
E-mail: cup@cuhk.edu.hk
Web-site: www.chineseupress.com

HONG KONG TRANSLATION SOCIETY
P.O. Box 20186
Hennessy Road Post Office
HONG KONG
Web-site: www.hkts.org.hk

Printed in Hong Kong

Contents

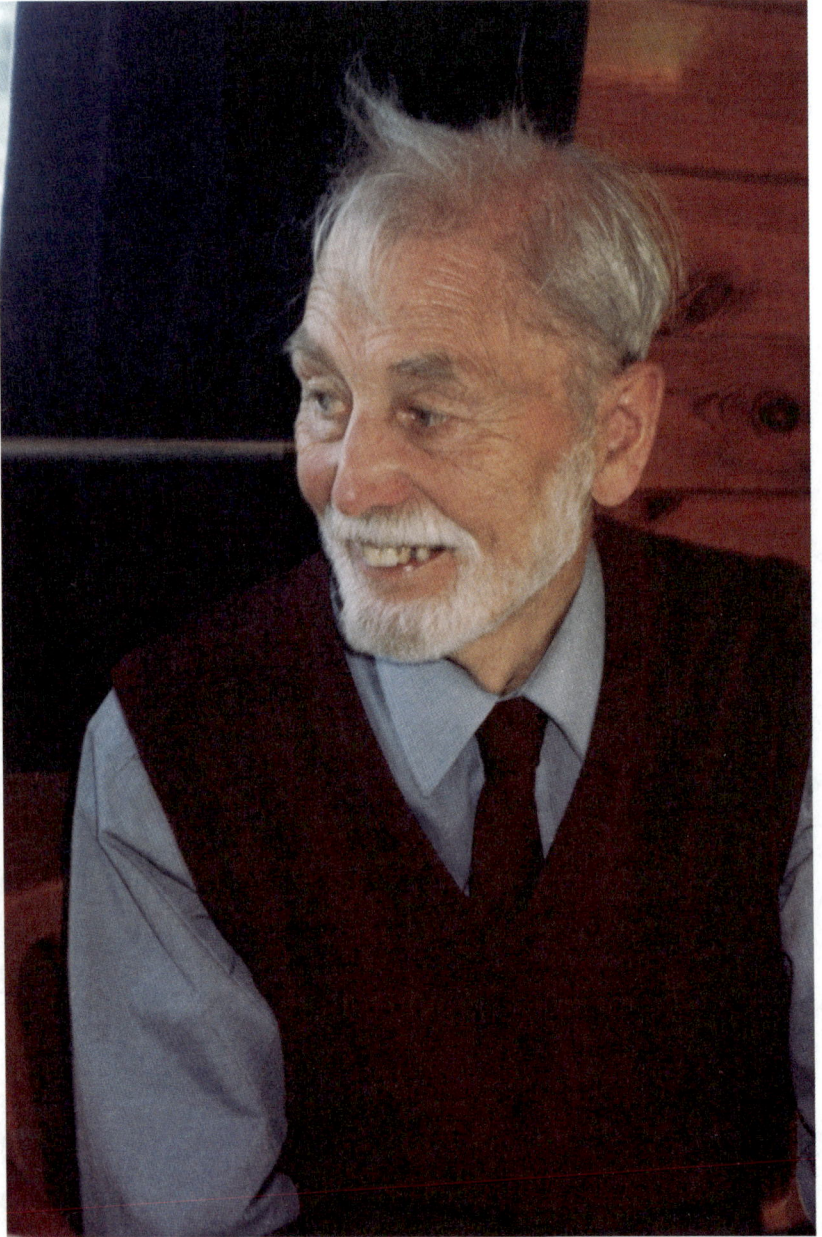

David, aged 76, celebrating his and Jean's Golden Wedding anniversary, Oxford, 5 May 2000.

Editors' Introduction

David is a very special person in our lives: father, father-in-law, grandfather of our children, teacher, friend, colleague, collaborator. Nearly two years ago, we decided to put together a book for his eightieth birthday on 6 July, 2003. We knew we wanted to celebrate a very important person and occasion, and we wanted to give other friends and colleagues of David's all over the world an opportunity to participate. From the start we called it a Birthday Book, not a Festschrift, as a way of letting people know that we didn't want to produce something stuffy or formal. This was partly because we liked the idea ourselves, and partly because we thought David would like it better that way too. Not that we consulted him … On the contrary, we have done our utmost to keep the idea a secret. (If he knows, he has also succeeded in keeping that a secret!) When we first started contacting people and sending out letters, we had no idea what to expect or how the book might take shape. But as the contributions started coming in, the book began to take on a life of its own. The whole process has been for us a rewarding and exciting experience.

There are some people we tried to contact about contributing to the book, but without success. (We offer our apologies if somewhere there is a thirteenth fairy we forgot to invite to the banquet!) Others have been unable to write because of pressure of work, or because of poor health, or for other reasons. C. T. Hsia, in a letter from New York dated 1 February 2002, writes of his "genuine admiration for [David's] scholarship and unsurpassed

wizardry as the translator of the *Stone*." A very old friend of
David's, Lo Hui-min, was prevented from writing by poor health.
His wife Helen wrote from Canberra on 21 August 2002:

> It pains me more than I can tell you to remind you that Lo won't be
> contributing the kind of rich, intellectual, emotional and gracious
> tribute that he would under normal circumstances have produced
> with the heartfelt respect he had for David.

Gary Snyder, prevented from writing by family circumstances,
wrote from California on 29 June 2002:

> What a lovely idea! I remember David well, and indeed he did ride
> on the back of my motorcycle as we shot around Kyoto.

Igor de Rachewilz in Australia asked that we include his name in
the Tabula Gratulatoria (I suppose this is the nearest we get to
having one).

Two old friends and colleagues of David's, who would have
wanted to contribute to the book, regrettably passed away as it
was being compiled: Piet van der Loon, and Raymond Dawson.

More than one contributor writes of karma, and there are an
astonishing number of such ties that bind this book together.
Many of them were expected — they arose from shared connections with the man, with his books (especially *The Songs of the
South* and *The Story of the Stone*), with his achievements as a
scholar and teacher, with everything he stands for in the
borderlands between sinology and the world of creative letters
that he has made so very much his own territory. But other more
unexpected connections emerged. To give but one example: no
less than six contributors (eight if we include ourselves) had
connections with Tientsin. David and Jean themselves stayed very
briefly in that city prior to their departure from China in 1951.

Or should it be written Tianjin? The two spellings seem to
conjure up two different cities. Both have (and are) a place. In
general, we have allowed minor inconsistencies to stand
uncorrected in the book, striving to achieve a minimum degree of
editorial uniformity without imposing a uniformity of voice.

We have had wonderful luck in our publisher, and in the sponsors of the book. At The Chinese University Press, our friends Steve Luk and Esther Tsang have made the process of editing a real pleasure. And C. C. Liu and Lo Chi-hong came forward with a generous and timely subvention from the Hong Kong Translation Society.

David may not be aware of the impact his work has had on others. Craig Clunas, from the University of Sussex, in a letter dated 24 February 2002, describes how he was affected by the appearance of the first volumes of the *Stone* translation.

> There was a stall in Cambridge market in the early 1970s which sold new paperbacks at reduced prices, then a very unusual thing, and I bought the first volume of David Hawkes' *Stone* there for 50p (I just checked inside the copy) in 1973. It was a stunning revelation to me. I *knew* the Chinese culture I had so wanted to study *must* be interesting, despite the best efforts of the Faculty of Oriental Studies to convince me otherwise, and I longed with a passion for the subsequent volumes to come out, buying them the minute they appeared and dropping all other reading to devour them.

David continues to write and translate, and continues to draw admiration the world over. We are enormously proud of him, and would like to add our own love and appreciation to that expressed in the pages that follow. Thanks Dad! Thank you David! And many happy returns!

Fontmarty, May 2003

Part 1

Personal

For David Hawkes

Vikram Seth

for David Hawkes

Happy the man who, not at Heaven's will,
At eighty sits, or stands, or lies down still;
Who, fugitive as moonlight on the pine,
Keeps to his whims, declining to decline,
Empty of self, yet seeing all in all —
Summer in frost, the scent of spring in fall..

Vikram Seth

CYRIL BIRCH

Tribute to David

I have always found particular amusement in names, perhaps because of the problems my own name has often caused me. I have been Cyrus, Si, Si-ril, Cecil (or Ceecil), I have been misspelled a dozen ways and I have received mail addressed to Miss Cyril Bitch. Our neighborhood "Mr. Luke the window-cleaner" made me smile when I was a boy and "Luke/look" were identical in the local pronunciation. Later I enjoyed discovering the shop-sign near Victoria Station proclaiming J. DeAth, Family Butcher. And many mornings I would pause to read the names of Asia historians on the School of Oriental Studies mailboxes — Ballhatchet, Pulleyblank, Basham and Twitchett: Dickens himself could not have invented a more imposing letterhead for a quartet of Gray's Inn lawyers.

It was Ted Pulleyblank himself who illustrated that even a classic English surname like Hawkes (remembering Old Uncle Tom Cobley) could pose a pronunciation pitfall. In the days before he left London for the Cambridge professorship both Ted and I belonged to the committee of the China Society. In the chair sat Lady White, whose late husband Sir Reginald had achieved Old China Hand distinction as Consul–General at Shanghai. (Another OCH and fellow member was Henry MacAleavy, who gave wonderful talks to the Society. It was unlikely however that Henry would ever ascend to the committee: in the thirties he too had worked in Shanghai, as a young lawyer. In one way and another his work had taken him into most of the bars of the city, and according to his own account he had been thrown out of at least half, no doubt in some instances on the orders of Sir Reginald himself).

The committee floor was open to suggestions for possible future speakers.

"Haahx," said Pulleyblank in his native Canadian.

"I beg your pardon?" said the chair, who may have thought he was clearing his throat.

"David Haahx, of Aahxford."

"Hacks? Hocks? How do you spell it?"

Secretary dutifully spells it out for the chair.

"OH, HAWWKES!" (Vowel sound in Lady White's deepest Kensington, emerging through rounded lips from back of throat, the result somewhere between Hooks and Hoax).

It was not long before David published his *Songs of the South* and became the closest to a household name of our generation. These superb translations of the lush, myth-shrouded poetry of early southern China were in large part, I suppose, the fruit of his years of study in Beijing, where he had the privilege of being liberated. David and I had had little contact, as was all too common, alas, between Oxford and London, yet he had responded with great generosity to my appeal for his help in securing a visa for me to join him in Beijing on my upcoming sabbatical leave. China entered the Korean War, David's efforts on my behalf proved abortive, and the only slight return I could make for his kindness was to meet his ship in Hong Kong when he came out of China late in 1950. David can never have been described as fleshy or corpulent, but when he came down the gangplank I could see that he was gaunt and pallid from his years of study in Beijing, and positively emaciated from his storm-plagued voyage down the China coast. But I suppose that at that time a great many of his ideas about the *Chuci* were already in his baggage, or certainly in his head. If he had not published his *Songs of the South* in 1959 I do not think I could have undertaken the anthology I made, for any selection had to include the *Chuci* and no one else could have translated them at that time.

I could not foresee then that David would be the one to undertake the daunting task of the *Hongloumeng*. I had myself fallen under the spell of this great work, to the extent of turning over in my mind the problems that a commitment to translating it would involve. I remember finding myself, one day in the fifties, in conversation with Arthur Waley, of whom I was always in awe, and summoning up the chutzpah to ask him why he had not translated it himself. His high-pitched voice rose in a tone of plaintive self-defense as he replied, "Well, I did do *Genji*!"

So he did, and *Monkey* and so many other marvellous things. But he went on to say that he felt *Hongloumeng* was "too uneven". I remembered this comment years later when David, half-way through his monumental task, complained in a letter to me that he was fast wearying of the innumerable routine passages in which character X walks from one room to another, through this garden court and along that passageway, adjusts his or her dress, sits down, gets up, sends a maid with a message to so-and-so and receives a page on an errand from such-and-such a place, looks out at the rain, sits down again — all just a chattering flow of a sort of logistical prose.

I think however that what deterred Waley was more than the drudgery of ploughing through overly detailed narrative. It was the strongly romantic essence of the *Hongloumeng* in its nostalgia for lost youth and lost time. Waley had paid his debt to romance with his *Tale of Genji*. That accomplished, he preferred *shi* poems to *ci*, Bai Juyi to Li Bai, *Monkey* to *The Story of the Stone*.

In contrast, when I think of David I can't help recalling a line in a poem Zhang Chuanshan sent to his friend Gao E: *Yanqing ren zi shuo Honglou*, "It took a romantic himself to narrate the *Red Chamber*." "Likewise to translate the *Red Chamber*," I would add: Only someone with a very special kind of vision and courage would challenge the enigmas and obscurities of *The Songs of the South*, the very fountainhead of the Chinese romantic tradition, and then, the challenge triumphantly overcome, leap two millennia to tackle a masterpiece of world fiction which existed entirely in editions either incomplete or cobbled together by various hands after the author's death. (There was no completely authoritative text of the *Hongloumeng* — "Redologists" are likely to agree that when the Hawkes–Minford English version appeared we possessed a recension superior to any that already existed in the original language.)

And then, in order to provide the needed years of un-trammelled time, to relinquish nothing less than the Oxford chair — surely this had to be the act of a true romantic. But an act of sacrifice that was triumphantly vindicated. David of all people had the learning, the wit, and the command of the aristocratic culture to meet the challenge set by Cao Xueqin. His translation is fully equal to the subtleties of the relationships within this supreme Chinese novel of manners. Dialogue is perfectly rendered to reflect familial and generational distinctions. The innumerable maids and pages are given delightful English names or sobriquets. The translation relishes the minutiae of daily life, the literary games and the exotic dishes, the garden designs and the furnishings of rooms and persons, and draws richly on the European (notably French and Italian) aesthetic vocabulary with its chignons and torques, its *portières* and loggias and cassolettes and niello-work. A neat and amusing European parallel is a recurring joy in David Hawkes' writing, as when he describes "Red Inkstone" as "just the kind of pseudonym that an *homme galant* would choose (dashing off a comment or two with a lady's lipstick, perhaps, in between sips of champagne from her slipper)." Even more impressive is the command of style that could reproduce such verse as the riddle-poems of the fifth chapter virtually as products of the English Augustan age, from the dignified pen of a Pope or a Johnson.

I could go on listing the delights of the *Stone*, but there is space only for one last comment. David did more than just translate a great novel. We can see that he embraced the whole ethos of the *Dream*, even to the extent of converting the project into a genuine family enterprise, the Gao E role played by his son-in-law, with Jean and daughter Rachel, doubtless, heavily involved as well. It is a pleasure and a privilege now to offer warmest best wishes to all the family in happy birthday tribute.

RED CHAN

Literature and Translation, Life and Love

It took me a long time to say hello to David. Ever since I first became a student of translation, David's name and works had always been a source of great inspiration and admiration. But I never imagined there would come a day, when I would sit down with the great man — and his wife — engaging in the warmest, most delicious moments of afternoon tea, casually chatting about everything under the sun while sipping tea and eating cakes and biscuits.

Life has brought me good luck and numerous surprises. Not only was I fortunate enough to have embarked on a DPhil programme at Oxford, I sometimes found myself in the same room as David, listening to talks and seminars given at the Chinese Institute. Yet I never found enough courage to introduce myself. I simply felt too insignificant. Two whole terms had passed without an encounter. Then, one day, I received a hand-written letter of invitation for tea at his home. I was overjoyed. Could this be real!

I still remember the first phone call I made. Jean answered and said: "Hello, Jean Hawkes here ..." I was tongue-tied. I wonder how I even managed to finish the short conversation with Jean and David, in my feeble effort to make an appointment! I remember feeling rather disappointed with myself after I put down the phone. I thought I must have said something silly, although I could not remember exactly what. Apart from "Thank you," I did not seem to have been able to say much at all!

Knowing David is also knowing Jean, since I came to know them both at the same time. Their profound love and understanding of each other shows itself in every way. Often David starts an account of something, perhaps a past event, an encounter, a book, a place, then Jean adds relevant details to the story. It is simply a joy listening to David and Jean telling what they have been through together, past and present, big and small. They are such living proof of great love. Spend a few minutes with them and you feel the gentle but profoundly affectionate love and harmony between them. Indeed, from knowing David and Jean I have learned more about life and love than about translation and literature.

Once David showed me a photo of himself and two friends in China. Sitting on the front steps of a typical, old-style Peking house, they are each holding a cigarette and looking very relaxed. David is sitting in the middle, his face radiant with youth and confidence. He is smiling, perhaps over something funny. Looking at his gesture and expression, one sees a man of vigour — he may be intense but he also has a strong sense of humour; he is sharp and critical, but he also has the amazing ability of being patient and accommodating. Plus, there is always time for friends and a good smoke (although not the latter any more these days!).

It is such an honour to know this man. What I have learned from him (and from Jean) will always be a guiding light in my life, however far I go, however old I become …

David with Hetta and William Empson in Peking, 1947/8.

ARTHUR COOPER

Four Poems, & Extract from a Letter to a Jungian Friend

The four poems and extract have kindly been supplied by Steve Balogh, who is custodian of the Arthur Cooper archive, and who welcomes any initiatives to publish as much of it as possible. We were very glad to be able to include something by Arthur in this book for David, since the two of them were old friends. To our knowledge, none of this material has previously been published.

Of the four poems, only one of them, *From the Icelandic*, is dated. There were three different versions of the poem *Galileo*, one with the title *The Fourth Nature*, another (possibly the earliest version) dated 1966. The poem *Autumn* has been punctuated by us. Arthur's pencilled instructions to an unknown person, on his typewritten copy of the poem, were: "Punctuate at will, but I think it needs lots of pauses." — *Editors*

Autumn

This little weeping willow
Whose curved boughs make, in summer
A pool, of cool, green shade —

Now gleams a frail pavilion
Glinting, magic, in the sunlight
Fragile, house-walls disarrayed
As the narrow arrowy leaves
Faded pink, faint gilt, or silver
Beneath, in a wreath, are laid.

All too soon show those bared branches
Golden house, green pool, no longer —
They but trace, fine-drawn, the space by winter made.

Response to the Sirens

Can, like the sand, is yellow,
Will, a deep pool, is like wine,
Shall lies, a still shell and hollow,
In a pit in the plimsoll line:

Vowels and Consonants follow,
Rinsing the Consonants white,
Consonants dance, dance in the shallow,
Breaking into rainbow light,

While Gesture and Reminiscence
Play, under my palate's dome,
Till my mind, in half light,
Listens, to sand in the sunlit foam;

And the parts of speech that follow
Can shape, so, an envelope,
Putting Man's Room in a hollow,
To hear, see, and then to grope —

I see Shall roll in the shallow
Again like a sea-chased shell;
May run till the billows swallow;
Must stay like the seaweed smell;

For I see, see your Truth, Nature:
No longer there's you or I,
But one articulate creature,
Alone, laps under the sky!

Galileo

A hooded shadow slowly came
across the pavement of a man so lame
he couldn't flee, he couldn't chase
but only stand in the same place,

and where the spectre leaves him stand
holding the matches in his hand
touch with his mind
the fissures of his ground
for mystic images once just found
by eye and hand,

till the eye in his blind
all-eye and a guttering flame
no gales ever curb, make flinch or tame —
will they not find,
timely in the game,

how far the rays of a man made sun
reflect too in night another one,
a not-beginning
and un-
begun?

From the Icelandic
(Pall Olafsson, a nineteenth-century peasant poet)

Time, how thrifty with each hour of my existence:
As on a staff is stretched the carded skein
So you draw out each separate pain.

Do you then have to reel and spool it all,
My very thread unravel too,
Guide it in the heddle, the reed draw through?

And then do you have to cut and knot it all,
Tread the treadle and work the reed
Back and forth to shoot my thread?

Do you then have to snick and sew it all,
Make of me something to be worn
Until in the end I'm tattered, torn?

And then do you have to patch and mend it all?
That is the eschatology foretold,
But I think my stuff will be too old.

(1966)

Extract from a Letter to a Jungian Friend

Haregrove,
Cranham,
Gloucester

(He was formerly local GP, then went to Zurich to learn Jungian Analysis. Over the years he has been interested in my work on the Chinese script. We meet occasionally for a pub lunch. This letter tries to summarize results, likely to interest him, of the work to date; with some recent developments in it)

Arthur Cooper

13. xii. 83

The discovery that I think may interest you, that is now as it were coming upon me in my work looked at overall (as I now have to do), is the extent to which the contrast of YIN and YANG underlay the Chinese view of the world from the earliest times and so the whole of their language: initial consonants of the monosyllables fell into the two groups, as did the vocalism (vowels, diphthongs, triphthongs) forming the core, and again the final consonants! This emerges from approaching the language semantically through the script, seeing that as 'ideo-etymological' as I have been doing; rather than 'phonetic' and to be approached by conventional philogy appropriate to other ancient languages without such a script.

Conventional philology, as with those languages, has two main aims: (1) discovering affinities and etymologies of words within a language or language family; (2) relating languages or language families to each other, with a view to the contribution that might make to human prehistory.

(1) in the case of Chinese, thanks to its script, is unnecessary; putting the cart before the horse as the semantic affinities and etymologies of the monosyllabic words was information that the script itself gave, and not their exact pronunciation; (2) as an aim I think should always be distrusted; with good reason when one thinks of how it led to the Aryan myth, and how that was used in Germany! But again in the case of Chinese it is putting the cart before the horse: what Chinese in fact shows is something much more fundamental than the relationships of mere words to each other within a language group (as in Indo-European languages, Semitic languages, or in a supposed Sino-Tibetan group); it helps to show how words were made in all these language groups and how much that process had in common despite the fact that the languages might be unrelated to each other in sound as much as, say, English and Chinese!

2.

To give but one example out of very many that could be given, the philologists tell us (e. g. in the Oxford Dictionary of English Etymology) that English 'god' is derived from an Indo-European verb *ghu- meaning 'to invoke', as its past participle: 'go-d' for '(one) invoke-d'. The Chinese for 'god' is 'shĕn', which does not have and never had any relation in sound with our word; but is shown in the ancient ideo-etymographic script to be an image of a man with arms raised 'invoking' (repeatedly, shown by the device of doubling the image, drawing it also upside-down). This image alone meant 'to repeat prayers, to invoke', just as apparently the Indo-European *ghu- did. As 'god', the one invoked, it is written with the addition of the sign for 'divine' in order to show the exact sense and word intended. It is written with other such signs added to it (called determinatives) for other derivatives of the idea of 'invoking the divine': for instance with the addition of the sign for 'weather', drawn as a precipitation from the sky, it is 'lightning' suggesting the presence and power of the gods; a word that in Chinese speech was related to that for 'god' but not pronounced the same. The script concerned itself with ideas and etymologies rather than with exact pronunciation; and, as with 'god', the ideas and etymologies can often be seen to be shared with words in other languages, of which the pronunciation was in no way related. ('Lightning' in English does not, of course, have a derivation similar to the Chinese word.)

[Modern characters in margin]

申

神

電

飛
機

電
話

[Images may indifferently face right or left]

Man invoking (ditto, repeatedly)

(Divine)

God

(Weather)

Lightning

It could only be for a language that retained a strong sense of the origin of the words it used (a language in the 'poetic' phase, as Vico would have called it), that such a system could have developed for the writing of it. This meant too, of course, that the language employing such a script had to be exceptionally homogeneous: it would need to be one disinclined to take into itself words from neighbouring languages, as most languages do, because they would lack evident etymologies in the mother tongue. Without such 'borrowed' words, there was no necessity to develop a phonetic script for writing them; whereas native words could continue to be written ideo-etymographically even after their origins had become forgotten. Chinese continues today to prefer to make up its own words for new ideas and innovations from abroad; and no serious attempts have been made to substitute a phonetic system of spelling until recent abortive endeavours by the present government to introduce the Western (Latin) alphabet, now virtually abandoned. New characters in the native script are very seldom invented because very seldom needed: new words, like most in the language now, are polysyllabic and composed of the old monosyllables combined; like the monosyllable for 'flying' and that for 'machine' making a two-syllable word for 'aeroplane', which could have no better way of writing it than the old one. Or that for 'telephone' combining 'lightning' (see above) for 'electric' and 'speech' as two syllables, easier to grasp, shorter and neater than the foreign word. (This is a diversion from discussion of the ancient language and script, but justified for showing that an ancient and different system of writing need not mean an out-of-date and inefficient one, as Westerners generally suppose.)

It should be obvious that such a language, recorded since ancient times by such a script as this, will benefit from philological studies dissimilar from those required for languages recorded only phonetically. Indeed, for the light that such an ideo-etymographic script may throw on ancient mental processes of word-making, these might lead to a new kind of comparative philology: one that took more account of the 'poetic' (as Vico said) creation of language instead of basing itself principally on the phonetic material resulting.

3.

Philologists of Indo-European languages see in them an ancestral verb *bh(e)r- with meanings like 'to be strong enough, to carry', as exceedingly prolific in the creation of words in the various languages. In English we have 'to bear' in its various senses of carrying, being strong enough, enduring; 'borough', originally for a strong place (cf. German 'Burg'); the same meaning in 'fort' from the Latin form of the verb, which also gives 'fero', 'I carry' and numerous English words from that: 'proffer', 'offer', 'prefer', 'suffer', etc. In Chinese there seems to have existed a verb of similar meaning to Indo-European *bh(e)r- and similarly prolific in the creation of words, but unrelated otherwise to the Indo-European word; that is, of course, unrelated phonetically. It is written with a profile drawing of a hand, bearing:

山 (以)

[A bear:　　; flesh, physique　　deer]
(see below)

能 (肉, 鹿)

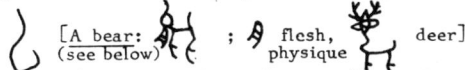

It was used like a preposition 'with (an instrument), by (means of)'; and was also used in the writing of many words with appropriate additional signs (determinatives) to show which derivative of it was intended: all these words can be recognized as related semantically to the idea of bearing, being strong; and phonologically, I now believe, to each other and to the verb written as a drawing of a hand bearing. What is particularly interesting is that two of these derivatives are used for the name of the animal, the 'bear', which is found in English and in other Germanic languages but not supposed by philologists to have any relation to the verb! One of these, which adds 2 determinatives (for 'flesh, body, physique' and for a 'deer, large animal'), besides meaning a kind of 'bear' in the ancient language, is also used today for the same Chinese word in the sense of 'strength', 'being physically able'. The part played by the bearing hand in the written character for a bear was recognized nearly two thousand years ago in an early Chinese dictionary; but has unfortunately been dismissed by recent scholars who see the bearing hand as the head & ear in what they suppose to be a strange and 'primitive' (!) drawing of a bear; which then, they suppose, was borrowed for merely phonetic use as a rebus to represent a word that happened to have the same pronunciation, used for physical strength and ability. (Similarly, the drawing we have illustrated for 'to invoke repeatedly', hence 'god' and used in writing the word for numinous weather, 'lightning', is now taken to have been a drawing of a flash of lightning; then used as a mere rebus in the other characters where it is seen: a rebus that would have been of scarce practical value to the reader — these words could never have been pronounced alike!)

also

能 (cf. 雄)

*Note deer's feet!

One word relating to that written with the bearing hand, illustrated above, is differentiated from it not by the addition of a determinative but by a line across the arm above the hand, drawing attention to that; a device that is to be seen elsewhere in the ideo-etymographic script:

九

This was used for the number 'nine'; but the addition of determinatives to it shows that this also had a 'bearing' sense, as both the drawing and the phonology would lead one to expect. For instance, with the addition of the determinative for 'cart, chariot', it was used to write a word, of related but different pronunciation, for the axle of a cart or chariot; hence also the distance between the wheels, and the ruts, tracks they made. Another meaning written with this etymograph is a place where several roads meet, just as spokes of a wheel meet at a hub: both being named as sorts of 'bearing'!

軌

尥

As the number 'nine', written without the addition of a determinative, this representation of a 'bearing arm', is of special interest; since the number

4

易經

'nine' is used in contrast to the number 'six' (nobody seems to know why)
as names respectively for the YANG and YIN, male and female principles,
in the ancient classic, the I Ching or Book of Changes which builds a view
of the world and system of divination on the contrast of these principles.
The number 'six', I have found, also related in archaic Chinese to the same
idea of 'bearing, being strong'; but in a passive sense (cf. again 'Burg' and
'fort'). It was written in the most ancient Chinese script with a drawing that
was identical with that for a 'house':

六   [As 'house' it has become
                                                 宀, but used only as part
陰   of other characters; as 'six',

In the I Ching the divided line — — , standing for the female principle,
YIN, is given 'six' as its name; whereas the undivided line ——— , which
stands for the male principle, YANG, is called 'nine'. The etymologies, which
the ancient script reveals of these names for the two kinds of line, show that
a numerical sense, which has always been inexplicable, was not intended; but
that they symbolized respectively female power by the enduring house(strength
passive), and male power by the bearing arm (strength active). Shchutskii, too
typically of scholars, accounts for 'six' and 'nine' (= YIN and YANG in the
I Ching) as 'number symbolism'; without accounting for that. But scholars do
not generally think of abstractions, like numbers, as having inevitably concrete
origins in language-making like any other words; however forgotten they may
become. [In Chinese 'eight', for instance, was pictorially a 'division' and as
a spoken word was related to various words with that sense; 'eight' being a
much divisible number as two cubed; 'two' in Indo-European languages had an
origin as divided; whereas 'three' in both Chinese and Indo-European seems
to have related to words for passing through (adding something between two).]

陽

八

三

Chinese tradition, ascribing a mythical origin to the I Ching, sees it
also as a founding creation of their civilization, giving it a traditional date
in the fourth millennium BC; but recognizing that the interpretations and
commentaries, of which the book now largely consists, are the work of later
hands – among whom they suppose the founder of the Chou dynasty at the end
of the first millennium and Confucius in the fifth century. Except for the fact
that the compilation is obviously by various hands at various dates, modern
scholars are generally agreed in dismissing such traditions, though not in
much else – especially about dates. But the two fundamental technical terms,
'six' and 'nine', if I am right, would suggest a very early origin.

'I' in 'I Ching', 'Changes' in the Book of Changes, is a word written in the
earliest Chinese script as a crescent moon with a shadow beside it, light and
shade:

易

                              [Evolving to   ]

陽

陰

YANG and YIN also stand for light and shade, and are indeed respectively
written as the bright and dark sides of a hill. From later forms of the above
drawing, as often happened probably arising from reinterpretations of rapidly
written forms of it, it came to be seen differently: so as a lizard; recently
by some scholars as water transferred from one vessel to another. None of
them seems, curiously, to have given attention to the earliest versions of the
image, as above; or to have seen its aptness in the title!

It is a difficult book, partly because it has been a tool for professional
dealers in the occult, and a plaything for interpreters and commentators;
but particularly, I think, for the modern Western mind because of the nature
of the associations and 'changes' of them that its authors saw. Underneath

5.

all things, all creation and occurrences, were to be seen combinations of the forces of YIN and YANG. These were represented diagrammatically in the I Ching by —— —— and ——— respectively; combined at first into the eight trigrams possible with permutations of the two symbols but later combining pairs of trigrams, each with its own significance, to make sixty-four hexa-grams. Further refinement made some lines in a hexagram dominant and some subservient, and some to undergo a 'change of sign'; in which case the original symbol and its opposite had each a part to play when the hexagram was analysed. The hexagrams themselves, however, showing arrangements of YIN and YANG forces, dominant or subservient, fixed or changeable, were never to be constructed by reasoned analysis but to be independent of the human mind and will. They were therefore to be constructed by playing, against oneself as it were, an elaborate game like patience or solitaire (but with solemn ritual to assist receptiveness); in which the gods, or as we should now say mere chance, had entire responsibility for the constructions, which could then provide 'objective' answers to questions put. In fact, such are often capable of clarifying the mind, removing an obsession, and making new thought possible by introducing an unwilled and unexpected view that might otherwise never occur; so it was, as you will know, much admired by Jung.

吉
哲
斤

Things that we regard in a positive way as good, for example good fortune and wisdom, can sometimes be seen by the way they were written in ancient ideo-etymographic script as thought of negatively: good fortune expressed by a vessel emptied of contents (also 'new' of a moon); wisdom by an adze or mattock, which was the etymological base of the word for it, the tool for clearing unwanted trees and scrub. 'Philosophy' is still expressed by-a-word by a word using this for writing it, though its origin may have been lost to those who see it. It may, however, help understanding of how the Chinese through the ages were able to regard the I Ching as their first Classic of Philosophy; even though to our minds its method may seem only irrational.

栖
(棲)
灣
(亂鬪)
西
詹
甬

A great difficulty encountered today when dealing with languages of what Vico called a 'poetic' phase in their making (of which ancient Chinese seems a prime example) is that they tended to compare things and group them into categories sensually ('poetically') rather than semantically in what we should regard as a more 'logical' way. One thus had, in ancient Chinese, words that can mean 'to rest' or 'to go busily to and fro' (clue: the image of a bird's-nest); 'to be calm' (clue: phases of a shaman's trance); 'good order, government' or 'disorder, confusion' (clue: 'ravel', of a thread; to which the Oxford English Dictionary gives such opposite meanings, quoting Shakespeare). All these examples involve patterns of action, behaviour, which speaker, hearer both know; so can be taken as similes: like a bird and nest; like a shaman; like winding a thread. Such is indeed the way words have to be created in the first place: branches spreading in all directions from a very few trees, the primary vocables which were perhaps oral (accompany-ing other) gestures. Evidence for that is seen by looking at the part played by the word-making ideas of YIN and YANG in the ancestral Chinese language (for which the objects of simile, as in the examples above, were illustrated in ancient ideo-etymographic script: a bird's-nest; words in a cave for shaman; hands winding — or unwinding — thread; but each is regarded by scholars now as no more than a rebus, without significance except for the resemblance of its sound in speech to that of the word indicated by its presence. What has, of course, put them off the scent are the wide dissimilarities in meaning of words sharing the same image in the script).

What I have been coming gradually to realise, and only recently very fully, was the part played by two fundamental and opposing ideas in the making of the ancestral Chinese language: namely the YIN-ness or the YANG-ness of any thing or any action.

6.

乾 ☰☰ and ☷☷ (all 'nines' and all 'sixes' respectively)
☰☰
（坤）

*Instead
of <u>stream,</u>
later as
<u>earth +</u>
<u>worship.</u>

These are the first two hexagrams in the I Ching, the all-YANG (creator,
father) and the all-YIN (receptive, mother). They have other significations,
such as sky and earth, and the names for them (originally written with images
of a staff and a stream*) are typical representatives of Chinese words that I
have called 'K — N' type and 'K — W — N' type. I long ago observed, as
many must, that words of the second type, with the inserted '-w-', tended
to have meanings such as 'round, around, bending, yielding, weak, flowing,
soft, warm'; but I was slower in allowing myself to see the absence of the
'-w-' in words of the 'K — N' type as forming another and contrasting group
of associations: 'direct, straight, firm, strong, rigid, hard, cold'. (I then
made two easily pronounceable English syllables 'ken' with a neutral vowel
as in 'taken' and 'kwen' as the same inserting '-w-', and asked a few people
which they would choose for 'male' and 'female' and various other meanings:
their answers mostly agreed with the Chinese, but the experiment needs to
be done with a greater number and more strictly by someone who does not
know what answers to expect).

In what I have called the Chinese 'K — N' and 'K — W — N' types of
word, I used 'K' to stand for various Chinese velar (k, g, ng, &c), laryngeal
(such as ', the 'glottal stop') consonants, which were grouped together by the
great Swedish scholar, Bernhard Karlgren, in his pioneering studies of early
Chinese phonology and script. Similarly, I used 'N' to stand for various
dental (d, t, n, &c) consonants. Karlgren, in his Analytic Dictionary (1923),
called such grouping of consonants 'homorganic' and believed that what he saw
as the essentially phonetic nature (phonetics and phonology were his interests)
of the ancient Chinese script could be understood, if it were accepted that its
makers had not generally distinguished 'homorganic' consonants — that is to
say, consonants produced by the <u>same organ</u>, like teeth, throat, lips — from each
other, so not matched sounds to the degree that an alphabet attempts. (Why a
script should ever have been made on such a principle, and what particular
value it would have to writer or reader, do not seem to have been considered).

It seemed that various 'homorganic' consonants found in words written with
the same so-called 'phonetic' element would be better understandable if that
were seen instead as 'etymographic'; and the words having the 'homorganic'
consonants were such as would have been recognized, by writer and reader,
as related etymologically, that is, all related to the simile or metaphor that the
drawing in the etymograph indicated. What had caused the variety in the
homorganic consonants, what speech mechanisms for word-making, I could not
tell; but in that I was not worse off than those who regarded the script as
merely phonetic.

I was therefore very happily able to accept the homorganic theory as more
than compatible with an etymographic one. But grave trouble soon arose for
the homorganic theory itself: although consonants in <u>most</u> words sharing the
same 'phonetic' (or as I should say, etymographic) element were homorganic,
I began to find more and more that were not so and difficult to make fit the
theory without speculation about conceivable ancient pronunciations for which
the script provided no evidence. On the other hand, though not homorganic,
it could be seen that there were limitations in the interchangeability of these
consonants and I ended up with three groups: labial (m, p, &c); lateral (L
and R, which seem not to have been among the basic word-making consonants
but infixed with the vowels); and the rest, velar, glottal, dental and sibilant.
Eliminating the laterals, there seem then only to have been two groups or
classes of word-making consonants in the ancestral Chinese language. If

7.

one then looks for something physical to distinguish the two groups, it will be noticed that one group (m, p, &c) involves closing the lips and that the other does not.

Turning again to what I have called the 'K — N' type words (associated with the YANG) and the 'K — W — N' type words (associated with the YIN), where the difference is in the vocalism, without or with an inserted '-w-' sound, Chinese philologists call this distinction 'open' or 'closed mouth' (開 ㅁ or 合 ㅁ) because in the latter the lips approach and nearly close. This vocalic distinction in fact matches that between the two groups of consonants, as above; and when one looks at words with initial consonant of either group or with final consonant of either group in ancient Chinese (changes in pronunciation over the centuries have largely obscured the distinctions, especially in northern dialects) it will be found that a similar distinction of 'open mouth' consonant for YANG and 'closed mouth' consonant for YIN can be detected in the meanings of the words. For instance, words meaning 'to (en)close, to shut, darkness' and the like, and words with such meanings as 'to go into, to go through' (one of which is the number 'three' already mentioned) and the word YIN itself, all ended with 'closed mouth' consonants, '-p' or '-m'. Words beginning with 'p-', 'b-' or 'm-' meant 'to stretch (over), cover, shut off, divide, part' and meanings derived from those ideas; the ones beginning with 'm-' mostly for 'stretching, extending (over)' and those beginning with 'p-' or 'b-' more often for 'dividing, parting'. There are many kinds of variation of the basic 'closed mouth' and 'open mouth' consonants, as well as in the vowels of the same two categories, multiplying and narrowing the meanings that could be expressed and distinguished but all relating ultimately to the basic ideas of YIN and YANG.

The effects on the direction of meaning made by this or that variation are not easily qualified, but these effects can be quantified to some extent by the etymographs in the script: whether or not words were felt to be sufficiently closely related to share an etymographic element in their written characters. Variations caused by voicing, aspirating or nasalizing homorganic consonants (e.g. k-, g-, k'- [=k followed by a breath], ng-) were commonly written with the same etymograph because the etymological relationship was clear; and so are regarded as sharing the same phonetic element by Karlgren and others who accept that theory. However, variations, especially in initial consonants quite often include non-homorganic consonants (e.g. t- against k-); yet words with any of these still could share the same etymographic element in writing them. For example, I have mentioned an adze or mattock as etymological base of the word for 'wisdom' and this may be seen by the way this word is still written. Although they were pronounced evidently like kien and tiat respectively, the script recognized their etymological kinship from the poetic age of language-making, when the consonantal variations must have originated. Between YIN consonants and YANG consonants, however, there was no such exchange, but there are a few interesting examples of the vocalism changing: the staff, 'K — N', very symbol of the YANG, when it is revolved, which is a YIN verb, is etymograph when writing words for a rotating staff, such as a crank handle or stick used in washing clothes, both 'K — W — N'; in the vocalism of the word for a staff, it was like a grammatical change from YANG to YIN to describe one kind of action with it. That every word in the ancestral Chinese language related to the notions of YANG and YIN perhaps may seem less extraordinary when one thinks of languages in which all nouns are either masculine or feminine!

斤
哲

乾
斡
澣

日
月

Comparison of genders is interesting:

⊙ Sun
(*ńiĕt)

☽ Moon
(*ngiwǎt)

8.

were respectively related to the 'K — N' and 'K — W — N' words for YANG
and YIN (the Sun is called 'T'ai Yang', the Supreme YANG), just as they are
respectively masculine and feminine in Greek, Latin and other languages. No
support can be drawn from this, however, for Jungian concepts of a 'collective unconscious' or universal 'archetypes' as causing the agreement between
the languages; because the genders are the other way about, for instance,
in the Germanic words for Sun and Moon, whilst peoples as far apart as the
Japanese and the South African Bushmen conceive of a Sun Goddess and a
Moon God. Again, though it will have been noticed that the all-YANG hexagram in the I Ching signified also Sky and Father, and the all-YIN hexagram
Earth and Mother, support cannot be drawn for the Earth Mother as an idea
to be found universally in the 'collective unconscious'; because in Ancient
Egyptian the genders are reversed and they conceive of a Sky Goddess and
an Earth God, Earth Father rather than Earth Mother! It is evidently not
the similes and metaphors that are universal in the human mind, but the
human mind's poetic faculty that will always make similes and metaphors for
thought and communication; here agreed only in making Sun and Moon, Sky
and Earth like pairs of opposite sex. Human minds need to relate things
creatively, like poets, but not all to make the same poem.

Chinese seems to be an extraordinarily 'self-made' language, showing
little tendency past or present to take into itself words from outside its own
language-making system. As a result, and as a result of the method of
writing adopted for it while it was still in its 'poetic' phase of language-
making, I believe it must have much to tell us about mankind's most important
gift, as well as about our own ancestors.

CLARE GOLSON

A Small Personal Tribute

I offer this small personal tribute to David Hawkes as someone of whose Oxford world I became a part, by accident, in 1951. He was not there at that time: he had already graduated from Oxford, and was in China as a research student at the National Peking University. Jean had joined him there. By the time they returned to Oxford, I had already left. I did not meet him, as far as I remember, until 1979, when, with Jean, he visited his daughter Rachel and her husband John Minford in Canberra.

In 1949 — as a second-generation New Zealander (on my mother's side) of Chinese descent, and a State Registered Nurse — I was offered a position in the Medical School at Lingnan University in Guangzhou, close to my family's place of origin. This was in the immediate aftermath of the communist accession to power and I was refused permission to take up the position. Instead, I went off to Europe with a New Zealand pakeha [i.e. white] friend from nursing days: this (according to my husband Jack's friend and former colleague, Douglas Yen) set an example to New Zealand Chinese girls, to break out of the traditional mould.

New Zealand-trained nurses were in high demand, and in due course we found ourselves at the Radcliffe Infirmary in Oxford. What an exciting and optimistic time and place it was, especially for two young women from the other side of the world! We moved in a multitude of circles that hardly overlapped, and we made friends with people whom we would come across years later in different parts of the world …

— On one occasion, I found myself giving an injection to the New Zealander Dan Davin, of Oxford University Press, who some years later saw the first edition of David's *The Songs of the South* into print.

— I became friendly with Bernard Kay, a B.Litt student working on Chinese poetry under Wu Shih-ch'ang, the scholarly commentator on *The Red Chamber Dream*. I got to know Wu and his wife well and, years later, after they had returned to China, tracked them down in Peking during a visit with Jack in 1982.

— At the Wu's place in Oxford, I used to meet Chiang Yee of *Silent Traveller* fame and Hsiung Shih-i, author of *Lady Precious Stream*, who would go off together minnow catching and return full of excitement, whether they had caught anything or not.

— Graduate students of Chinese like Willie Willetts and Hugh Dunn came and went …

During the time I spent in Oxford, I always heard David spoken of with affection and respect (mingled with some awe), and the same has been the case in my subsequent experience elsewhere. The high opinion of him all stems, of course, from the modesty, the humour and the kindness that are typical of the man I came to know on his two longish visits with Jean to Canberra. These same qualities inform his scholarship — classical, modern and humane.

ROBERT HIGHTOWER

To David Hawkes at Eighty

David, greetings from an established octogenarian to a newcomer. By this time we have become accustomed to count by decades as the years run together. For the past ten years you have, I trust, been able to do whatever you want without transgression. Confucius left us with no guidance for what comes now. Though lacking the authority of the Master, I can offer some first-hand pointers.

As my doctor once told me during a physical examination, after eighteen it's all down hill. It still is, only more so. You could have guessed as much. But there are compensations. With practice one acquires a certain tolerance of the loss or diminution of one's faculties. If you can't read any more you can listen to tapes of other people reading. They bring revelations, such as how Faulkner's Mississippians sound, or Scott's Scots. I don't get to live concerts, but there's lots of recorded music at the library and on the radio. I can cook and I enjoy eating. So you see there's still life after eighty, just less of it.

When Rachel's letter about your impending birthday arrived, I began to recall the history of our acquaintance. We just missed meeting in 1948 when I left Peking at about the time you arrived. It didn't happen until the early 1950s, on the occasion of the Congress of Orientalists in Cambridge. We nearly missed meeting even then, for you avoided both the Congress and the subsequent meeting of the Junior Sinologues in Durham to work on your thesis. You had sent word by one of your colleagues that you would like to see me, and I stopped off in Oxford to pay you a visit. I showed you the paper I had read at one of the meetings. I forget the subject, maybe something about *Chuci*. You returned it without comment, which I took to mean disapproval. You more than made amends by taking me to dinner at Pembroke, Christ Church being closed for the summer. The Irish whiskey I provided for the occasion made you sick, but in spite of it all we established a sufficiently cordial relationship that we were able to plan to exchange places for a year.

It wasn't exactly as the academics do in David Lodge's novel of that name, for we brought our respective and by that time numerous families with us. You arrived in Auburndale a few days before our departure for Oxford, so there was time for me to give you a driving lesson before leaving you to cope with Nash, our large, soft, very American vehicle that had seen better days, lots of them. I was terrified when you seemed about to run us off the road down an embankment and onto the railroad tracks, and recommended that you practice in a vacant parking lot. You must have done so, for later you drove your family to Washington, something I would never have attempted in that car.

When we moved into your house in Woodstock Road there was a British-style (i.e., very small) refrigerator in the dining room. A few days later a scruffy individual arrived in a van to announce that he had come for his fridge. He departed with it in his arms. I immediately went to Elliston and Cavell, Oxford's largest department store, and bought a new one, charging it to you. It was on sale. I realized it was on sale because it was a large (American) fridge and there was no local demand for such a monster. Some years later, when I visited you in your newly-purchased house off the Iffley Road, the first thing I saw was the refrigerator, a white and imposing apparition. When I opened it, there was inside a lone liter of milk.

After we had returned to our respective homes we corresponded but did not meet again until you came to teach at Cornell for a year and spent a few days in Auburndale. When I was next in Oxford, this time for a conference at Ditchley Manor,

I don't remember seeing you and believe you must already have moved to Wales. Some years later, after I had retired, I visited you at Bryncaregog in the dead of winter. You picked me up at the train station in a four-wheel drive military-style vehicle of Soviet manufacture and drove me, most skillfully, some miles up a single-track dirt road to a stone house you and Jean had bought and now inhabited. It was idyllic and in many respects primitive. Water had to be pumped each day to a retaining tank, heat was provided by the kitchen stove and a fireplace in a small room off the dining room; the upstairs bedrooms were not heated. Going to bed under a mountain of bedding to find the warmth of a hot-water bottle thoughtfully placed at the foot of the bed took me back to childhood winter nights in Colorado. The pleasures we miss by being too comfortable! I was impressed by what the two of you were doing in this bleak, lonely, and beautiful place — Jean with her goat's milk, you building, repairing, gardening even, your books still in packing cases.

You took me to visit your nearest and only neighbors, a Welsh couple about a mile up the road and nearly at its end. You practiced your Welsh, and I got the recipe for the scones we were served. Back home I made a batch, but they were not the same.

Snow had fallen the day you drove me back to the village for my train. It was an unnerving ride, and I appreciated the need for that kind of car. Jean came along and did her week's shopping. Coming down out of the hills meant entering a different and less hostile climate, so I was sorry but not surprised when you left Bryncaregog to live in the village of Penuwch.

For the last ten years or so we have corresponded annually. Your long letters have for the most part detailed your activities and news of your children. Mine have been mostly about children and grandchildren, as I no longer travel and my daily life is a routine varying only with the seasons and family visits.

Confucius, you will recall, wrote of the pleasure of a visit from a friend who lives far away. I can no longer be that visiting friend, but hope you might bestow such a pleasure on me if your travels at some time bring you in my direction.

LIU CHING-CHIH

Notes of a Musical Traveller

Beethoven and *Jean Christophe*

It was my elder brother who introduced me to European classical music when I was eleven years old. He was interested in vocal music and took part in his school choir in Peking (or Beiping as it was then called) during the late 1940s, when my father worked in Tientsin. In 1946, the Japanese residents of Tientsin put their long-playing records of European classical music on sale in the streets at very low prices, before they were repatriated to Japan. My brother used to purchase recordings of vocal music, such as Franz Schubert's Lieder, and orchestral works, such as Beethoven's Fifth Symphony and Schubert's Unfinished Symphony. I have no recollection of the names of the singers of the Lieder, nor of the names of the conductor and the orchestra performing Beethoven's Fifth Symphony.

My brother could only stay in Tientsin during the winter and summer vacations. During term-time he was required to live in his school hostel in Peking. It was during the terms, when my brother was away at school in Peking, that I started listening to his records. I was terrified by the outburst of emotions in Beethoven's Fifth. I remember the melancholy mood of Schubert's Unfinished Symphony, and the tenderness of his Lieder. On reflection, I can see now that these works of classicism and romanticism from nineteenth-century Europe were a bit alien to me. At that time I was not yet ready for them — culturally, musically, or emotionally.

I was attracted to these works nonetheless and listened to them continuously during my senior primary and junior secondary school years.

I also remember that when I listened to the records, I was at the same time reading Ba Jin's trilogy, *Family*, *Spring*, and *Autumn*, and thinking a great deal about the plots of Ba Jin's novels. During the post-war years, the late 1940s, primary and secondary school pupils could enjoy a relatively easy life as compared with their counterparts nowadays. After school, I spent almost all my time reading novels and listening to my brother's records on my manually operated record-player. These were my most enjoyable pastimes. I continued this leisurely life when my father was transferred from Tientsin to Hong Kong in May 1948, and I entered Pui Ching Middle School, on Waterloo Road, Kowloon.

During my first two years at Pui Ching, I became more involved in European classical music as well as in the literary works of the "May Fourth" writers, including Lu Xun, Mao Dun, and Lao She. But my greatest discovery was Romain Rolland's *Jean Christophe*, translated by Fu Lei and published by the Shanghai publisher Luo Tuo (Camel) Press in 1948. I purchased a set of four volumes at the Qian Jin (Forward) Book Shop in Nathan Road for HK$40 in 1949, which was in fact very expensive at that time. The novel definitely had a profound influence on my character formation, as well as on my sense of values and my philosophy of life. From the time I purchased *Jean Christophe* in 1949 to my graduation from Pui Ching in 1953, I went through the novel five times from cover to cover, all four volumes of the Chinese translation. In the fifty years since then I have flipped through certain chapters time and time again. Now I am in possession of six different Chinese editions, one English edition and one French edition of *Jean Christophe*. And I have to date acquired more than fifty publications, in both English and Chinese, on Beethoven's life and works.

My passion for *Jean Christophe*, for Beethoven and for European classical music has always been at the centre of my life, although as the years went by, the passion became more rational.

Musical Reviews and Musical Tours

I was obliged to take up another profession, and music became my after-work pleasure. Although my profession, i.e. my livelihood, has never been in the field of music, my passion for European classical music has never diminished. In 1979 I started writing reviews for the "Music Weekly" section of the *New Evening Post* on musical performances, books and musicians, and later for several other publications. Writing musical reviews has required me to attend many musical performances over the years, in Hong Kong and elsewhere. In the early 1980s, I concentrated on musical activities in Hong Kong. Later I did some concert-going in London while attending academic conferences in the United Kingdom. During the 1990s, my musical travels extended to Taiwan, China, and continental Europe, and to a limited extent to New York and Boston in the United States. At the invitation of the Japan Foundation, I visited a number of universities and conservatories in Japan in 1978, but I only attended two orchestral concerts of western music, one given by the New Japan Philharmonic, performing works by Ravel, Bartók, and Brahms, and one given by the famous NHK Symphony Orchestra performing works by Arnold Schönberg, William Walton, and Andrzei Panufnik. To my ears, even the well-known NHK Symphony Orchestra sounded rather mechanical and monotonous. After all, I concluded, European classical music is alien to the Japanese people, although these were talented Japanese performers and conductors.

The United Kingdom

From the mid-1970s onwards, I have been a fairly regular visitor to the United Kingdom, especially London, Oxford, and lately Glyndebourne. At first I was mainly interested in orchestral concerts, but later my interest extended to ballets and operas. The cost of going to an opera performance or an orchestral concert was, and still is, quite expensive. But the qualities of the performances were so good that they justified the high admission fees. I have always learned something from these performances. For example, in 1985, I went to see Stockhausen's opera *Donnerstag aus Licht (Thursday)* at Covent Garden. The curtain rose at 4 p.m. and fell at 10:15 p.m., a total of six hours in the opera house, listening to ultra-avant-garde electronic music. My eyes suffered from the lighting. Watching the composer from above, operating a huge computer, was quite an interesting experience. It gave me the impression that composing electronic music was a different kind of creativity altogether, one which required a diversification of knowledge into the fields of computer science and electronic engineering. But to be absolutely honest, I did not derive any enjoyment from this opera.

Stockhausen was an exception. My experiences in watching traditional Italian opera at Covent Garden, the English National Opera, and Glyndebourne were most enjoyable. Through the performances at Glyndebourne, I came to know more about opera traditions other than the Italian one — Czech operas, the operas of Handel and Gluck.

My recent visit in June 2002 to the Symphony Hall in Birmingham was a surprise — at the quality of the acoustics, and at the design and the comfort of the Hall. Sir Simon Rattle has indeed left a magnificent legacy to the people of the city of Birmingham. I remember it was an afternoon concert, starting at 2:15 p.m., featuring Wagner's *Rienzi* Overture, Liszt's First Piano Concerto in E Flat, and Beethoven's Second Symphony in D Major. I was also surprised at the good attendance, almost eighty percent, mostly retired people. I have observed over the years that there are a large number of loyal and devoted concert-goers in the United Kingdom. They are the products of a good music education and of a good cultural environment.

Once, in 2001, I attended the Edinburgh Festival and it left a very deep impression. The whole city is involved in the Festival. The people, residents as well as visitors, all seemed to enjoy the occasion thoroughly. The programme I enjoyed most was an all-Beethoven concert — one overture, two symphonies, two piano concertos, and one mass, totalling four performing hours. I have never attended such a long concert and have never enjoyed a

Beethoven concert as much as I enjoyed this one. For me, the four hours passed quickly. I wished the experience would never end.

The Edinburgh Festival audience was totally different from the audiences at Glyndebourne and at the Bayreuth Festival, both of which require black tie and provide a three-course dinner with Champagne and wines. The Edinburgh Festival audience were a care-free, happy lot — they wore whatever they felt like and they dined informally in the lobby of the theatre where Wagner's *Walküre* was being staged. Nowhere in the world have I found an opera audience as relaxed as the one at the Edinburgh Festival.

Italy: the Arena di Verona and the Teatro alla Scala

I have been to Verona many times since 1991, when my friend Mr. Dennis Constantine, a portrait photographer, introduced me to this magnificent city and we drove from his home in Salford Prior via France to Lake Garda in Italy. We watched three performances: *Rigoletto*, *Turandot*, and *Nabucco*, and the impression was overwhelming — the huge stage, the floodlights, the chattering audience, the typical Italian style of the whole occasion. The acoustics were so good, I could not help admiring the talented Roman architects of so long ago. The chorus of the final act of *Nabucco* and the arias of *Rigoletto* are deeply engraved in my mind.

The production and performances at the Arena di Verona are unique — the vast stage, the superb acoustics, the audience and the open air atmosphere. There is no opera venue throughout the world which can be compared with the Arena, for the production and staging of the "big" operas like *Aida*, *Carmen*, and *Nabucco*. For more intimate works such as *Rigoletto* and *Tosca*, the stage at the Arena is a bit too big.

The Teatro Alla Scala in Milan is one of the most prestigious opera houses in Europe, with a long history of staging Italian operas and with a string of celebrated opera conductors and singers, such as Arturo Toscanini, Maria Callas, etc. To keep abreast of the Metropolitan Opera in New York, the Opera Bastille in Paris, the new opera house at Glyndebourne, and the renovated and refurbished Covent Garden, La Scala is now undergoing a three year major renovation and refurbishing.

The museum in the Teatro alla Scala is a valuable addition, an outstanding feature other opera houses do not have. In 1999, I watched Rossini's *Barber of Seville*, a refined and modern production; and in 2000, I attended *Peter Grimes* and the ballet *Amarcord La Strada*. The La Scala audiences were considerably more conservative in dress as well as in behaviour, when compared with the audiences at Covent Garden and the Opera Bastille. In general, I have found that audiences in Milan, Salzburg, Bayreuth, Vienna, and Switzerland are more conservative than audiences in the United Kingdom, the United States, and France.

Paris

The timing of my visits to Paris has never seemed quite right for musical performances other than operas. I have visited Paris some twenty times altogether and never once have I attended an orchestral performance! I have been to the Palais Garnier several times, to the Opera Bastille three or four times, and to the Opera Comique only once for the performance of the Italian version of *Tosca*. As an opera house, the Opera Bastille is much better than the Garnier, though its surroundings are not that pleasant. I saw superb productions and staging of *Don Giovanni, Rigoletto,* and *Norma* at the Bastille. Although the Palais Garnier looks beautiful from the outside, especially after the recent renovation, the interior still looks over-used and in need of a complete overhaul and refurbishing. The stage is a bit too small for modern productions.

Paris is first and foremost a city for the visual arts. There are indeed many venues for musical and opera performances. But it is the visual arts that dominate the cultural scene in this beautiful city. There are over a hundred museums and art galleries. But when it comes to museums for composers and performers, Paris has very little to offer — of all the French composers, only Ravel has a whole museum dedicated to him, and that is two hours by train from Paris. Debussy's house is now shared by a Tourist Office downstairs and the Debussy Museum upstairs. As for

Coupérin, Saint Saens, Berlioz, and Chopin, I found nothing! I was very surprised at the heartlessness of the Parisians towards their musicians, both French and visiting ones.

Vienna, Salzburg, and Breganz

The first time I visited Vienna was a rainy, cold day in December 1976. It was a Saturday too, and the following Monday was a bank holiday. I had to leave for Münich on Tuesday, which meant that I could not see anything in the way of museums and operas. Nor could I listen to anything since there were no concerts that weekend. My first visit was a badly organised one!

My subsequent four visits were more successful as they took place during weekdays and the weather was much better. I had done my homework, and was able to enjoy Berlioz's opera *The Trojans* at the Vienna Opera House during my second visit and an orchestral concert during my fourth visit in 1995. I spent time visiting the museums dedicated to Haydn, Mozart, Beethoven, Schubert, and Johann Strauss. I also went to Beethoven's birth place in Bonn during my extensive study visit to Germany in 1976, and to Machelen and Louvain in Belgium where Beethoven's father and grandfather had lived before they moved to Bonn. I followed the route of the Beethoven family from Machelen via Louvain to Bonn and followed Beethoven to Vienna where he lived and composed and became a great artist.

The Chinese Communist Party has always asked artists and writers to experience life so that they can write better and more thoroughly about the life of the ordinary people, in other words the life of the peasants and workers. In actual fact the great composers of Europe never "went down" to the factories and countryside to experience the hard life. They nevertheless wrote great music. Bach always lived in Germany, and Schubert and Beethoven spent the greater part of their lives in Austria. Mozart was an exception. Even Haydn went to London only after he had already written most of his works. Schumann, Brahms and many other composers travelled little. But their music was capable of reaching the heights of artistic perfection.

If we attribute Bach's greatness to his belief in God, if Beethoven's greatness was due to his strong will and noble character, then what is it that made Schubert so eternal? What made these great musicians so infinitely resourceful? Where did they draw their inspiration from? The achievement of these composers renders Mao's *Talks on Literature and Art at the Yan'an Forum* meaningless. Their masterpieces have become the shared treasure of mankind. Their musical inspirations were the cumulative results of human creativity.

I visited Salzburg several times, but only enjoyed the Salzburg Festival once — the cost of attending it was simply too high. In 1996, Abbado's choral and orchestral concert, featuring Schönberg's *Gurre-lieder* and Beethoven's Egmont Overture and Fourth Piano Concerto, with the Gustav Mahler Orchestra, was quite an experience to me, with over a hundred choral members and over a hundred orchestral players. It produced a shattering effect. Boulez's performance of Mahler's Seventh Symphony was another rare opportunity for me to see the composer/conductor's participation in the Festival in person.

I have only been once to Breganz, to attend a performance of Bizet's *Carmen*, on the lake behind the Breganz Opera House. It was August 1991, and we were on our way back from Verona to England. It was drizzling and we had to wait until the rain stopped. However, it was a superb production, with horses galloping on the floating stage on the lake and smugglers climbing up and down the man-made mountains.

The Austrians I have encountered so far have all been good organisers and business people. They are polite, firm, clear-headed and smart. They all know what they want and what their clients want, and they price their commodities a little higher than they are worth. For example, in 1996 all the hotels in Salzburg charged room-rates one grade higher than their actual grading; while the highest price for a ticket to Beethoven's *Fidelio* was around US$270, much higher than prices at the Bayreuth Festival, Covent Garden, or Glyndebourne. People nevertheless came and the Festival had a full house. Very successful and smart business people, the Austrians.

Germany

I made my first visit to Germany for two weeks in October 1976. As I said, I paid a visit to the birth place of Beethoven in Bonn, which was very impressive. My second visit to Bonn was twenty-six years later on Wednesday 26 June 2002, for one hour only. Bonn is now a much more prosperous, noisy and crowded city, with a lot more buildings, traffic and people. I could hardly recognise the birth place of Beethoven, which is now surrounded by shops. The ground floor is now a souvenir shop and a lecture room. The arrangement of the exhibits is not the same and a few of the items displayed in 1976 have been removed. I was very disappointed.

After a lapse of two decades, I resumed my liaison with Germany in 1995 for the Wagnerian cycle of music dramas, the *Ring*, and other operas. I went back in 1999, 2000, and 2002. My first visit to Bayreuth, in 1995, was a cultural shock. No audiences in other European countries behave like the Germans at Bayreuth — all dressed up in black tie, sitting up straight; no movement or breathing seemed to take place during the performance! There was no air-conditioning in the Auditorium. Imagine — wearing a stifling tuxedo in mid-summer! People stared at you if you tried to take out a handkerchief to mop your forehead. It was as if you were not behaving properly in front of God, i.e. Wagner. If you were late arriving and trying to get to the middle of a row before the curtain went up, you would be stared at as if you were committing a serious crime. It was my impression that, despite all the great philosophers, writers and composers, Germans on the whole at Bayreuth are pretty rude as compared with the Italians, the British, the French, and the Scandinavians in their opera houses. A very strange phenomenon.

But the singing and the orchestral playing are so beautiful that I am prepared to put up with all the inconveniences, and I visit Bayreuth from time to time whenever I can. There is always a price for everything, and there is nowhere in the world where you can see such superb productions of the Wagnerian music-dramas. A German-speaking lady from Zurich once told me that she had attended the Bayreuth Festival every year since 1962! She is a donor and proud of it. She said that it was important to help the opera house so that Wagner's music could be perpetuated.

The United States and elsewhere

In December 1988, after a visit to Harvard University, I stayed in New York for three days, at Columbia University. The Lincoln Centre was my prime target and I managed to attend an opera performance at the Metropolitan Opera and a rehearsal of the New York Philharmonic Orchestra. The Metropolitan Opera House was magnificent and the production and performance were first class. It is the most modern opera house I have ever seen, quite a contrast to the traditional ones in Europe. The pleasure of my musical travels (I do not have the space here to mention cities such as Prague, Budapest, and Belgrade) is something I owe to the writing of musical reviews. I have been extremely fortunate.

Music and Translation

While music has taken up a good part of my after-work hours, it is translation that has helped me to make a living. It was also due to my association with translation that I had further opportunities to enjoy music in Europe, and was able to get to know Professor David Hawkes in 1998, when we were arranging the publication of the facsimile edition of the note-books he kept while translating *The Story of the Stone*. The Lingnan University Centre for Literature and Translation finally brought out the facsimile in May 2000. David, I discovered, is also a keen music lover. He told me that he loved Verdi's *Un Ballo in Maschera*: "I grew up knowing one of the arias from it," he wrote in his letter of 22 July 2000, "and I was quite impressed when I saw it at Covent Garden half a life later. I love the *Ring*, but perhaps *Tristan* even more, and *Parsifal* for the music. I saw *Parsifal* performed quite creditably in Tokyo in 1967 or 8." For David, "*Pelléas* is the greatest operatic experience, though I suppose Debussy wouldn't have called it an opera." With David's abundant knowledge of European music, I fear that my scattered observations may not sound "creditably" interesting. But I hope he will not mind reading my Musical Traveller's Notes to while away a few moments on his eightieth birthday.

LIU TS'UN-YAN

Green-stone and Quince

It has been my great honour to count Professor Hawkes among my friends for nearly half a century now. Ours is a friendship that has grown through different times, and in different places. Our very first encounter was in Oxford, on the afternoon of August 13th, 1957. We had corresponded before then, concerning my proposed visit to Oxford's Bodleian Library, to inspect some rare Ming editions of traditional Chinese fiction. Books cannot be borrowed from the Bodleian, they have to be read on the premises, and before they can do this readers have to go through the procedure of registration. On the morning of the day in question, I had already made my first exploratory trip to the library, and when I went to call on Professor Hawkes that afternoon, it was a purely personal visit, a chance for me to express my feelings of respect and admiration — feelings which have continued over the almost half century of our deepening acquaintance. I had been thrilled that morning to see for myself the ancient Bodleian Library (a century older than the Fan family library in Ningbo, the famous Tianyige); but I hardly need say that I was more thrilled by far that afternoon, to meet David Hawkes in person.

That year I myself was nearly forty years old, and Professor Hawkes was a bit younger than me. He seemed rather thin, but had a lively air about him. He looked about thirty-three or thirty-four years old. Before long our conversation turned to a discussion of certain minute details of scholarship, what Chinese scholars like to call *douding* 餖飣, scraps of knowledge, especially the sorts of scraps relating to the questions of "dating and authorship" that preoccupied us both at the time (see the Preface to his *Ch'u Tz'u: The Songs of the South*, published in 1959). I recall his asking me a question about something he had seen when he was in northern China: people carrying paper fans with no decoration on them (no paintings, no poems) other than calligraphy consisting of four large characters: *jiu* 酒, *se* 色, *cai* 財, and *qi* 氣. He no doubt asked me about this because he knew I had done some research into the connection between the deities of Buddhism and Taoism and traditional Chinese fiction. At the time I answered without a great deal of reflection, basing my reply on my childhood experiences in Beijing: "Oh, they must have been 'True Ones'!" I went on to explain that it was a common practice in northern China, during the early years of the Republic, for merchants to wear long gowns of plain grey cotton, with black cloth jackets over them. By traditional custom, merchants were not entitled to wear silk, this indicating that, however wealthy they might have become, they were always to be regarded as lowly people in the Confucian scheme of things. This attitude began with the Han Emperor Gaozu, when he decreed that merchants should "neither wear silk, nor ride carriages". Some of these merchants created semi-religious popular organisations or guilds of their own, which were called Truth Sects *lijiao* 理教, the believers or members being called True Ones *zaili* 在理. They used these four characters as emblems of their livelihood, as articles of their faith. At the time, this seemed like a casual conversation. I did not know that having completed his translation of *The Songs of the South*, Professor Hawkes had already formed a plan to translate *The Story of the Stone*. Nor did I know that he had a great interest in Yuan drama. If he had indeed mentioned Yuan drama that afternoon in Oxford, my thoughts might quite possibly have turned to the several Yuan plays that deal with members of the Taoist sect known as Quanzhen Taoism. In the collected writings of the seven Golden Lotus Founders of the Quanzhen Sect (Wang Zhe and his six disciples), we also encounter these very same four Chinese characters. Anyway, in his article "Quanzhen Plays and Quanzhen Masters", published in 1981, in the *Bulletin de l'Ecole Française d'Extrême Orient*, Tome LXIX, Professor Hawkes has spelt out this background very clearly. (He translates the four characters as "the snares of drink, sex, money and anger"). It is my belief that the Truth Sect of the Late Qing/Early Republican period in northern China was a popular sect in its own right, and not necessarily a latter-day descendant of Quanzhen Taoism!

Many of my readers will probably know that over a longish period of time my friendship with Professor Hawkes had a lot to do with the fact that his daughter Rachel and his son-in-law Professor John Minford came to live in Australia, in the city of Canberra. (I myself live there still!) This relationship of ours, when I come to think about it, is rather a complex one. In fact, there seems to me almost to be some inexplicable element of karma involved, some form of predestination at work. To this day I am not sure if my understanding of this is correct or not. I do remember that on that afternoon when I first met Professor Hawkes in his home, in his drawing room I saw one of his daughters — she must have been six or seven at the time. I did not ask her name. Many years later I came to know that Professor and Mrs Hawkes have three daughters and one son, and that it was their eldest daughter, Rachel, who married John Minford. I have often wanted to ask her if she was indeed that little girl I saw — a smiling little girl, telling a story! Certainly the dates "match"! If indeed my calculations are correct, the little story-teller is now an accomplished novelist in her own right!

My friend John Minford came to Canberra in 1977, with the support of a Commonwealth Scholarship, to continue his researches into *The Story of the Stone*, at the same time completing his part of the joint project to translate the whole novel for Penguin Classics (his part consisting of the last forty chapters). He arrived in April of that year, and stayed until August 1980. This was when I came to know him and his wife. Gradually our acquaintance became closer. This too was part of our shared karma. Minford himself had come to Chinese studies from a background in the Greek and Latin classics. Professor Hawkes must have looked on him with approval as the person to complete his *Stone*, as the right person to play the English Gao E to his English Cao Xueqin. There was a certain inescapable logic to this arrangement. Although to the outside observer, the *Stone* has all the appearance of a finished novel, and although for more than two centuries after its appearance as a book, no one questioned its integrity as a work of literature, subsequently, the intricate scholarship of specialists and the discovery of new relevant materials have established beyond doubt that in actuality the last forty chapters are a continuation. And yet, despite all of this, even so fastidious a scholar as the late Bernhard Karlgren was still able to write an article stating that the language used in the last forty chapters was indistinguishable from that used in the first eighty. From this we can see the need for the translator of the "continuation" to study the translation of the first eighty chapters with enormous care, if his continuation is to "connect with" rather than just "reflect" the work of his predecessor. I personally also detect a certain homogeneity in the tone of the two parts, a certain shared emotion. Minford spent two periods here in Canberra, and during both of these periods his father-in-law came to stay. There is something here over and above family loyalty and affection. In 1989, Minford came to an agreement with the famous Hong Kong Martial Arts novelist Louis Cha, to translate his last novel *The Deer and the Cauldron*. This translation has now appeared in three volumes (1997–2003). In his own Preface to the first volume, Minford wrote: "My dear friend David Hawkes has contributed many chapters of the translation, and I cannot adequately express how much I owe him for his unstinting help and guidance over the years." Why did Hawkes do this? My guess is that he did it partly out of a feeling of friendship, partly for the sheer fun of keeping his hand in! Happily, Louis Cha himself had the vision to understand and appreciate this, and in his own Author's Preface expresses his personal gratitude for the generosity of this fine scholar, adding that he himself had once hoped, "when he was at

Oxford University, to be one of Hawkes' students, but he (Hawkes) had already retired into the Welsh hills!" How right Louis Cha was in his use of the word "retired", with its echoes of the great hermits and recluses of the Chinese past! The sublime tone and inspiration of David Hawkes' work lie beyond this troubled world.

I have already mentioned Professor Hawkes' two visits to Canberra. I had the good fortune to be present on the occasions when he lectured for our colleagues and students. His first visit was in 1979. He arrived on the 17th September of that year. Long before he and Mrs Hawkes came, towards the end of September of the previous year, I had received a letter from my friend Stephen Soong 宋淇, Director of the Research Centre for Translation at the Chinese University of Hong Kong, and editor of the journal *Renditions*, telling me that he thought Professor Hawkes might be passing through Hong Kong some time the following year, and asking me if I thought it might be a good idea to organise a translation symposium in Hong Kong to coincide with his visit. I made some enquiries, and ascertained that indeed Professor Hawkes was due to visit Canberra in the last three months of 1979, and might very well be passing through Hong Kong on his way. I did not imagine the symposium would present any problems. Stephen Soong and David Hawkes were already in correspondence. Stephen had started writing (in Chinese) a series of interesting and valuable articles about the first volume of the *Stone* translation when it first appeared in 1973. Several of these essays were put together in book form and published in Taiwan in September 1976. The book was entitled *The Stone's Journey to the West*, and was written using Stephen's pen-name Lin Yiliang 林以亮. Stephen asked Professor Hawkes to contribute a short introductory Preface to the book, which he did, writing with touching sincerity:

> Each time I read these criticisms, I feel a mixture of different emotions. For a foreign translator it is a somewhat alarming experience to have his work subjected to such thorough scrutiny by a Chinese

expert; at the same time it is a source of pride and satisfaction to be thought worthy — however misguided or erroneous — of so much attention. Then again, there is a sense of pleasure in meeting with criticism that is so well informed — criticism that may eventually lead to real improvements in the translation. But I think the feeling that prevails over all others is one of gratitude — I would even say of comradeship, if Mr Soong would not object to such a term — because, of all my readers, I can be sure that, whether he approves or disapproves, Mr Soong always knows what I have done, or tried to do, and why I have done it; and to be understood is better than to be praised.

In the opening words of this essay, I intimated what an honour it has been for me to count Professor Hawkes as my friend, as a friend who "knows and understands" — *zhiji* 知己. Here Professor Hawkes himself talks of Stephen Soong and their spirit of comradeship in a similar way. In the Preface to the third volume of the *Stone*, Hawkes refers to Stephen once again, with gratitude and respect, as "that indefatigable *Hong lou meng* enthusiast", thanking him for his generosity. Stephen, in his own Preface to *The Stone's Journey to the West*, writes with candour:

> In his very first letter to me, Mr Hawkes called me his friend *zhiji* 知己. Normally an author or translator will tend to regard his critic with circumspection, or downright hostility. The critic tends, after all, to be seen as the "opposition". And it is true, however scrupulous and careful a critic may be, he will almost inevitably have differences with his author. In our direct exchange of ideas, Mr Hawkes has never been concerned with such things: he has never been on the defensive. He has always considered our shared love for the novel to be something that enables us to transcend such petty considerations. He has urged me to show him no mercy, never to let myself be restrained by sentiment, but to point out whatever distortions or errors I find in the translation. Such contributions of mine could even have some use, he suggests. He refers to himself wih great humility as C. C. Wang's "junior", and even goes so far as to say that in some respects, especially in terms of the narrative, he finds C. C. Wang's version superior to his own. He asked me to convey his respects to

C. C. Wang. All of this shows the bigness of the man, the breadth of his vision.

These words of Stephen's express the shared feelings of all those who have been fortunate enough to be Professor Hawkes' friends.

I don't think the Hong Kong translation symposium ever took place. But when Professor Hawkes came to Canberra in 1979, he gave three public seminars (on the 11th October, the 8th and 21st November), and all three were on subjects connected with the *Stone*. By then the second volume, *The Crabflower Club*, had already been out for almost two years, taking the novel to the end of chapter 53. And in the previous year, 1978, the first two volumes (chapters 1–80) of the Foreign Languages Press translation by Yang Xianyi and Gladys Yang, under the title *A Dream of Red Mansions*, had also appeared in Peking. Although Yang Xianyi insisted that he was "just a translator" and not a textual scholar, the Publisher's Note to the first volume of their translation states that their translation of the first eighty chapters was based on the Qi Liaosheng transcription of the Qianlong era, photolithograhically reproduced in 1911 by the Yu-cheng Book Company in Shanghai, while their text for the last forty chapters would be the printed edition of Cheng Weiyuan. It also states that other texts were consulted, to rectify certain minor errors and omissions. All of this was to draw to the attention of the reading public the continuing debate concerning the various editions of the novel, and the intensifying controversy over the existence of an "early version" prior to Cao Xueqin's own work. In the course of 1979, in the inaugural issue of the Harbin Normal College journal *Beifang luncong*, a scholar by the name of Dai Bufan published an article entitled "Unravelling the riddle of the authorship of the *Stone*". Dai argued that there was indeed an "earlier version". Any talk given by Professor Hawkes would be bound to be "news" on campus, and there was a very good turn-out for these three seminars — several times the size of our normal audience. Professor Hawkes spoke in his usual careful, scholarly manner, arguing in a leisurely and unhurried fashion, never losing his sense of objectivity or departing from his scrupulously empirical and detailed examination of the facts. It had been eleven years since our last meeting (I had visited Oxford again in 1968). During those eleven years, he had resigned his prestigious Oxford chair, in order to concentrate on the task of translating the *Stone*, and had retired to the Welsh hills, to live in a remote farm-house. I found myself gazing at a much older man, grey-haired and bearded — a man of the Tao. I suddenly thought of the conclusion of the poem "After prolonged rain at Wang River estate", where the Tang poet Wang Wei refers to the Taoist sage Yang Zhu, "the old rustic" who, in the words of the book of Liezi, has come to the realisation that he no longer needs to "compete for his place on the mat".

We had another chance to meet when Professor Hawkes visited Canberra again in February 1994. Minford had himself resigned his professorship at Auckland University a couple of years before, and was with our East Asian History department as a Visiting Fellow. On the 10th March Professor Hawkes telephoned to invite us to join them at lunch the following day at the Great Wall restaurant (a place we often frequented), for *yumcha* 飲茶. This was how I learned the excellent news that he was in Canberra, on a private visit. He would not be giving any seminars this time. Minford's last two volumes of the Penguin *Stone* were already out (they appeared in 1982 and 1986). I always thought that using this title was a big gamble in terms of sales (since the book had always been known by its alternative title *Hongloumeng*, under one translation or another) — but the Penguin version certainly seemed to be making a name for itself. When Professor Hawkes and I met up again, we soon found ourselves discussing one or two perfunctory scraps of scholarship, tackling the latest items in *Stone*-studies, almost as if we were solving a literary puzzle. One day during this visit of his, Professor Hawkes asked me about a passage in the Preface by Qi Liaosheng. It was a passage we had discussed once before — inconclusively. It contained several literary allusions, and

Professor Hawkes asked me if I had formed any new ideas about their provenance.

In this passage, Qi Liaosheng compares Jia Baoyu, his obsessive "lust of the mind", and his combination of sentiment and Zen enlightenment, with Lixia Langya 歷下琅琊; and he goes on to compare Lin Daiyu, her over-sensitive jealousy, her sincere love and deep compassion, with Sang'e Shinü 桑娥石女. I recalled that we had discussed this passage once back in 1979, on the occasion of one of Professor Hawkes' seminars. Afterwards I had written a couple of letters communicating my own thoughts on this matter to two friends, Wu Shichang in Beijing, and Pan Chonggui in Taipei, asking them for their views. The allusions in Qi's Preface are multiple, and susceptible of several interpretations. Mr Wu argued that Sang'e refers to the "mulberry-picking girl" in the Han Ballad "Mulberry on the Bank" *Mo shang sang* 陌上桑; as for Shinü, Wu referred me to the biography of Shi Chong in the *Jin Dynastic History,* and to Shi's much-loved concubine Green Pearl. I myself had no argument with either of these interpretations, but Pan Chonggui had other ideas on the subject. In his view, Shinü alludes to the story of the officer of Yangxian District in the collection *Youminglu*; and Sang'e alludes to two lines in the "Rhapsody on Parting" (*Wenxuan, juan* 16) by the Liang-dynasty poet Jiang Yan. In these two lines both of the words (*sang* and *e*) occur, which makes Pan's argument more convincing, and the allusion less vague. In fact, Jiang Yan himself is using a prior allusion, from the *Book of Songs,* the poem "Sang-zhong" in the Airs of Yong. Perhaps I should not be too critical of the helpful scholarly endeavours of my "understanding friends"! But I cannot help being a little sceptical of Wu Shichang's explanation of the allusion in Lixia Langya. He argues that this refers to the story of Sun Chu in the Western Jin period. Sun Chu's biography is to be found in the *Jin Dynastic History, juan* 56. Sun hailed from Taiyuan. Lixia and Langya are both places in Shandong. Now, although Sun Chu did accompany the Valiant General Shi Bao (Shi Chong's father) to Shandong, he had no close connection with Shandong. Both the biography in the *Jin History* and the collection of anecdotes *A New Account of Tales of the World* (section four, "Letters and Scholarship") refer to the story of Sun Chu removing his mourning clothes after having completed the mourning period for the death of his wife, and to the poem he wrote on that occasion, which moved his good friend Wang Ji to say that "words are born of feeling; feeling is born of words". But I can see no particularly convincing reason to connect this story with that of Baoyu and Daiyu. Besides, if we look at the exact wording of the passage in Qi Liaosheng's Preface, just as the two elements Sang'e and Shinü are separate, so Lixia and Langya must be too. I remember saying this to Professor Hawkes in 1979, and having to leave the matter in this inconclusive state, to everyone's great disappointment. Here we are more than twenty years later, and I am still unable to resolve the problem in a satisfactory fashion, am still obliged to disappoint my friends. From my present repertoire, all I can offer by way of solace is the following scrap, also from *New Account* (section XXIII, "The Free and Unrestrained"): "As Wang Qian climbed Mount Mao, he wept bitterly, saying, 'Wang Qian of Langya will finally die because of his romantic passions!'" Wang Qian's biography can be found in the *Jin History, juan* 65, appended to the biographies of his grandfather Wang Dao and his father Wang Hui. Such stories relating to the prominent Wang family of Langya are worthy of our attention.

When writing this little memoir, I learned that Professor Hawkes will soon celebrate his eightieth birthday. In these troubled times, when all the talk is of the turmoil and chaos of war, to have had a friendship that has lasted half a century is something to be treasured. When Professor Hawkes came to Canberra for the first time in 1979, he gave me a very beautiful wooden spoon, which had carved on it a depiction of stories from the Arthurian story-cycle. It is what the Welsh call a love-spoon, and holds a very special and deep significance for the Welsh people. I am glad to say that I now have a piece of good news to give Professor Hawkes and his dear son-in-law, my friend Minford. I have recently been reading a full-length novel from the late-Ming/early-Qing period, a book only recently reprinted, entitled *Jin Yun Qiao zhuan* 金雲翹傳. The literary quality of this novel is certainly inferior to that of the *Stone*. But there are elements in it that may possibly be of interest to *Stone*-scholars investigating clues to the novel's possible precursors: we encounter a Department of Star-crossed Love, a Poem of Heartbreak, a series of ten songs with three-character titles, and even a young lady charged with administering Star-crossed Love within the Realm of the Heartbroken.

May I be permitted to conclude by turning on their heads two lines from the *Book of Songs*, with the addition of one or two characters of my own, as my way of wishing Professor Hawkes many happy returns of this joyful occasion?

> You cast me a green-stone;
> I would requite it with a quince!

Translated by John Minford

GÖRAN MALMQVIST

Nine Home-made Haiku for David

蝌蚪們做夢，
叭嗒地跳入池塘！
聽到麼，芭蕉？

The tadpoles dream: Ho!
We jump into the pool! Plop!
Did you hear, Basho?

太陽耍戲法：
Hocus-pocus! A crocus!
（韻是借來的）。

The sun's a wizard!
Hocus-pocus! A crocus!
(The rhyme is borrowed).

十三陵山谷：
深藍色的天空下，
淡紅的柿子。

The Ming Tomb valley:
   under the deep blue heaven,
   pale red persimmons.

鄰居燒葉子，
風正向我這兒吹來：
我耙子在哪兒？

My neighbour burns leaves.
The wind is blowing my way!
Quick! Fetch me my rake!

冬天的池塘：
蛤蟆呱呱的聲音
也凍冰了麼？

The pool in winter:
   has the croaking of the frogs
   turned into ice too?

三杯過崗了！
白額大虫何所似？
空虛的錦囊。

Three cups passed the ridge!
What's the man-eating beast like?
An empty cloth bag!

有人開大門：
灶邊的老貓豎耳，
懶得睜眼看。

Someone's at the door:
   the old cat pricks up her ears,
   too lazy to look.

松鼠嚇壞了！
秋天最後一片葉
在枝上發抖。

The squirrel panics!
Woe! The last leaf of Autumn
    trembles on the branch!

嘩啦拉一聲！
風把小小的橡子
吹落到地上！

What terrible noise!
The breeze has brought to the ground
    a tiny acorn!

To celebrate
David's Eightieth Birthday

Wishing you
Fortune as vast as the Eastern Sea,
Life as long as the Southern Mountains

Dorothy Liu

恭賀

大衛仁兄八十榮慶

福如東海

壽比南山

程蔭拜祝

PANG BINGJUN

Following in the Steps of Karma

Less than twelve months after the Mao–Nixon meeting in October 1971 we were all recalled to the university's main campus from the so-called May 7th School in the city's southern outskirts, where we had been made to stay and remould ourselves into brand-new staff members. The return from the limbo of the School and rejoining the Foreign Languages Department had at least the advantage of making the reading of English a legitimate part of my job as a teacher of English.

At that time the main library and the Department's reading room were in the painful process of recovering from the impact of the unprecedented GPCR [Great Proletarian Cultural Revolution]. New accessions and subscriptions, particularly in the field of the humanities, came literally only in trickles. Luckily my supply of English reading materials was eked out with parcels of new books and magazines which a colleague of mine, an American lady who had chosen to stay on with her Chinese husband and family after the changeover in 1949, was able to receive from abroad. She was happy to share the pleasure of this reading material with me.

Among these borrowed books one stands out distinctly from all the rest. It is the first volume of *The Story of the Stone*, translated by David Hawkes. Even to this day every time I think of first opening the book and starting to drink in this delectable and delicious English version of the Chinese masterpiece, I can't help reliving the joy, the thrill and the wonder I experienced, then and ever so many times later on. The Chinese original and the English rendition are such a perfect fusion that one could imagine a reincarnated Cao Xueqin would have written exactly like David Hawkes and a reincarnated David Hawkes would have written exactly like Cao Xueqin.

As a result of decades of isolation from the academic world outside China, the name David Hawkes was completely unknown to me, nor did I have the means in those days to find out anything much about him. As much as I admired his miraculous achievement and as much as I wondered about personal contact with him, I knew for a certainty that the chance of meeting the legendary scholar–translator was not slim, but non-existent. At that time if someone had predicted that about ten years later I was going to meet him and spend days together with him at his home in Wales I would have dismissed the idea as a pipe dream.

One evening in late autumn, 1980, I was invited by a close friend of mine from my university years to meet two English colleagues of hers at the city's Foreign Languages Institute. The young English couple I was introduced to were John and Rachel Minford, with their two-year old son Daniel. When I was told that Rachel was David Hawkes' daughter and John his son-in-law, I had a momentary sensation that the world had suddenly shrunk considerably for me. The great translator, who had so far only existed in my imagination, seemed magically brought in front of me, through the magic looking-glass of his close relations.

In my subsequent conversations with John I learned much more about David Hawkes' work on *The Story of the Stone* than I could have done from any other possible source available. He also told me about his own involvement and share in the translation of the *Stone*. In those days, conditions for contact between Chinese and foreign staff members could hardly be described as encouraging. But we still managed to see quite a bit of one another, for interesting and seemingly never-ending discussions on translation, cross-cultural understanding etc., as well as mere socialising. Very soon a firm friendship had developed between us. Towards the end of their stay in the city John presented me with a cassette tape on which he had recorded his reading of

Matthew Arnold's "Dover Beach", one of my most-cherished English poems. In a sense it was the choice of this poem that served to clinch our mutual understanding and friendship, a friendship that has stood the test of time over more than twenty years.

In the mid 1980s, I was offered a research fellowship at Oxford University. While in the UK, I had the privilege of meeting with David and Jean, and also the pleasure of spending quite some time together with them as their guest. Our first meeting was arranged by Rachel and John and took place at the Welsh seaside resort of Newquay. One afternoon David and Jean drove over from their home near Lampeter to join us for a picnic on the beach. Because we had already heard so much about one another, the meeting was totally relaxed. We engaged in random conversation over our food. One of the topics we discussed, I still remember to this day, was language maintenance. David asked me how I managed to maintain fluency in my spoken English in a Chinese-speaking environment. I said by practising reading aloud as much as I could. He said that reminded him of what Lord Chesterfield advised his son to do in one of his letters to the boy. When it was getting late David and Jean drove away home.

Later that same year, in winter, I was invited to spend a few days at David and Jean's house in the Welsh hills, with them and two of their grandchildren. When I arrived at the railway station they were already there to meet me and drove me back home. Theirs was a typical Welsh house in the country, not even connected to the main electricity grid and far away from the local hospital. There was a spacious study-studio, but the bookshelves that lined the walls were emptied of their books, which had been donated to the National Library of Wales in the nearby town of Aberystwyth. In this house they lived in seclusion from modern society. They built their own stone walls, grew the potatoes they consumed, and stored summer rain in a water tank for household use. In winter they even collected kindling for their fireplace from the surrounding country.

In the evenings we would sit round the fireplace (Jean, David, the grandchildren, and myself) and chat about whatever topics occurred to us, ranging from David and Jean's years in China, to English dowsing-rods and Chinese copper or porcelain bed-warmers (*tangpozi*)! It was such a delightful experience listening to David's wonderful conversation. His erudition, his sense of humour and his frequent wisecracks in both Chinese and English made him one of the best conversationalists I had ever come across. I couldn't help remarking to myself: Here was a great scholar-cum-writer-cum-translator, one of the greatest of our time, who had absolutely nothing snobbish or pretentious or self-seeking about him. His largeness of mind, his quiet self-assurance, combined with a sincere modesty, and his amiable, approachable mien — all made him a perfect gentleman-scholar, both in the English and Chinese senses of the word. He reminded me of the Confucian saying: "The gentleman is easy and broad of mind, while the small man is always full of insecurity." There is another Chinese saying which could be said to characterise the reclusive side of him: "The peach and plum grove does not speak, but a well-trodden path appears beneath."

Our friendship was further strengthened by reunions later on in other parts of the world. In the summer of 1990 (according to the seasons of the southern hemisphere) David and Jean came to Auckland to visit John, Rachel and the kids. They were also the very first visitors to the new apartment my wife and I had just moved into. Except for a couple of rustic garden benches there was not a stick of furniture in the house on that occasion. But they were too unconventional to mind the bareness. It was at my insistence that they complied to go to a nearby restaurant for an Indonesian meal. Seven years later, in March 1997, David and Jean came to Hong Kong on a family visit. Again we were able to join one another for a day's adventure on the small outlying island of Ping Chau.

From the first time we met each other in 1986 to the time we said goodbye to each other in Hong Kong in 1997 was roughly a period of ten years, during which we were able to gather together four times, the average interval between the reunions being two and a half years. This frequently makes me wonder: How many of my other close friends and relatives have I been able to see with the same frequency during the same ten-year period? None! Not a single one.

When a golfer sends a golf-ball flying and it lands miraculously in the desired or destined hole, some call it a matter of maths and physics; others call it perfect skill; still others call it pure magic. When certain human beings are brought together on a trajectory not exactly totally under their control, some may believe it to be a matter of causality; others may believe it to be human chemistry. But I believe it is karma, or *yuanfen* in Chinese. Hence the above story. Of course, there is no end to this story. As long as the karma is there, the story goes on and on.

JACQUES PIMPANEAU

A Walk in Blenheim Park, and Afterwards

When I arrived in Oxford at the beginning of the academic year in 1963, I phoned Professor David Hawkes, whom I had heard of but never met, for an appointment, since he was to be my director of studies. I was surprised to hear him suggest taking me to visit Blenheim Park the following Sunday. A French professor would have given me an appointment at the end of one of his lectures and would have received me standing for a few minutes. On the Sunday morning, it was pouring with rain. When I came down for breakfast in the college where I was staying, I said to one of the students: "I have an appointment with the professor of Chinese to visit a park; in weather like this, surely he will think that I am an ass if I phone him to ask if the appointment has been cancelled."

"Is this professor English?" asked the student.

"Yes," I answered.

"Then he will not even realise it is raining."

And sure enough, Professor Hawkes arrived in his car, we visited the park, not the palace, in the rain, and he talked about the trees as well as about Chinese studies.

I recall this incident not because of the amusing exchange about the rain but because it was my first experience of a different relationship between teachers and students. In France, this relationship is very distant; teachers protect their privacy like a fortress. It was only after becoming a colleague that I entered the homes of French professors, and then only of a few of them.

Of course, through the unique lectures of David Hawkes on

Chinese poetry and through his tutorials once a week (tutorials are an institution non-existent in France), I learnt much about Chinese literature; but I had also learnt from other teachers, in France and in China. The great discovery was a new approach to teaching. I was surprised to see that the level of the students was much higher than that of French students in the Ecole des Langues Orientales in Paris, where I had first studied. But here in Oxford, the teaching method was also quite classical: studies of texts, use of some tapes, nothing different from what was then used on the other side of the Channel. Since then, in Paris, new methods have been tried, one more modern than the other; new textbooks have been used, one supposedly better than another, but the result has always been disappointing — probably because methods of teaching are like washing machines: it is not necessarily the latest model which is the best. Thanks to my experience with David Hawkes, I understood that the superiority of English students was due to this different relationship between teachers and students. In France, students are obsessed with marks; they are not in a university to learn as much as possible but to pass exams, and they are only interested in what they might be asked in an exam. A teacher is first and foremost a judge. I discovered by going to David Hawkes' lectures that examinations never came into consideration, that you were offered certain knowledge and were free to do whatever you liked with it, that you were entirely responsible for your studies, you managed them at your own speed, you developed your own personal interests. During his tutorials, you were discussing with an equal (it took me some time to get used to this), the only difference between you being that he had some information and points of view you did not have and that he was willing to share them with you. In France, specialists have a tendency to jealously keep for themselves the best of their knowledge, like private property. I was astonished how the former attitude could make you draw the best out of yourself. When I came back to teach in France, I always thought of David Hawkes as a model in this respect. Even if by the end the French system got the better of me, at the beginning at least I also used to invite students to my home, before there were just too many of them. I tried to be severe during the year because of the French system, in order to be lenient at exams. I even caught David Hawkes' illness, of judging young people at exams on the basis of a few papers: to break them by failing them made me sick right up to the end, and one of the pleasures of retirement is to have escaped this duty. I often remembered something David once said: "We laugh at tribes with their cruel initiation ceremony, but we do the same with our doctorate: after it, you are one of us."

The other thing I learnt from David Hawkes was a certain kind of humility. Every time he taught you something, he almost seemed to be apologising. The sinologues I had known before spent all their time criticising their colleagues, but in David's case that jealousy was replaced by consideration! One day, David Hawkes came to see me with his new book, *A Little Primer of Du Fu*, saying that it might be useful to students. I thought to myself: that is the kind of book which I would like to write and which I might be able to write; not a book for specialists, but one which might be interesting for students and common people, which gives access to texts.

I don't know if teachers realise where their influence lies. They probably think that it is through what they teach, while in fact, for better or worse, it is much more through their personality. How many teachers have put students off their subject or led them down blind alleys through their attitude! In my case, I was lucky: I had met the man who opened up a whole way for me by his behaviour, never by instruction. I do not mean that David Hawkes shaped my personality — thank God, he was never a guru; but he made me realise possibilities in myself, which I then preferred to develop rather than others. I could have tried to make a career; ambition is always a temptation. After those two years in Oxford, I decided to limit myself more to the role of a primary school teacher, teaching Chinese language and culture in the Ecole des Langues Orientales: the students there start from scratch. Feeling a bit ill at ease in the French system of education, I seized the opportunity of a gift from Mr. Kwok On in Hong Kong to create a small museum; I had dreamed of this museum as a place to introduce some aspects of Asian cultures, as an annex to the regimented world of university teaching, as a kind of centre for the general public and not only for future specialists. For me, such a museum was not a place in which to keep rare and precious objects and to show only some of them, but an entirely didactic place that at the same time would excite the imagination. I added to it a puppet troupe to complement the teaching on Chinese theatre, thinking that students would learn as much by trying to adapt a Chinese play for a French audience with Chinese puppets as by listening to theoretical teaching. The idea was not to train actors or puppeteers: we performed only a few times on the streets for fun, and passed round a hat to collect enough money to have a good dinner together afterwards.

I collected objects only if, through them, it was possible to introduce what constitutes the popular culture of different Asian countries, the visual aspects of the stories which are known there by all classes of society. I was not interested in fine arts and archaeology; there are already museums for that. So, I was led to exhibit anything connected with theatricals, masks, costumes, musical instruments, and with myths, paintings, engravings, rubbings, as well as their evocation in religious rites. Why did I choose stories as a subject? Because I like stories, but also because to transform anything into stories is a characteristic of the human mind: while we sleep, our brain transforms physical impressions into dreams, discomforts into nightmares, hormonal changes into erotic dreams; the revolutions of stars and planets gave rise to myths; and science is probably the last story that man tells himself. There is a French saying: "Tell me what company you keep, and I shall tell you who you are"; one can also say: "Ask a culture which stories it tells and you will understand it." If an Asian student wanted a first acquaintance with Western civilisation, he could start with Greek theatre and Shakespeare plus some stories from the Bible. Sometimes students thought I was not very serious since in class I used to tell Chinese stories and act them out a bit to make them more palatable, but I was glad to hear them saying later that, once in China, they found that the knowledge of these stories was most useful: they had a common language with the Chinese that went further than being able to say "Give me a beer" with a perfect accent.

But I could never convince French bureaucrats of the interest of the Kwok On collection, which they classified as folk art — that is to say, something inferior, without great value. This is the reason why finally the entire contents of this museum ended up in Lisbon, Mr. Monjardino, the president of the Foundation Oriente, having had the intelligence to immediately realise the interest of this collection. But I am also grateful for the contempt that I met with in France; it obliged me to think about this term folk art.

What does it mean? Art created by "the people"? But "the people" do not create, only individuals do, even if they remain anonymous. It probably is this artist called Anonymous who has created the largest number of works of art. Does folk art mean art created by artists coming from a low social class? To adopt this position obliges us to call the Sistine Chapel and the Moses in the church of Saint Peter in Chains folk art, since Michelangelo came from a poor family. From the point of view of art and creation, the term folk art has no meaning. A real artist, whoever he is, for whomever he works, always goes beyond his social origin. As Diderot said of himself and his father, "I do not descend, but ascend from a barrel-maker."

But it is true that we can talk of two kinds of art. On the one hand, we have works done with the aim above all of making art, of showing a personal approach to reality, an individual eye on the world. This is the reason why such works are signed. It is what is called in Chinese the art of scholars. On the other hand, we have artists who work rather in the spirit of artisans, who do not want to create Art, but who care for a job well done. When we consider what they do, we realise that in fact most of their work is related to religion, so that, instead of Fine Arts as opposed to folk art, what is relevant is religious art as opposed to secular art, which does not mean that spirituality is absent from the latter. In Europe, this difference is obvious over time: in the art of the

Middle-Ages, a statue or a painting of Christ was first of all Christ before being a statue or a painting; and in the art of the Renaissance, a painting or a sculpture became first of all a work of art and was considered as such. The policy of museums is misleading: when they exhibit Fine Arts, they only show real works of art; when they exhibit folk art, they mix paintings, sculptures, and engravings with pots, baskets, tools, and utilitarian objects. But art, be it folk or not, is only art when there is a thought behind it, even if this thought, as in contemporary art, is a will to destroy art.

In China, these two kinds of art existed and, in a way, still exist together: the art of scholars survives even now although many contemporary artists prefer to compete with modern Western creations where cultural differences tend to disappear, the same types of works being done in New York, London, Tokyo, and now Peking. But there is also a religious art, still alive in villages in some regions, which, because it is classified as folk art, is neglected in the histories of Chinese art. If we take the religious statues or paintings of deities for temples and family altars, we immediately see a difference in style with the traditional art of scholars. While the art of scholars is enclosed in the rules of a certain code of aesthetics as defined by Xie He, Zhang Yanyuan or Shitao, religious art has to obey other rules: the artists have to paint or sculpt deities in order to make them present, to give them a shape in order to make them tangible, so that they can be venerated. They have to follow rules that are neither the rules of chiaroscuro or perspective, nor the norms of *The Mustard Seed Garden*, nor the different types of strokes used in calligraphy; but Guan Yu must have a red face, the God of Wealth must hold an ingot, the God of Earth must look like an old man, so that each deity can be identified. Such works have to be gods before being works of art, and this is also true in tribal art and in Western religious art (the Virgin Mary must have some characteristic so as to be recognisable).

Because this religious art creates the supernatural, its realism has nothing to do with what is usually called realist art. Within the rules just mentioned, it enjoys a freedom of imagination and of humour that the representation of the visible world cannot have. The consequence is a unique charm not found in other types of art, which is clearly visible for example in the popular woodblock prints called New Year pictures. As a painter friend said after visiting an exhibition of traditional Asian folk art, "When one sees these works, one realises that Picasso did not invent much." Thanks to ethnographers, collectors, and now even museums, tribal art has started to be considered on the same level as the Mona Lisa; but what is called folk art in China as well as in other parts of the world is still looked upon as a marginal curiosity, probably because it is disappearing and has become a cheap production for tourists. Since the coming to Paris of a *dixi* troupe from Guizhou, the masks of that region are now made on a large scale, at high speed, just to sell as decorative objects. When we remember that this folk art was in fact a religious art, it is not surprising that it follows the destiny of religion and cannot survive as such when the gods tend to die.

It is true that folk art is not always religious and sometimes has a purely decorative aim, which is also the case with the paintings decorating the Palace of Versailles or the entrance halls of some modern hotels. The Chinese woodblock prints representing scenes from novels or operas, or flowers, and the paper-cuts to be stuck on windows, these cannot be classified as religious art. But at the same time religion is rarely absent even in this decorative art. To understand the paper-cuts made by villagers — not the very fine ones just made for sale — it is necessary to know some of the beliefs of these village women, as Professor Jin Zhilin demonstrated in his book *The Good Luck Dolly*. The woodblock prints of scenes from novels or operas show heroic characters who, in popular religion, are considered to be incarnations of stellar powers. Some motifs are chosen for the way they sound in Chinese: fishes are chosen because the word fish is homophonous with prosperity; cocks and halberds, because the words for these are homophonous with auspicious; peaches, because the Queen Mother of the West in her heavenly garden cultivates them, the peach being the fruit supposed to grant immortality; pomegranates, because of their many seeds, alluding to the wish to have a large descent. These motifs, which could seem entirely decorative, are in fact the expression of wishes posted as prayers to the gods for a good destiny and they illustrate the Chinese creed that words create things, that words call forth reality. It is this belief which leads to the fourth floor being omitted in some lifts, because the word four is homophonous with death.

If, rather than talking of religious art, we want to keep the term folk art in order to distinguish it in China from the art of scholars, then we have to admit that it refers neither to the spirit in which it is done, nor to the origin of its creators, but only to the people for whom it is intended. The art of scholars wants to seduce a public made up of other scholars, of rich or powerful people who pretend to have a monopoly over good taste. Having the upper hand in society, they dictate fashion, they call what they collect Fine Arts, and they despise all the rest; and the bureaucrats, who are their servants, naturally follow their prejudices. Folk art then only means art that is made for common people, and as such it respects their creeds, their way of thinking, their imagination. But the two types of art are not as antagonistic to the other as they may seem; there have always been cross-currents and influences between the two, and the scholars and the élite have to admit that what they call folk art is also part of their culture, even if they have the regrettable tendency to look down upon it from their snobbish heights. The history of Chinese poetry shows that once a poetic genre had said all that it could say, the poets turned to folk songs for inspiration. In the case of Chinese literature, one has to be cautious: what is officially called popular literature often in fact consists of novels or plays written by scholars <u>for</u> the people. *The Story of Yingying* by Yuan Zhen transformed into the play *The Western Pavilion* is not folk art; it was adapted to drive morality into the minds of people expected to be obedient subjects of the State. There is a real folk version of that story, which I found in Shanxi Province: it ends tragically like the story by Yuan Zhen, but with a magical atmosphere peculiar to folk literature.

Call one folk art or religious art, and the other Fine Arts, as you prefer; but each has to be judged with different criteria, they have to be considered as the manifestation of two kinds of spirit. From an aesthetic point of view, which is another approach, both are seen with the same eye, and both include more or less beautiful works; but élitist art should not prevent us from appreciating works whose only fault is not to have been made for the so-called élite. Since I created the Kwok On Museum to introduce the popular culture of different Asian countries to a Western public, it was natural to have collected folk art. I had a satisfying experience the other day. I organised an exhibition of Chinese woodblock prints in a gallery otherwise devoted to the most modern art; the workers who came to help with the installation said it was the first time they had actually liked what was exhibited there. It is not surprising: there is an extraordinary kinship between the folk arts of different civilisations. Paper-cuts are to be found from Japan to Portugal, and if you were to put them next to one another it would be difficult to identify the origin of some of them. The same experiment could be done with other genres. The conclusion is that the differences between social classes within a single culture are much more important than the cultural differences between one country and another. This was what struck me the first time I went to China. Communication with a Chinese teacher or artist was immediate, much more so than with a French peasant or worker. Leftist intellectuals boast of knowing the common people; ask them how they know them and they answer that it is because they talk to taxi drivers. We brought a group of peasants to France who performed shadow theatre. They performed in the Guimet Museum; the bourgeois audience looked at them with sympathy but just as if they were animals in the zoo. They were then taken to French villages. The local peasants immediately invited them for dinner and, in spite of the language barrier, they were all on the same wavelength. The most amusing incident was when the Chinese peasants were looking wide-eyed at the TV, and the French villagers asked them what they liked best. "The naked girls in the ads," answered the Chinese. "That's what we guessed," answered the French, "so we have already recorded them for you. Here is the tape." This incident helps us understand why ancient feasts (I mean ancient festivals, not the boring degenerate ones of today) and moments of revolution such as the events of May '68, create such nostalgia: they are the only moments that unite those who believe in heaven and those who don't.

I failed in France — I could not convince the local bureaucrats of the interest of introducing stories through objects, of a museum intended for a Western public. I have chosen to present my defence in this volume in homage to David Hawkes because, with his open-mindedness, his sense of humour, his taste for art and literature never enclosed in élitism, he may agree with this small point raised by a former student.

MARGARET T. SOUTH

Images of Xi'an, 1984

In the autumn of the year one thousand nine hundred and eighty-four I travelled to Xi'an, the site of the former Tang dynasty capital, Chang'an. On arriving at the railway station I found the city enveloped in thick mist and although I knew that, except for the Greater and Lesser Wild Goose Pagodas, nothing of old Chang'an remains, I still could not help peering about, hoping to catch a glimpse of a famous landmark, an Imperial palace, a Chief Minister's mansion, a courtesan's dwelling, a poet's abode. Next morning, when the sun came out, I could see plainly that such no longer existed. Nevertheless not everything had changed. The poet Du Fu once wrote:

> The state is in ruins but the mountains and rivers still remain.

This line embodies an enduring truth. The grand man-made structures of Tang Chang'an may no longer exist but, in the surrounding countryside, the fine natural landscapes noted by literary men of that time can still be observed, the broad sweep of the Wei river, the extended range of the Southern mountains, the emerald ripples on the Taiyi lake, the white stones in the Wang stream.

In the ensuing months, as I went about the city or wandered in the countryside, I came to realise another truth: that modern Xi'an was not after all so very different from Tang Chang'an. Whereas the appearance of the city may have changed, essentially the people were the same, going about their business and performing their daily tasks very much as they had always done, their shoes coated with the same dust, their carts impeded by the same mud of which their Tang ancestors had so often complained.

Recently, when sorting through a box of old papers, I came across some poems I had written recording this period in my life. Remembering that an old friend, the retired scholar David Hawkes, is about to celebrate his eightieth birthday, I have selected eleven of the poems to present to him. I have written this preface for them and have entitled the collection *Images of Xi'an, 1984.*

෩

Within the Passes

On a mild morning in early autumn I am distracted from my study of the early history of this area by a large bee hovering just outside the insect screen.

Western Zhou lies on my desk,
Guanzhong before my window.
Cicadas sing as in the Ya,
Crickets chirp as in the Feng.
Beyond the wall men dig and shovel,
Within the wall women sweep and dust.
Past and present, where does the difference lie?
Perhaps I'll ask this yellow bee.

On Buying a Kettle

East street is always full of people,
In the bicycle enclosure there's never any room.
The Department Store appears more crowded still,
The aisles are narrow and it's difficult to move.
I want to buy myself a kitchen kettle,
The whole of Shaanxi Province gathers round.
One by one the kettles are brought out,
Unused to buying kettles I am troubled and confused.
An old man from the countryside then speaks,
Taking a kettle in his calloused hands.
"This," he says, "is a kettle from Zhongshan,
No better brand of kettle to be found!"

The Greater Wild Goose Pagoda

Continuous rain, six days and nights,
Suddenly the sun, a warm clear morning.
From eaves and gutters water drains away,
On paths and steps mud powders into dust.
Crowding balconies, umbrellas drying out,
Dividing courtyards, lines of airing bedding.
Boiling my kettle I look out the window,
Between two trees the top of a pagoda.

In Search of Double-Happiness

Winter begins with several falls of snow,
Fearing the cold I purchase extra bedding.
From the quilt store, cotton dense and thick,
In the cloth shop, damask smooth and sleek.
Phoenixes or love birds, difficult to choose,
Green or scarlet, not easy to decide.
I like the red but am shown it will not do.
"Double-Happiness, old miss, is clearly not for you!"

The Chinese Hen

Outside our gate some peasants selling hens,
Brought by bicycle, they hang by their feet.
Though upside down their heads are twisted up
To keep their combs from trailing in the mud.
They know that this is not their natural state,
But spare our ears vain squawks and cacklings.
Tucked in a basket or suspended from a stick,
They quietly submit to whatever be their fate.

The Canna

A large cock struts by the courtyard wall,
This way and that it shakes its fiery comb.
But why I wonder are its feathers green?
Tossed in the wind a single scarlet bloom.

The Eight Immortals

Climbing in the mountains south of Xi'an, I come across a small cave.
Inside it, behind an iron grill, eight painted figures representing the Eight
Immortals are crammed together in a small space.

Long had I heard of the Eight Immortals,
Now, by the path, an Eight Immortals' shrine.
Seeking herbs they wandered among clouds,
Drinking dew they rested beneath pines.
People feared they followed a capitalist road,
Seized and questioned, their views were criticised.
Closely confined they huddle in a cave,
Firmly restrained they languish behind bars.
Peasants offer incense and fresh flowers,
Better to give them room to move about!
Now policies have changed to "Open door",
Can't someone come and let the Immortals out?

The Woodcutters

Taiyi Lake is hidden in thick mist,
Even the clouds no longer can be seen.
Seeking shelter we come to a woodman's hut,
Father and son kindly invite us in.
As we eat our lunch we watch them both at work,
First with a square, then with an inked string.
Trimming the bark, each log clean and white,
Planing the knots, each pole smooth and straight.
Daughter-in-law runs to fetch us tea,
Anxious to please she brings three thermos flasks.
Grandfather waits by the open door,
Again and again he offers cigarettes.
A straggly beard, no hair on his head,
A toothless smile, hands calloused and brown.
By means of signs we manage to have a chat,
And before I leave he tries on my fur hat!

The Pig

Walking in the mountains south of Xi'an I come across a peasant family
preparing to salt a large pig they have just killed.

Remote indeed the peaks of the Southern mountains
A place for hermits among the floating clouds.
Climbing high through intermittent rain
I rise above the city's dust and grime.
The sound of water flowing over stones,
A glimpse of sunlight slanting through the pines.
Of these I've read in many ancient poems,
For these I've left my daily cares behind.
All I lack is a small thatched hut,
And a rustic table on which to set my wine.
But the one I find it seems I'll have to share
With a stuck pig and a vat of steaming brine!

The Dog Market

Passing through a village near Mawei slope west of Xi'an, I notice a number of large dogs congregated. Upon enquiry I find it is the day of the weekly dog market.

If you need protection, why not buy a dog?
Fierce and loyal, it becomes a family friend.
When past its prime you can slaughter it for food,
The flesh is eaten, the skin goes on the floor.
But a dog, they say, is difficult to kill,
Sensing its fate, tears form in its eyes.
When strung by the neck at the end of a rope,
It may struggle for days until finally it chokes.
If your wife objects, then sell it at the market,
She'll thus be spared its look of hurt reproach.
The people are poor, no cash for gun or bullets,
But how can they smile when telling me about it!

Eternal Spring

Walking in the countryside south-east of Xi'an we stop to look at some tomb mounds near the village of East Five. Falling into conversation with a Mr Song whose given names are Yongchun (Eternal Spring), we ask him how old they are.

Descendant of Qin is Song Yongchun,
His native place the village of East Five.
Father, grandfathers all born here,
Sons and grandsons till the neighbouring fields.
Flanking the road, the tombs of ancient kings,
Hidden in grass, figures of weathered stone.
Who cares if they are Qin or Han?
Past and present here in this one man!

MICHAEL SULLIVAN

The Spanish Doctors

We called them the Spanish Doctors, although none of them were Spanish. But all but Mann, who had been in a German Concentration Camp, were doctors, from Germany, Austria, Poland, Czechoslovakia, Hungary, Roumania and Bulgaria. Communists and Socialists, they had volunteered for service with the Republican army in Spain, and when the Republicans were defeated by Franco, ended up as refugees in a camp in the south of France. There they were discovered by the China Campaign Committee in Hong Kong, looking for doctors to work with the Chinese Red Cross. They were brought to China, and went out with Red Cross units to front-line hospitals. But as the war dragged on, the fighting died down, the front line melted away, and the units were withdrawn one by one. More and more of the Spanish Doctors (who in any case were politically suspect) found themselves languishing at Red Cross Headquarters outside Guiyang, with nothing to do; bored and restless, it was getting harder and harder for them to keep up their morale. This was not what they had come to China for.

What was I doing there? My stint driving trucks for the International Red Cross had come to an end — a large contingent from the Friends' Ambulance Unit had taken over — and I was working on the designs for a new brick and tile hospital to replace the crude mud and thatch blocks put up in haste earlier in the war. The identity of the Chinese girl referred to may be guessed by some of my readers.

❧

There was a shuffling of feet in the narrow passage between the rooms. The door creaked open and Lao Wang, the soldier-servant, came in with a dirty paraffin lamp which he placed on the table in front of Kriegel, who had been reading for some time in the gathering dusk. Outside it was raining, and Lao Wang's gray padded coat with its long-armed red cross on the chest glistened wet in the lamplight. Kriegel looked up, thanked the boy with a curt *xie-xie* (thanks!), and went on reading. There was something massive, intense, and a little oppressive about Kriegel, with his easy mastery of languages, and his air of assumed authority over the rest of the Spanish Doctors. Lao Wang was terrified of him and gave him an uneasy look as he slid out, the door grinding on its wooden hinges. The room became quiet again.

The dormitory for the foreign doctors, occupying one end of a long thatched building, comprised four small rooms separated by thin wood partitions. There was no privacy. Over the partitions and through cracks in the planks you could see into the next room. No movement, no whisper, was secret. If anyone went out or came in, you heard it; if they had anything to eat, washed their hands, pulled a suitcase from under a bunk, you knew it. So we were silent in our movements, till Kriegel's deep voice, or Coutell's high tenor, reached over the partition to someone in another room.

One of the rooms was reserved for the women doctors, and the doctors' wives. It was Manya, the small, compact Roumanian, who looked after most of the men. In the evening her shrill voice would call out that the coffee or the peanuts were ready; there would be a scraping of stools, doors would swing open, and six or seven men would crowd into the little room and eat and drink hungrily.

But now, the room was quiet. Manya and some of the men were down in Guiyang, buying wine and cakes for a party. The other two women sat silent in the room. Courtney, the English doctor, was poring over a book with the air of dry efficiency that she always wore. A masculine woman, her body was lean, her face strong, her hair short and straight. Two years of medical work in India had given her an insight into Hindu mysticism that contrasted strangely with her practical, downright manner. She took no interest in her appearance, unlike Manya, who was proud of her breasts, massaging them with cold water every morning, and wearing tight clothes that embarrassed the Chinese staff.

The other occupant of the room, a Chinese biologist, seemed not to belong there. Young, slender, lively, with a certain child-like beauty, she was working in the physiology laboratory, and carried about her a seemingly care-free air that contrasted with the rather charged atmosphere that surrounded the Spanish Doctors, and became heavier as the year drew on. They would have been less than human if they had not envied her.

Condemned to idleness by official jealousy and their some-times less-than-diplomatic protests at official corruption and inefficiency, the Spanish Doctors knew that they would get no more work at the Red Cross. Coming to China with almost missionary fervour, Courtney had had no work for ten months; Kaneti, the romantic young Bulgarian, had not been out for a year. Mann, the young German with the memory of Dachau, where he had always been cold, was dragging out his days in futile chemical experiments in a hut, lavishing all his pent-up affection on his decrepit old dog, Le Vieux Pétain. Fat, curly-headed Baer, Jungermann, suave and doctrinaire, and a few others, were still at the Front. They were the lucky ones.

Across the passage Mamlock, gentle, smiling, soft Mamlock was fussing over something — an electric torch, or a microscope, it was hard to tell what. Generous, willing, and hopelessly incompetent, he was the butt of the group, and its slave. He could be heard muttering and exclaiming to himself, like a child with a toy.

The silence deepened. Outside, it was quite dark. The thin rice paper flapped in the windows, and, as the thatch became soaked, water began to drip from the roof in two or three places; slowly and dully onto a bed, flatly onto the floor, and after a few minutes,

striking a tin basin with a sharp sound. One felt only sounds —
the water dripping, the paper snapping in the window. And
gradually one became aware of the sound that was to accompany
us through the night — the rats. They were timid at first, gnawing
quiet holes in inaccessible places under beds and behind boxes.
But as the night wore on they would venture out across the floor
in the flickering lamplight at our feet. When the lights were out,
they would run madly about, chasing each other with hysterical
shrieks over tables and beds, up walls and along shelves,
knocking over tins and toothmugs, dropping again with a thud
onto our beds where they would suddenly stop, sitting up on their
haunches. They ate soap, and candles. The paper in the windows
afforded an excellent paste, as did the backs of books. Combs and
buttons were gnawed, and if we were foolish enough to leave
anything edible in a coat pocket or under a blanket, holes were
drilled till it was reached. The night was theirs, and unless the din
was enough to wake us, they did as they pleased.

I had somehow got hold of a rat-trap, and with foolish
gallantry had set it, attached to a chain, under the bunks in the
women's room next to the one I shared with Kriegel, Mann and
Coutell. Often in the night we would be woken up by a rattle of
the chain, a squeal, and a cry from Manya: "Herr Sullivan! Herr
Sullivan! Noch ein Ratte!" accompanied by more squeals and the
sound of the chain dragged across the floor. I would get up, go
next door, grope around under her bunk for the chain, drag out
the trap, remove the rat and take it out to end its days in a bucket
of water; then set the trap again, and go back to bed. An hour later
would come Manya's cry again, "Herr Sullivan! Herr Sullivan!" and
the ritual would be repeated. I cursed the day I bought that trap.

The time was seven in the evening. There was a sound of feet
on the path outside. Manya came in, dapper in high boots and
riding-breeches, then Coutell, carrying two stoneware bottles of
Maotai, the powerful wheat and sorghum spirit of Guizhou,
cunningly lashed together with string. Behind him came sturdy
little Freudmann, with the serious frown of a schoolboy,
handsome Kaneti, and Mann, who had not shaved for several

days, giving his face, with its prominent nose and heavy jaw, a false suggestion of dignity and command. Old Pétain trotted in behind him, and the cakes and peanuts were dumped on the table. The Chinese girl smiled, then got up and went out quietly. They hardly seemed to notice that she had gone, and started to prepare the feast.

Kaneti was singing, leaning back on his bunk, staring at the charcoal glowing in the brazier on which his feet were resting. Mamlock's eyes were glistening. He was slightly drunk, and thinking, I imagined, of his mother. He wasn't used to Maotai, and the fiery spirit made him want to giggle. Mann, Coutell and Friedmann sat on the bunk opposite Kaneti. Manya was rocking herself back and forth on a stool, while Coutell was looking at Courtney with some concern. The party was for her. She was touched, but rather at a loss, for they sang in Russian, German and Spanish, never in English.

The remains of the feast lay on the table — an odd assortment of cups and mugs, crumbs, coarse brown paper and peanut-shells. Kaneti was singing the haunting Russian song *"Serdtse"* ("Heart") and at the chorus they all joined in — except for Courtney, who didn't know the song, and Mamlock, who was tone-deaf— Coutell's high, clear tenor, Kriegel's resonant bass, Mann's coarse nondescript bellow, and Manya, singing stridently through her nose. Then it was Mann's turn. He gave a raucous rendering of several rude students' songs (*"Es war ein Kuh ..."* I forget the rest), and the recruits' song beginning:

Der Hauptmann, der Hauptmann kam geritten, geritten
Auf einem weissen Bok.
Es meinten, es meinten die Rekruiten,
Es war der liebe Gott.

> The captain, the captain he came riding
> Upon a snow-white goat.
> They thought — did the recruits, the recruits —
> It was the Lord God himself.

But now their mood was sombre. They sang, as always on these occasions, *"Die Moorsoldaten"*, the forbidden song of the concentration camps, with passionate feeling, as if they themselves were the prisoners — as in a sense they were. I only remember one of the verses, and the last:

Auf und nieder geh'n die Posten,
Keiner, keiner kann hindurch.
Flucht wird nur das Leben kosten —
Vierfach ist umzäunt der Burg.

> Up and down go the guards.
> No one — but no one — can get through.
> Flight will only cost you your life.
> For the camp is surrounded fourfold.

But when they came to the last verse, with the hope of release, their singing became almost heart-rending.

Doch für uns gibt es kein Klagen —
Ewig kann's nicht Winter sein.
Einmal froh wir werden sagen
"Heimat, du bist wieder mein!"

Dann ziehen die Moorsoldaten
NICHT MEHR mit den Spaten
Ins Moor!
Dann ziehen die Moorsoldaten
NICHT MEHR mit den Spaten
Ins Moor!

> Yet for us there's no lamenting;
> Winter cannot last for ever.
> One day, with joy we'll say
> "Home — you are mine again!"
>
> Then, never again will the Moorsoldiers
> Trudge spade in hand out onto the moor. (repeat)

That night the group was making a deliberate effort to be

more cheerful, for Courtney's sake. After nearly a year doing nothing, she had just received orders to go east to Zhejiang Province to work in plague prevention on which, coming from India, she was thought to be an expert. She was ecstatic, very flushed, and talking all the time through excitement rather than fear. She was a person of great physical courage. Courtney had not been in Spain, and so was not considered politically suspect by the Guomindang officials. She was spared the supreme irony of the Spanish Doctors who had come to China to fight, as they thought, for democracy against fascism, only to be placed under what amounted to house arrest as enemies of the state. Courtney had arrived in Guiyang believing in the Empire, the menace of Communism, and Theosophy. The Spanish Doctors had got to work on her, methodically and without reserve, and turned her into a passionate Marxist. She was perhaps too willing to sit at their feet. Of the whole group, only Coutell was sensitive enough to see that she had something to give — Coutell, who as a boy had symbolically burned his bible — and under her influence he had undergone a subtle change, or perhaps she brought out an aspect of his personality that our degraded life had left no room for. There was in his half-French, half-Lutheran upbringing an intellectual refinement that the others seemed to lack, and there had developed between him and Courtney a purely platonic attachment that was oddly touching in the emotional wilderness in which we lived.

There had always been long discussions after the singing, on China and the iniquity of the government, on economics and imperialism. When I told them I thought that India was not yet ready for independence, they all stared at me in disbelief. They had never encountered an unrepentant British Imperialist in the flesh before. Often the talk was about Soviet society, when some rather starry-eyed views were expressed; there were reminiscences of the Spanish Civil War, stories of life at the Front, and occasionally dry, intense debates on philosophy. These had become more frequent since Courtney's coming, and had taken a different turn. But that night she seemed to be feeling the effects of the Maotai. She looked feverish, a sore had inexplicably opened on her foot, and the party broke up. The men went back to their rooms talking among themselves, and went to bed. The Chinese girl came in — she always seemed to know when to come back — and undressed. The lights went out one by one, leaving only the candle by which Kriegel continued, as usual, to read far into the night. Soon the rats were gathering under the table in Manya's room, fighting noisily over the peanut-shells. Courtney tossed on her bunk, and mumbled in her sleep.

Next morning, she was still feverish, and unable to get up. She complained of pains in her head and neck. Through the day, she got worse. Towards sunset she became delirious. At eight o'clock one of the Chinese doctors came in and made a lumbar puncture; he was astonished to find that the spinal fluid had thickened to such an extent that it could barely enter the needle. But there was no doubt about the diagnosis: meningitis.

Coutell and Manya were busy in the small room. Curious people — soldiers, servants and others — crowded round the door gazing with a detached fascination at the body of the strong foreign woman breaking down. Her eyes, wide open, stared at the ceiling. The sound of her breathing filled the room. It would slowly become louder and more stertorous till it reached a rasping cough, then lapse into a silence so profound that she seemed to have stopped breathing altogether; then gradually the harsh note would come and the crescendo begin again. At intervals, she muttered "Plague! I've got plague!" in an anxious and pitiful voice. She never closed her eyes, but stared fixedly upwards.

There was nothing to be done. Coutell, Kriegel and Manya stayed in the room, watching the shrinking figure on the bunk. The Chinese girl had slipped away to make room for them, and the rest of us were silent in our rooms, reading or trying to read, or thinking of nothing.

Ten o'clock passed, then eleven, and the rats came out on their nightly forage. They were bolder than usual — the place was so still. Only Courtney's breathing, and an occasional sound as someone shifted on a stool, broke the silence.

Now Courtney was choking, and it seemed that someone (most likely Coutell) put his hand over her mouth, and that eased her breathing, which was coming faster and faster.

Towards three o'clock in the morning the silence became so deep that we thought her breathing had stopped. No one moved. Under a bunk, a rat was gnawing something, but there was no other sound.

Coutell said something in a low voice. Kriegel answered. Then it sounded as though Coutell had moved. Suddenly, from the depths of her unconsciousness, Courtney uttered two quick, tiny cries, "Ah! — Ah!" It seemed to us listening that for a brief moment before death she was aware that she was dying, that she struggled up to the surface of conscious life by a great effort, remained there an instant, and then sank back into the darkness. At that moment she died.

For a long time no one moved. Then Coutell sighed deeply, got up, and closed Courtney's eyes. Kriegel came into our room and told us what we already knew: "She is dead."

The shrunken body was disposed decently. Manya covered Courtney's face, then got out her tin basin and washed her hands. Coutell came in, and undressed slowly. He was silent for a long time, sitting on the edge of his bunk. Then, half to himself, he said, "*Sie war ein guter Kerl*" — "She was a good sort" — and put out the light.

GÜNTER WOHLFART

Bergerie de Chauvette

Do you know the Way? You don't? Never mind. I don't mean the "Great Way", I only mean the small way to our mountain cottage, the "Bergerie de Chauvette". Sometimes people come and visit us here in Southern France near **Tu-chan** (a sinologist's hyphen) because of our **home products**. Our home products: that is, the fine woollen textile Barbara produces out of the mohair of our mountain-goats, not the crazy texts produced by me, the would-be mountain-man from Mount Tauch.

Well: one day David and Jean and the young birds of passage John and Rachel made their long way up to our white-cloud-cuckoo-land on Mount Tauch. It was Jean and David's first visit to our mountain refuge. To find us, you have to take the "Route de Faste". After a time you reach "Notre Dame de Faste", the ruined and deserted "Ecclesia de Fausta" (Latin, **Faustus**?). It's a **favourable** place to pick wild asparagus and think quietly about "Heavenly Questions", for example those from *The Songs of the South*. Beyond our Lady's place, the way starts to get difficult. The autumn floods destroyed parts of it and made free and easy wandering <u>un</u>easy. Nevertheless, the wayfarers arrived.

We sat outside in the open and "broke the crust" together. John and I were joking about hermits on "cold mountains" — our cottage faces north-east. David, looking far away, mentioned the old Greek "Garden-philosopher" Epicurus — you know — the one who said that we should laugh and philosophize at the same time. This brought us to his contemporary, the Chinese Epicurean who, according to Wang Wei, did nothing but stroll around in his Lacquer Garden counting trees ... We concluded, like *Candide*, that "il faut cultiver notre jardin"....

David stood to one side, silently regarding our mountain refuge, saying quietly: "Isn't it a real *shanzhuang*," thus bringing old Master Zhuang to Mount Tauch. This was the Chinese baptism of our Bergerie de Chauvette as *xiaoyao shanzhuang*.

So we chatted about mountain-goats, mountain-paths, and the difficulty of free and easy wandering (*you*); or should I translate it as "free and easy <u>floating</u>"? — since our way had been partially flooded.

Talking about floods and rivers brought to mind the story of that big gourd, a gourd much bigger than the stuffed one we ate together with David, Jean, and the Minfords at Fontmarty. You remember: the old boy Zhuang recommended using it as a great tub, so that one could go floating around in it on the rivers and lakes instead of worrying about its uselessness.

By the way: doesn't this story go well with the "poetic" interpretation of the Chinese character *xin* which is explained as a man in a boat, loosening the oars? Couldn't the man in the boat be David practising *xin zhai* and *zuo wang*???

Anyway: David sat to one side facing due south, as if he was "sitting and forgetting"... I looked at him and was a bit worried about his *wu xin* — state of mind — but suddenly he looked at me as if he wanted to say: Never mind!

The others were drifting aimlessly along in their conversation about the wild life in the Tuchan outback.

Entre chien et loup our visitors decided to make their way down. When they were gone, I looked back thinking of David, saying to myself: "I had expected to meet an author, a well-known translator who has made a name for himself, but I met more. I met a man who knows how to transcend his name, a wayfarer who has left name and fame behind — and 'arrived': *zhi ren wu ming.*"

The following foolish little "chinglish" Haiku is dedicated to David:

loosened oars
free and easy floating
of course

Günter, der große Hohlkopf vom Tauch

LAURENCE WONG

The English Stone
For David Hawkes, on His Eightieth Birthday

黃國彬

說英語的石頭
賀霍克思教授八十華誕

多年來，大家都以為，青埂峰下
只有石頭一塊，用中文刻成。
然而，你在牛津退隱多年，
在英國的江湖久無消息；
再出現時，攜來另一塊石頭，
說的是英語，頻率與漢語相同。
於是，大家才知道，媧皇補天，
留下的石頭有二：一中一英。
說英語的，由你，在牛津隱遁後，
跟閔福德往大荒山無稽崖尋回。

For years and years they spoke
Of a single Stone
At the foot of Greensickness Peak,
A single inscription carved in Chinese.
But after years in your Oxford hermitage,
Little heard of on River and Lake,
You re-emerged with another Stone,
A tale told in English,
On the same frequency as the old one,
The Chinese one.
And that was when we knew:
Nü-wa, when she repaired the sky,
Had left not one Stone, but two,
Two blocks unused,
A Chinese and an English Stone.
You fetched the English one,
And from your hermitage
Set out upon your quest,
With that young disciple of yours,
Back to the Incredible Crags
Of the Great Fable Mountains.

Translated by John Minford

Part 2

Essays

Rock and Flower Midstream

Pieter Holstein

To David
in recognition and with love
pieter and marianne from quintillan

STEVE BALOGH

Under the Shadow of the Bomb

Life and Entertainment in Newly Liberated Peking

In 1949 the Chinese Communists had every reason to dislike and
distrust the U.S. It was the U.S. that had helped Chiang Kai Shek
on many occasions during the civil war and had declared its
hostility to Communism. The U.S. government in turn thoroughly
distrusted and disliked the regime of Mao Zedong. The Americans
were hurt, angry and frightened by the Communist victory. They
were hurt because they felt they had done much for China and
were receiving no thanks for their pains. Their missionaries had
for a century regarded China as their own chosen field of activity.
Money had been poured into hospitals and orphanages. Now, in
1949, it was clear that sooner or later the missionaries would be
expelled. American money had been invested in Chinese
industries. It was equally clear that the businessmen would be
expelled. The Americans felt that their atomic bombs had
delivered the Chinese from the Japanese invaders. But there was
no gratitude for their efforts. They were frightened because in
1949 it seemed that Communism was spreading to every part of
the world: all of Eastern Europe had become Communist since
1945, and now the most populous country in the world had a
Communist government, and their Soviet allies were about to
become a nuclear power. American–Chinese hostility was to
remain a constant theme of Chinese foreign policy for decades.
The American occupations of Japan and South Korea, like the
French colonial administrations in Indochina, were explicitly anti-
Communist, and were based largely on pre-existing bureaucracies

of collaborators detested by their fellow countrymen, and on Japanese nationals with undisguised right-wing credentials. When on 24 July 1948, after a bogus election in South Korea, Syngman Rhee became the puppet leader of a repressive regime and the Stars and Stripes were hauled down and replaced by the new flag of the South Korean republic, General MacArthur, gauleiter of Japan, made a bellicose speech in which he told the Koreans, "An artificial barrier has divided your land. This barrier must and shall be torn down." When an attempt was made to fulfil this very same aspiration a couple of years later (by the North Korean and Chinese forces), the U.N., now devoid of any Soviet representation, because of their refusal to recognise the Peoples' Republic, mobilized first U.S. and British, then Australian, and finally Turkish forces to frustrate it under MacArthur's very command!

Up to and throughout the War of Resistance to Japan the Comintern had, in remarkable consonance with the U.S. State Department and most other agencies that might have provided the Eighth Route Army with the means to fight, insisted on an alliance with the K.M.T. This was despite Chiang Kai Shek's avowed determination to eradicate Communism from China before turning the offensive on the Japanese. Thus the only arms with which the Japanese had been opposed during upwards of a decade of occupation, were those that had been captured either from them or else from K.M.T. forces sent against the Red Army. It is not surprising really that after Hiroshima/Nagasaki and the suddenness of the Japanese capitulation, the Red Army was seen as the only force to have taken the field against the Japanese occupation, or that the greater part of the population rallied to their leadership in liberating the country.

By 1949, when Stalin announced the U.S.S.R.'s first atom bomb test, Chinese assessments of the world situation were as follows: firstly, they needed to be steeled for the universal condemnation that would follow the military defeat of the K.M.T. and the expulsion of those who would not repudiate it; and secondly, they should take into account, perhaps considerably in advance of the rest of the international community, the fact that nuclear weapons transform the situations of all parties, not simply of those who possess them and those they threaten with them.

There were still in China a number of westerners who were neither missionaries nor businessmen, but teachers, doctors and journalists who because of their commitment to Liberation were not facing expulsion. In the years of privation during and following the Japanese occupation they had, in the absence of any forms of public entertainment, acquired the habit of making their own. Some of them took the opportunity offered by the first ever National Day, to create an entertainment which sought to indicate to a (predominantly intellectual) audience, the machinations and conspiracies that the newfound Chinese autonomy might be expected to encounter. The photograph on page 11 shows David Hawkes with William Empson and Hetta Crouse, his communist sculptor wife; Hetta, together with a number of friends, created the puppet show illustrated on the following pages.

When he arrived in Peking David Hawkes was accommodated, along with other single foreign teachers and students at Bei Da, at a purpose-built Japanese interrogation unit for POWs, Dong Chang prison which had been converted to a hostel. Empson held a British Council subsidized post. Linda Greer the British Council chief in Nanjing had had Empson moved north so that, during the siege of Peking, Empson had cycled between Bei Da and Qing Hua (where he also gave classes), crossing enemy lines there — and back!

Hetta also gave English classes and together with Ronnie Parker put together a puppet Shakespeare. She was a renowned sculptor and made a bust of Pannikar, the first ambassador representing India to the People's Republic. She, Walter Brown and the New Zealander Max Bickerton (who could do some of the funny voices) collaborated on an ambitious puppet show celebrating the victory of Communism in the Far East and lampooning the schemes and subterfuges of the imperialists.

MacArthur was in the lead role and Syngman Rhee and Chiang Kai Shek in supporting parts, while the Man from the Foreign Office and General de Gaulle provided some subsidiary business.

MacArthur was by far the biggest puppet, and the Mikado the smallest, dangling from MacArthur's swagger stick. In some scenes there is a Japanese Doxy (with voice by Max Bickerton). She was almost as big as MacArthur and she wore a full-on Geisha outfit that must have made her very difficult to handle on-stage.

Beside the forces of Liberation there was also a Nuclear Genie who sprang, like a jack-in-the-box, out of a black trunk marked Top Secret. Facing one way it was a devil with a death's head, but its reverse side was an angelic figure — supposedly the Workers' Bomb — the first successful nuclear device to be exploded in the U.S.S.R. earlier that year.

Korea was around the corner, when MacArthur would threaten his enemies with atomic weapons. Dien Bien Phu was a little further on down the road. The use of the bomb on Japanese targets had meant that the Japanese occupation had collapsed very suddenly which left the Red Armies in the field with a huge advantage over the Nationalists. The K.M.T. had neither engaged with the occupation forces, nor were they therefore in any position to take over the strategic vantage points the Japanese abandoned.

To the Yan'an leadership waging the war of Liberation, it must have seemed as if nuclear weapons had transformed the nature of warfare. Perhaps they were the first to realize exactly how radically this was in fact the case. I do wonder what the script for the Nuclear Genie's part actually was, but I have been unable to excavate anything by way of dialogue for the pictures reproduced here. David himself recalls that the sound effects, which must have been dominated by choruses of the Internationale, included a wind-up gramophone for which the only record they had been able to find was the Moonlight Sonata!

Note on the Photos and the Surviving Puppets

These photos are not the sole evidence for this talented collaboration; the smaller puppets still exist and were given to Linda Queen by Hetta. The MacArthur and Geisha puppets have vanished. I am grateful to Linda for the loan of both puppets and photos. I wrongly believed the photos were an early example of colour photography until it was pointed out to me they had been painstakingly hand coloured! Clearly, they were not snapped live in action during a performance, but were carefully posed and carefully lit for a session expressly devoted to recording the achievement for posterity. The captions for the photos are mine, and tentative.

An interesting sidelight on the puppet show is to be found in a contemporary diary, an entry written during August 1949, by a young officer from the Royal Corps of Signals, based in Japan, on "special duties" in Peking:

> *Friday fifteenth*... In the evening we were invited to some puppet show, something to do with the British Council I think it was, but went to see "Flying Down to Rio" instead, but spoiled by some clown letting off an air raid siren.

> *Saturday sixteenth*... Tommy went to the puppet show and had much more fun. Came back with black eye and minus a tooth. On a charge, but in the meantime one of his horrendous hangovers. Apparently a fight broke out between the Yanks and our boys, but it wasn't as bad as I had feared. One of the Yanks threw a puppet at the bloke we call Lord Muck, but the effigy of Uncle Joe caught Tommy in the eye and he tripped and knocked his tooth on the table. Uncle Joe in smithereens. Another feller from Blighty with long beard goes berserk and bops the Yank. General mayhem, tables turned over etc. Tommy not sure who won...

It is fascinating to discover that by this time the show included Uncle Joe. And as for the "feller from Blighty with long beard", one assumes that he must have been William Empson!

An earlier puppet show — from which I also have some of the surviving puppets — is referred to in the following extract provided by John Haffenden, William Empson's literary executor and successor at Sheffield University:

> In the first weeks after 1st October 1949 the Empsons set great store

by the prospect that the United Kingdom would presently recognise the PRC; and the infectious enthusiasm of their many social contacts — gatherings with Chinese and foreign friends alike — sustained the hope ... Max Bickerton, whom Empson had last seen in Tokyo in 1933, turned up in Peking and jumped at the offer of a teaching post at Bei Da. Similarly, Hetta Empson happily took on a regular class in English Conversation — "So I do four hours a week of gossiping with the students," she reported. "They are really quite good. I have twenty-six and the English Department got a better enrolment than people thought likely ..." Out of class, she and Walter Brown spent a good deal of time making the puppets for a "real Punch and Judy show, because we discovered that Max Bickerton can do the manipulating and talking"; and Ronnie Parker built a "fine booth, six feet high and three wide ... with lovely red and white stripes, and it folds up." Typically, Bickerton could not resist a little mischief: "Max made the Doctor say to Punch, 'I can't waste my time on lower middle class cases like yours.' So Punch poked him in his lower middle until he was dead." The upshot might have been predictable: when they presented their show at the Peking Club, a number of tots had to be carried out screaming; and Mrs Clubb, wife of the U.S. Consul General, commented with splendid ambiguity: "We should have asked more adults." (Later they proposed to go around the countryside, like a traditional Chinese travelling puppet show, though with a repertoire of "some new Chinese plays".)

Photographs: A Peking Puppet Show

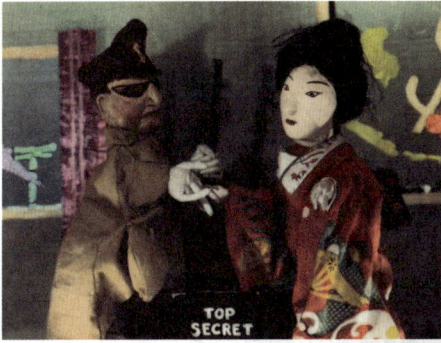

1. MacArthur hectoring his Japanese Geisha: "This here is my secret weapon and gives the U.S. power to do a Hiroshima any place…"

2. MacArthur gives Syngman Rhee his marching orders: "You do what you're told, buster, or I'll turn you over to the Communists, see?"

3. The Mikado dangling from his baton, MacArthur forces the Geisha to kowtow to both of them: "This little guy is your emperor, poppet, and I'm his boss, see—so lick my boots!"

4. Chiang Kai Shek gets a drubbing from MacArthur (the Geisha listens in): "You're a general? —so where's your army? You're just a puppet generalissimo, and when the gloves are off, it's always someone else props you up!"

5. and 6.

MacArthur interrogates his Nuclear Genie.

"A-bomb, A-bomb in my trunk
Why is Truman in such a funk?"

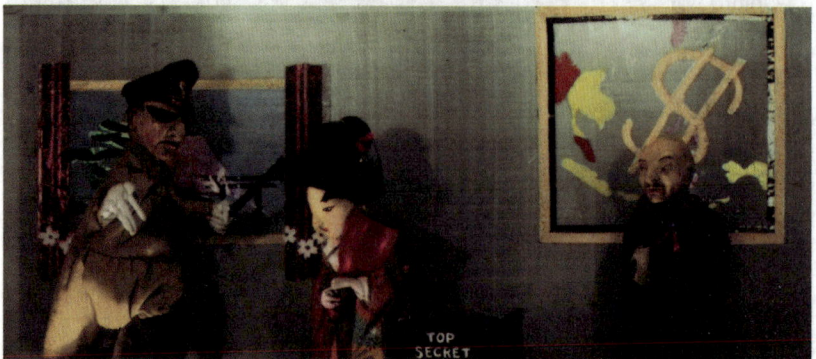

7. MacArthur outlines his wild-west plan for the Far East to the Geisha; Chiang Kai Shek listens in, rubbing his hands with glee: "Those goddam Commies'll have to capitulate or we'll drop an A-bomb on Shanghai!"

8. Syngman Rhee requests U.S. assistance for some dirty business: "The Communists will win the election unless we rig it …"

9. MacArthur and the man from the F.O. share a joke: "Nuclear weapons make the Opium Wars look like a puppet show!"

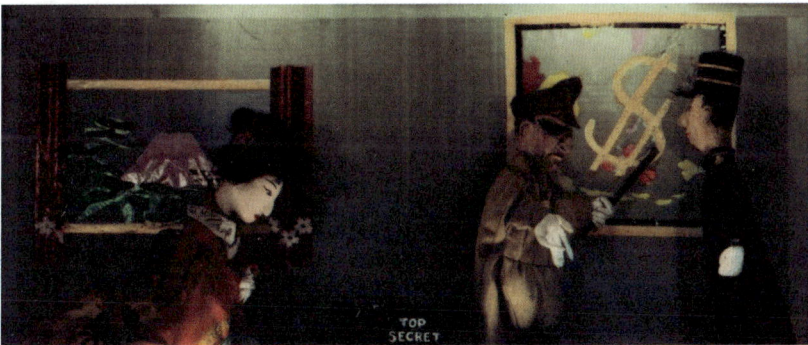

10. MacArthur has a go at bullying General de Gaulle: "Whatever you Froggies get up to in Indochina, you're on your own, Mon General …"

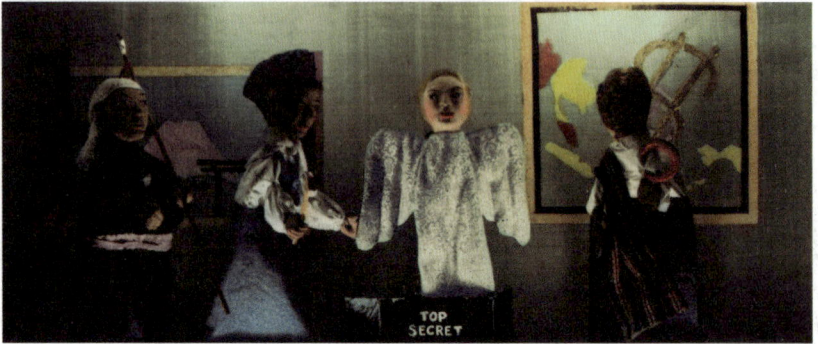

11. The workers, peasants, and subject peoples take possession of the Nuclear
    Genie: "Behold, under the stalwart leadership of Comrade Stalin and the C.P.S.U.,
    an atomic bomb has been developed to defend working people all over the
    world!"

12. And with It on their side,
    a war of Liberation is
    internationalised, and
    imperialism confronted
    wherever it seeks to
    establish itself.

13. The forces of Liberation arrest General de Gaulle, Chiang Kai Shek, and
    MacArthur's Geisha puppet government: "We know you're the dupes of U.S.
    world dominion, and up to no good!"

14. The workers despatch Syngman Rhee, MacArthur, and the man from the F.O.: "Oppressors! On your knees!"

15. The Bad Guys take a boo.

16. The Good Guys sing a Grand Finale chorus: "Arise ye starvelings from your slumber …"

CHOW TSE-TSUNG

The Origin of the Title of The Red Chamber Dream

Professor David Hawkes' attendance at the First International Conference on *The Dream of the Red Chamber* at the University of Wisconsin-Madison in June 1980 made the participants overjoyed that a major English translator of the novel and one of the best Sinologists was among us. As an organiser of that conference, I particularly appreciated his enthusiasm and effort to participate in all of the discussions and activities.

David Hawkes has spent almost his entire life studying Chinese language and literature. He even resigned his professorship from Oxford University in order to commit himself to translating the novel. Such devotion would have made the novelist Cao Xueqin feel honored if he were alive today. Professor Hawkes' English translation of another most difficult Chinese classic, *Chuci* 楚辭 (*The Songs of the South*), has also been universally acclaimed. Having had similar interests in Chinese literature and history, I admire Professor Hawkes' immeasurable contributions to his field, and treasure my longtime friendship with him. To celebrate his eightieth birthday on July 6, 2003, I am dedicating this article to him with my best wishes.

೧೪

Many scholars know that the earliest title of Cao Xueqin's novel was *The Story of the Stone* (*Shitou ji* 石頭記), but in his later years, Cao allowed the use of *The Red Chamber Dream* (*Honglou meng*

紅樓夢) as its overall title ("總其全書之名"). I gave a lecture on this subject at the National University of Singapore in 1987, and a revised version of the lecture is included in my book, *The Case of the Red Chamber Dream: Redological Articles of the Deserted Garden* [*Honglou meng an: Qiyuan hongxue lunwen ji* 紅樓夢案：棄園紅學論文集] (Hong Kong: The Chinese University Press, 2000).

Redologists have no difficulty in knowing how the title *The Story of the Stone* was formed, but as for the title *The Red Chamber Dream*, it is quite obscure. Although we may find in some poems and lyrics of the Tang dynasty that the ideas of "red chamber" and "dream" are closely connected, the closest similarity to the title of the novel only appears in a poem, "On the Cuckoo" ("*Yong zigui*" 咏子規), by Cai Jing 蔡京 of the Tang dynasty (circa 8th–9th century, not to be confused with the Song-dynasty chief minister of the same name, Cai Jing [1047–1126]). It is an eight-line "regulated poem" (*lü shi* 律詩) with each line containing seven characters. The parallel couplet of its fifth and sixth lines, translated roughly and literally, reads as follows:

> Frozen are its (the cuckoo's) tears along the Purple Frontier against the wind,
> (Its cries) Frighten and break hearts in the red chamber dream.

> 凝成紫塞風前淚，
> 驚破紅樓夢裏心。

> *Quan Tang shi* 全唐詩, *juan* 472.

One can easily recognize the phrase "the red chamber dream", appearing for the first time in the Chinese language in the second line of the couplet, but no one can be sure whether or not Cao Xueqin adopted the phrase from this poem for the title of his novel. When I read the first line more carefully, I came to believe that Cao definitely did adopt the title of his novel from this couplet.

Perhaps I should first clarify a few points in Cai Jing's poem. The bird "cuckoo" in Chinese is usually called *zigui* or *dujuan*

杜鵑, or simply *juan* 鵑. According to a popular myth, in ancient times a king in the area of modern Sichuan Province loved and had relations with a beautiful woman. Because of this affair, he was compelled to give up his throne, and was transformed into a cuckoo. As the story relates, the bird cried persistently until its beak bled. Other sources say that the cuckoo lived not only in western and southern China, but also along the Great Wall on the northern frontier. The term "purple frontier" (*zi sai* 紫塞) has been used by Bao Zhao 鮑照 (424–466) in his well-known *fu* 賦 which is anthologized in the *Wen xuan* 文選 (*juan* 11). It has been explained by annotators that the earth of the northern frontier was purple in color, hence it was called the "purple frontier". But, to my knowledge, the term's being related to the cuckoo appears merely in Cai Jing's poem as cited above.

Now, it is known that in *The Red Chamber Dream* (or *The Story of the Stone*), the heroine Black Jade (Dai-yu 黛玉) has a most intimate maid whose name is Purple Cuckoo (Zi-juan 紫鵑; David Hawkes named her Nightingale). Whereas many works have been devoted to finding the origins of the main characters' names in the novel, no one has provided a convincing explanation for the name of Purple Cuckoo. I am quite sure her name originated in the first line of Cai Jing's couplet quoted above. As a matter of fact, in Chapter 62 of the novel, Lady Xiangling 香菱 (Caltrop) has a discussion with Lady Shi Xiangyun 史湘雲 about the names of two major characters Bao-yu 寶玉 and Bao-chai 寶釵. Xiangling cries out, laughing, that she has found the origins of their names: "Both their names are from Tang poems!" ("他兩個名字，都原來在唐詩上呢！") This is the novelist himself revealing that the names of the characters originated in Tang poems. Thus, to say that the name Purple Cuckoo is based on a Tang poem may not be as far-fetched as we think.

If in fact Purple Cuckoo's name originated in Cai Jing's couplet, and no better sources can be ascertained, it is easy to accept that the title of the novel, *The Red Chamber Dream*, came from the same couplet. In my view, it cannot be a coincidence.

JACQUES GERNET

Sur notre perception du monde

En témoignage d'amitié, puisque c'est l'un de ses grands anniversaires, j'ai réuni ici pour David quelques textes de Wang Fuzhi (1619–1692), auteur chez qui on peut trouver des idées intéressantes et, d'une certaine façon, très modernes. Peut-être ne lisons-nous pas assez longuement et d'assez près les ouvrages des penseurs chinois. Nous n'avons pour cela qu'une excuse: ce qu'ils ont écrit est prodigieusement étendu et nous demande bien souvent de grands efforts de compréhension.

L'œuvre de Wang Fuzhi n'échappe pas à la règle[1] et, bien qu'on y reconnaisse partout la marque de son esprit, elle traite de sujets très divers: il n'est parfois compréhensible que grâce aux rapprochements qu'on peut faire entre différents passages de ses écrits. On sait bien que les Chinois ne cherchaient pas à donner un exposé suivi de leurs idées. Comme disait le grand missionnaire jésuite Matteo Ricci, mort à Pékin en 1610: "Comme c'est un fait qu'ils ne connaissent aucune dialectique, ils disent et écrivent toute chose non pas de façon scientifique, mais confuse, au moyen de propos et discours divers, autant qu'ils peuvent comprendre en suivant la lumière naturelle."[2] On peut penser cependant que, si les Chinois répugnaient à tout système, c'est parce qu'ils avaient un sens aigu des phénomènes vitaux: de même qu'on ne peut véritablement expliquer ce qu'est un être vivant parce qu'il forme un tout dont toutes les parties sont interdépendantes et parce qu'on ne pourrait expliquer pourquoi il vit une fois qu'il serait mort, de même les Chinois ne pouvaient exposer leurs idées en opérant sur elles cette mise en ordre systématique qui ne peut se faire qu'une fois qu'elles sont mortes.

Le thème que j'ai abordé ici très brièvement, en rapprochant des passages parfois très éloignés les uns des autres, a trait au décalage qui existe entre les témoignages de nos sens et la réalité de l'univers. Le monde que nos sens nous font connaître nous est particulier et fait partie de ce que Wang Fuzhi appelle "le Ciel de l'homme" *(ren zhi tian)*. Ce monde, dont le bouddhisme affirme qu'il est une création de notre esprit, mais dont Wang a tenu à montrer au contraire qu'il n'était ni absurde ni irréel, correspond seulement à l'image très particulière que nous pouvons en avoir et aux conditions de vie qui nous sont propres. Si imparfaits qu'ils soient, nos sens nous donnent la seule lueur que nous ayons sur l'univers. La différence des nôtres avec ceux des animaux serait à elle seule une preuve de sa valeur:

"Chiens et chevaux voient en pleine nuit," dit Wang. "Les hiboux sont aveugles en plein jour. Le dragon entend avec ses cornes, la fourmi parle avec ses barbes. L'ouïe et la vue n'ont pas (chez eux) de sièges définis; ce qui influence les perceptions et ce qui est perçu sont différents *(ganzhe yi er shouzhe shu)*. L'homme meurt dans l'eau, les poissons meurent sur la terre ferme … Goûts et profits diffèrent suivant les espèces. C'est pourquoi ce que l'homme sait du monde est pour lui son Ciel et ce que les animaux en perçoivent est le leur *(gu ren zhi suo zhi, ren zhi tian ye; wu zhi suo zhi, wu zhi tian ye)*."[3] Empruntant à des thèmes traditionnels, Wang revient sur cette extrême relativité des perceptions et des goûts entre les hommes et les animaux dans un autre commentaire:

"Lors du festin à la porte de Lu, les beaux airs de Yunmen et de Shaohuo firent s'envoler avec des cris plaintifs les oiseaux qui s'y étaient perchés: leur ouïe ne s'y accordait pas; à la vue de ces femmes si célèbres par leur beauté qu'étaient Qiang de Mao et Shi de Xi, les poissons se cachèrent au fond des eaux et les oiseaux s'enfuirent: leur vue ne s'y accordait pas.[4] … En dégurgitant ce qu'il a pris pour nourrir ses petits, le corbeau pense faire acte de sollicitude à leur égard; le hibou croit manquer à la piété filiale en ne dévorant pas en entier ses père et mère: désaccord sur le bien … Ce que Yao et Shun récompensaient, Qin le punissait de mort."[5]

De la thèse de Zhang Zai (1020–1078) d'après laquelle il existe une énergie invisible dont les combinaisons sont à l'origine de tout ce que nous pouvons percevoir, Wang conclut qu'il existe un au-delà de nos perceptions. "Comme la puissance des yeux humains," écrit-il, "atteint ses limites dans l'infiniment petit (*wei*), les hommes tiennent pour inexistant ce qu'ils ne peuvent voir. La capacité de l'esprit humain atteint ses limites dans l'immense, la puissance de la vue et de l'ouïe atteint ses limites dans l'infime."[6] Mais "ce que nos yeux ne voient pas n'en est pas moins doué des propriétés du visible. Ce que notre ouïe n'entend pas n'en est pas moins doué des propriétés de l'audible. Des propos que nous ne comprenons pas n'en (peuvent) pas moins être doués de sens. C'est pourquoi il est dit: 'Ce qu'on sait, savoir qu'on le sait, ce qu'on ne sait pas, savoir qu'on ne le sait pas, tel est le vrai savoir.'[7] Dans ce qu'on sait, il subsiste des choses qu'on ne sait pas, et savoir cela, c'est cela le vrai savoir. En procédant ainsi et en tirant toutes les conséquences de ce qu'on voit, l'aspect de ce qu'on ne voit pas apparaîtra clairement … Ne pas être arrêté par ce qu'on ne sait pas (parce qu'on ne le perçoit pas) et chercher à le connaître, c'est là qu'est la grande différence entre l'enseignement du grand sage et les doctrines hétérodoxes (qui, elles, se fondent sur les données vulgaires de la perception sans chercher au delà)."[8]

On ne trouve pas seulement chez Wang le relativisme typiquement chinois dont toute son œuvre est inspirée. Le plus remarquable est la conséquence qu'il en tire: si nos sens et ceux des animaux sont aussi différents, c'est que, contrairement à une idée naïve, notre appréhension du monde est inexacte et approximative. Dans un autre commentaire au *Daya* où Wang vise à réfuter la thèse bouddhique d'après laquelle notre esprit crée le monde, il termine sur cette remarque: ce que nous percevons ne correspond pas nécessairement à ce qu'est le monde. Ce qu'il est réellement est inaccessible à nos sens.

"De jour, nous ne voyons pas les étoiles, mais nous savons qu'il y a des étoiles. De nuit, nous ne voyons pas le soleil, mais nous savons qu'il y a un soleil. Quand bien même (nous ne les voyons pas), il y a des nombres (qui nous permettent de calculer l'emplacement des étoiles et la marche du soleil). Nous avons la certitude[9] que, même sans eau, l'antique miroir *fangzhu* peut recueillir la rosée, que, même sans être enflammés, sophora et mûrier sont inflammables. Quand bien même (nous n'en ferions pas l'expérience), il y a des associations constantes (*lei*) (qui nous permettent d'en être assurés)…[10] Ce que nous voyons, entendons, sentons par le toucher, percevons par notre esprit ne sont pas des choses que nous serions capables (de créer) par nous-mêmes:[11] tout cela vient du Ciel. Ce ne sont pas des réalités qui existent certainement dans le Ciel (la nature) (*fei tian zhi bi you shi*). Tous ces témoignages de nos sens sont (des réalités du) Ciel de l'homme."[12]

De cette idée d'une inadéquation fondamentale entre notre vision du monde et sa réalité, Wang Fuzhi tire une conclusion des plus audacieuses. L'homme tend tout naturellement à imaginer le monde d'après ses propres critères, à y projeter ses propres cadres mentaux. Mais ces critères n'ont de sens que dans les conditions particulières et relatives où il se trouve. Ils ne peuvent valoir pour l'activité de création et transformation incessante de l'univers:

"L'homme distingue les quatre points cardinaux afin de se repérer par rapport à ce qu'il a devant ou derrière lui; il se conforme à la distinction du passé et du présent, du commencement et de la fin pour donner un ordre à ce qu'il voit et à ce qu'il entend. Il en est ainsi assurément pour ce qu'il perçoit[13] et pour ce qu'il pense à la suite de ce qu'il a perçu,[14] mais du point de vue du principe d'organisation spontanée (*li*)[15] et des énergies (*qi*) (*yin* et *yang*) (qui sont à l'œuvre dans l'univers), il n'est pas vrai qu'il y ait un avant et un après. Dans l'absence de toute orientation temporelle ou spatiale du chaos (*hunlun hu wumen*) dans lequel le principe d'organisation dirige les énergies, le commencement est aussi la fin, le créé est aussi l'origine du créé, ce qui est au repos est aussi ce qui circule, ce qui se sépare est aussi ce qui s'unit. Il n'est rien qui ne commence, rien qui ne soit achevé."[16]

"Je ne sais comment le Ciel aurait une fin," dit encore Wang Fuzhi, "ni pourquoi la Terre aurait un commencement. Le commencement et la fin de la Terre et du Ciel n'auraient-ils pas lieu aujourd'hui-même?"[17] A quoi fait écho cette formule de Diderot: "Tout change, tout passe; il n'y a que le grand tout qui reste. Le monde commence et finit sans cesse; il est à chaque instant à son commencement et à sa fin."[18]

Chinese Texts

1. 犬馬夜視，鵂鶹晝闇，龍聽以角，蟪語以鬚。聰明無方，感者異而受者殊矣。人死於水，魚死於陸⋯⋯歆者異而利殊矣。故人之所知，人之天也；物之所知，物之天也。〔尚書引義卷一，皋陶謨，270–271。〕

2. 雲門、韶濩之音，饗爰居於魯門，而悲鳴去之，耳無適聲矣。毛之嬙、西之施，魚見之而潛，鳥見之而飛，目無適色矣⋯⋯烏反哺以為慈，梟以不盡食其父母之為不孝，心無適賢矣。唐、虞之所賞，嬴秦之所誅⋯⋯〔詩廣傳卷四，大雅，一九，論生民，451–452。〕

3. 人之目力窮於微，遂見為無也。心量窮於大，耳目之力窮於小。〔正蒙注卷一，太和篇，28。〕

4. 目所不見，非無色也。耳所不聞，非無聲也。言所不通，非無義也。故曰「知之為知之，不知為不知」。知有其不知者存，則既知有知矣，是知也。因此而求之者，盡其所見，則不見之色章⋯⋯不迫于其所不知而索之，此聖學、異端之大辨。〔思聞錄內篇，401。〕

5. 晝不見星而知有星、夕不見日而知有日；雖然，猶有數也。方諸無水而信其水，槐柘無火而信其火；雖然，猶有類也⋯⋯目之所見，耳之所聞，身之所觸，心之所覺，非己能之而皆天，非天之必有事而皆人之天。〔詩廣傳卷四，大雅，一，論文王二，438。〕

6. 東西南北者，人識之以為嚮背也。今、昔、初、終者，人循之以次見聞也。物與目遇、目與心諭而固然者如斯，舍所見以思所自而能然者如斯。要非理氣之但此為先，但此為後也。理之御氣，混淪乎

無門，即始即終，即所生即所自生，即所居即所行，即分即合，無
所不肇，無所不成。〔周易外傳卷七，説卦傳二，1078。〕

7. 夫天，吾不知其何以終也。地，吾不知其何以始也。天地始者，
其今日乎！天地終者，其今日乎！〔周易外傳卷五，繫辭上一，
992。〕

天地之終，不可得而測也。以理求之，天地始者，今日也，天地之
終，今日也。〔周易外傳卷四，未濟一，979。〕

Notes

1. Les œuvres complètes de Wang Fuzhi dans la dernière édition en 15
   volumes, le *Chuanshan quanshu*, publiée par le Yuelu shushe,
   Changsha, 1988–1996, comptent près de 13,000 pages, ce qui ferait, sans
   notes ni commentaires, quelque 30,000 pages une fois traduites en
   français, à supposer que cette traduction soit possible. Les textes de
   Wang Fuzhi sont cités ici d'après cette édition.

2. "Ma conciosiacosachè non sappino nessuna dialectica, tutto dicono e
   scrivono, non in modo scientifico, ma confuso, per varie sententie e
   discorsi, seguendo quanto col lume naturale potettero intendere." *Fonti
   Ricciane edite e commentate da Pasquale D'Elia S.I.*, vol. I, Rome,
   Libreria dello Stato, 1942, p. 39, paragraphe 55.

3. *Shangshu yinyi* I, *Gaoyaomo*, 270–271. [Chinese Text 1.]

4. On a ici des thèmes qu'on retrouve en particulier dans le *Zhuangzi*,
   chap. XVIII, le *Guanzi* et le *Xunzi*.

5. *Shiguangzhuan* IV, *Daya*, 19, poème 245, *Shengmin*, 451–452. [Chinese
   Text 2.]

6. *Zhengmeng zhu* I, *Taihe*, 28. [Chinese Text 3.]

7. *Lunyu* II, 17.

8. *Siwen lu*, note 2, 401. [Chinese Text 4.]

9. Le mot *xin* s'applique à tous les phénomènes dans lesquels on peut
   avoir confiance (*xin*) parce qu'ils se reproduisent de façon absolument
   régulière.

10. Puisque ce que nous ne pouvons pas voir n'en existe pas moins, cela
    justifie selon Wang ce que dit le poème sur le roi Wen des Zhou qui,
    d'après le *Daya*, se trouve après sa mort à gauche et droite du Souverain
    du Ciel (*zai di zuoyou*). Wang emploie ici le mot *lei* dans un sens plus
    large que le sens habituel d'espèce ou catégorie.

11. *Neng* est ici transitif. Wang reprend la terminologie bouddhique qui distingue le sujet (ce qui a capacité), *neng*, de l'objet, *suo*.
12. *Shiguangzhuan* IV, *Daya* 1, poème 235, *Wenwang* 2, 438. [Chinese Text 5.]
13. Littéralement: lors de la rencontre de ses yeux et des choses.
14. Pour ce qu'il est capable de penser par lui-même quand il laisse de côté ce qu'il a vu.
15. Cette tradition du mot *li* est déduite de tout un ensemble de textes de Zhang Zai et de Wang Fuzhi.
16. *Zhouyi waizhuan* VII, *Shuogua* 2, 1078. [Chinese Text 6.]
17. *Ibid.* V, *Xici shang, zhang* 1, 992. Même formule *ibid.* IV, *Weiji*, 979 : "La fin du Ciel et de la Terre échappe à toute conjecture. Mais si on cherche une réponse conforme à la raison, (on dira que) le commencement du Ciel et de la Terre ainsi que leur fin ont lieu aujourd'hui même." [Chinese Text 7.]
18. Diderot, *Le rêve de d'Alembert* (1769), Robert Laffont, coll. Bouquins, vol. I, p. 631.

ALAIN GINESTY

China's Way to the West

First of all, are we aware of how much we owe to China?

We can all name her inventions: the use of silk, dear to well-to-do Roman ladies; gunpowder, which we diverted from its festive origins for use as an instrument of death; the printing press, little used for poetry nowadays but rather for commercial ends; the compass (which however does not stop us from frequently losing our bearings!); porcelain, of course — not to mention the wheelbarrow. Over the centuries these inventions have fundamentally changed life in the West. But — leaving them aside — it would seem useful to try to define what our ways of thought owe to this civilisation which we imagine so remote, yet which in fact exerts an increasingly pervasive and irreversible influence on us, an influence of which we are largely unaware.

At the beginning of the twentieth century our forbears spoke freely with a knowing air of the "yellow peril" which they saw as a military invasion like those of Attila, Genghis Khan or Tamburlaine, spreading over Europe and leaving behind nothing but ashes, death and destruction.

This was a serious misconception of the way our Chinese friends think. At that time the general public had not yet come across the works of the master strategist Sunzi in translation. To infiltrate the enemy ranks, "entryism" in Marxist terms, was only a notion in Lenin's brain. (Incidentally, what became of that autopsy of Lenin's brain so long promised but never made public — if indeed it revealed anything of interest?)

In our opinion the second half of the twentieth century has been characterised by the borrowings we made from the Middle Kingdom. Fifty years ago very few people in Western Europe had recourse to acupuncture, in spite of the pioneering work of the Ricci Institute in this field (as in others where the sixteenth-century Jesuit scholar began the attempt to bridge the two cultures). Nowadays everybody feels competent to distinguish between the energy generated respectively by Yin and Yang.

Who knew anything then about the martial arts? Barely a handful of fanatics. And there were few practitioners. Whereas today the energies of any over-active child can be controlled and enhanced through Kungfu or Qigong without anybody raising an eyebrow — quite the contrary.

In 1950 how many Chinese restaurants were there in Paris, apart from the Latin Quarter? Certainly very few, whereas nowadays in France (whose cuisine is considered supreme, especially by the French ...) one restaurant out of every six or seven — around eighteen per cent — is Asian. And despite the large number of Vietnamese employed in their kitchens, the dishes most often served in these restaurants belong to one of the main Chinese culinary traditions.

And anyone of a reflective turn of mind must be struck by the contrast between the fall of the Berlin wall and the continuing rise of Shenzhen. Yet the two situations were very similar: it was vital to play down the attractions of West Berlin as compared with the poverty of East Germany, just as it was vital to play down the attractions of Hong Kong as compared with the poverty of revolutionary China at that time. The subtle Chinese did as Sunzi advises and exploited the strengths of their adversary, whereas the brutal Bolsheviks achieved only negative results in the long term: the break-up of East Germany and everything that followed — the collapse of the Iron Curtain and the dissolution of the former Soviet Union.

In the 1960s the Nobel Prize for Physics was awarded to a Chinese (working in the USA) because he had succeeded in jettisoning Aristotle and recognised that a thing could be itself and its opposite at one and the same time. This led the best minds in the West to recall their classical studies (the Latin poet Horace, after all, speaks of a divine infant being "albus et ater", both white and black). They rediscovered the Pre-Socratics and began comparing their philosophy with that of the Chinese. Enlightened sinologues such as François Jullien continue this process today.

We should not pass over in silence the new fashion for Fengshui, which, as the first Chinese restaurant proprietor to arrive here always knew, permits every lady of even the most modest household (thanks to hasty popularisation) to discover the virtues of geomancy, an ancient art long forgotten in the West, except among specialists.

We have already mentioned Sunzi, virtually unknown half a century ago, despite the translations made by Jesuits (the Jesuits again!) in the eighteenth century, and despite the fact that he was studied by the first modern dictator — I refer to Napoleon Bonaparte. Today Sunzi's teachings form the basis of many business management courses, not to mention the training offered by the French Military Academy, where they have finally acknowledged that he goes very much further than Clausewitz, the Prussian strategist most widely read in nineteenth-century Europe.

We cannot be sufficiently grateful to the best European sinologues, who have devoted their lives to making us familiar with the masterpieces of the Chinese spirit: Richard Wilhelm in Germany, Henri Maspero, Marcel Granet and many others in France, David Hawkes and John Minford in the Anglo-Saxon world (with their exemplary translation of *Hongloumeng, The Story of the Stone*).

We should now consider our immediate future: China's recent admission to the World Trade Organisation cannot fail to affect our material circumstances. Already our basic necessities are no longer manufactured in Taiwan or Korea but in mainland China where labour is considerably cheaper and probably more docile, even if technically "free". In this respect our dependence on China will reach unprecedented proportions, and the Chinese will certainly know how to squeeze the maximum profit from it — we may be sure of that!

But in our opinion the essential change has already occurred. It is enough to measure the degree to which western attitudes have changed in the past century. Western travellers no longer go to China to force the Chinese to trade with them (as in the first Opium War of the 1840s and its aftermath) or to "civilise" savages ignorant of the "true faith" and "true values" (our own, it goes without saying).

Until the early 1950s, China, subjected to unequal treaties and practically dismembered by the western powers (and her neighbour Japan, who showed little concern for her as long as it was possible to do so), saw no end to her long decline. But despite the tribulations worthy of a medieval hell which she went on to suffer in the second half of the twentieth century, we behold her now, ready to overcome all obstacles, thanks to the concerted intelligence and energy of her scattered peoples, her worldwide diaspora. Here we have one facet of one of those mysterious "plays of opposites" so dear to Carl Gustav Jung.

It might be appropriate to consider the role — perhaps unique on the planet — of this Chinese diaspora which, without "making waves", has quietly proceeded to acquire a dominant financial, economic and social position wherever it has taken root, an achievement unequalled in any other large-scale migration of the past hundred years. To take an example on a much smaller scale, the Turkish influx into Germany from the 1960s onwards, while displaying an impressive economic initiative, has not exerted a comparable influence.

We only have to think of Vancouver, in Canada, sometimes known as "Hong-couver", where the Chinese (around ten per cent of the population) have fundamentally transformed the atmosphere of the city. But to say more on this topic would go beyond the limits of these simple notes.

In my humble opinion, when it comes to the question of human cloning, it is more than likely that the current European indecision and American intransigence, based as they are on ethical considerations of venerable Judeo-Christian origin, will not hold out for long in the face of Confucian morality, which does not have the same respect for the life of the embryo in its early stages. Before very long, with advanced Chinese research into the medical utilisation of stem-cells of embryonic provenance, we shall see the Americans (and perhaps the Europeans too?) hastily reconsider their position for fear of losing so profitable a market — profitable not just for medicine and human health in general, but for the companies that invest in it....

We should certainly not imagine that the classical wisdom of the Tang or Song dynasties (not to mention their art and literature) is about to transform us at the touch of a magic wand! But if we can see beyond our prevalent monotheisms, which have been, and still are, so rigidly totalitarian — especially since September 11th 2001 — we may perhaps place hope in the Chinese sense of relativity, together with the Confucian sense of social obligation, in the serene tolerance of Buddhism and in the infinite profundity of Taoism (a spirituality so close to that of our Neolithic ancestors — here the link is Shamanism). We may perhaps hope that these influences will succeed in making us more receptive, more receptive especially to our own perennial values, values which we have at long last rediscovered from our Chinese friends, so far from our own world.

Just as the poet Horace, whom we have already quoted, observed of Greece, "Captive, she conquered her conqueror," so China is ready, twenty centuries later, to offer the New-born World (Count Keyserling's *Neuenstehende Welt*) another perspective and other values (a Way, or Meaning, as Keyserling would say) which it lacks at present.

Today the values of the Far West, unlike those of Chinese culture, are centred on an excessive individualism. This goes against the customs of our own traditional societies, which gave a more important role to the structure in which the individual lived — family (nuclear or extended), lineage, brotherhood, urban or professional community, historical nation, linguistic group, etc. Contemporary Western values tend to neglect the general interest, and to be confined to the furtherance of the material profit of their political and economic leaders.

We have great hopes that the Genius of China, as it gradually permeates and transforms us, may help us arrive at a better balance between the individual and society. Unless China, too, turns her back on her own history, dare I say on her destiny, and herself capitulates to current Western materialism?

Translated from the French by Jean Hawkes

JOHN GITTINGS

The Vegetarian Outrage of 1895

It was a steamy summer evening in the South China hills. They had walked out from the bungalows at Huasang, along a narrow little path on the side of the mountain, till they came to an open space looking over the valley. Stands of tall bamboo on the nearest slopes were touched by the setting sun which turned the tips of each branch into golden feathers. They were at the midpoint of an amphitheatre of great peaks, wrapped in soft purple shadow as the light receded. Far-down below through the foothills, the town of Kucheng sat next to the river with a pagoda on a small hill beside. The missionaries pointed out to their children, far in the distance, the silver band of the river, the little wood next to the mission compound beside it, and the paved track through the villages and the paddy fields which led eventually up to their holiday retreat here in the mountains.

Some distance from the town, over towards the hills on the other side, was a temple perched on a small crag. That evening they could hear, across the valley, the sound of flutes and drums, and just see the stage for opera performers.

"Don't they make such an awful screeching sound?" said Topsy Saunders. "I know my head would ache if I was down there. They go on in such an utterly stupid way!"

"Never mind about your headache," said Nellie Saunders severely to her sister. "Think of those poor sinners worshipping idols in their ignorance. You should be blaming Satan, not the noise."

Robert Stewart, the senior missionary in the group, moved away from his own family and from the sisters, walking along the bluff to exchange a few words with Mr Thomas, a young recruit to Fukien province also on summer furlough at Huasang.

"There must be several hundred of them down there," he murmured. "Vegetarians and riff-raff. We are lucky to be well away from town. The magistrate is weak-kneed and will do nothing."

Topsy caught a snatch of what he said. "We're not afraid of them," she cried out cheerfully. "We think they are silly old Vegetables, don't we, Nellie?"

Nellie looked stern and Mr Thomas cleared his throat, as he always did before speaking — it made Topsy giggle. "There is no call to be afraid, young ladies. You have menfolk to protect you and I venture to count myself in that number."

Herbert, the young Stewart boy, fidgeted and tugged his father's hand. "Papa, papa! Ah Cheng says they have spears, and swords, and they can talk to spirits, and they can smash stones with their hands!" He chopped the air sideways with excitement.

"They are heathens," said his father not unkindly, "and we must pray for them tonight." His wife shivered and pulled her shawl closer around the baby. "The air is getting damp. We must go back now to the house."

⚭

The opera stage had been built out on a raft of bamboo poles over a steep drop in front of the temple. Two performers with rouged faces and fans were carrying on a comic cross-talk, accompanied by a pair of clappers, but no one paid much attention. On the dusty ground between the stage and the temple, iron braziers filled with pitch-soaked reeds had been placed in a rough circle. Four young men were limbering up, snapping their muscles and kicking their legs in the air.

A dozen or more older men, barefoot but with heads wrapped in red kerchiefs, squatted to one side, talking quietly among themselves. Outside the circle a crowd of local peasants, including a few from the village of Huasang, also squatted in a restless way. "We've waited since noon for the magic," one of them shouted out as the darkness fell. "So far we haven't seen a fart!"

As if waiting for this cue, one of the older men stood up revealing himself at least a head higher than anyone else on the scene. Two of the others leapt up, ran to one side and came back with a large flagstone which they propped against the side of the stage. The tall man threw off his loose shirt and paraded carelessly around the circle, practising a few kick-jumps which made the peasants recoil. "What are you afraid of, stupid dolts?" he muttered and then declared, more loudly: "You have waited since noon? I have waited till dusk when the Spirit comes down from heaven."

He completed the circle, then casually launched a kick at the side of the stage, as if taking aim. The entire structure swayed on its bamboo supports: the two performers stopped in mid-sentence, and leapt to the ground.

He kicked again, this time hitting the flagstone with one heel. There was a moment of suspense, and then with a loud crack it split jaggedly into two pieces and keeled over. Very quickly he then lay down, and his two colleagues picked up the two pieces, stacking them on his chest. One produced a mallet from under the stage and smashed it down twice onto the stones which shattered into smaller pieces.

The tall man underneath seemed unaffected: they lifted off the pieces and he stood up, spitting into the nearest brazier. "Tonight we shall do great things," he announced, "and those who dare can join us. Those who do not dare, go back to your wives and your pigs."

∽

Huasang was the missionaries' summer retreat — they called it the Sanatorium — but it was still oppressively hot. Every day Nellie rose early to study Chinese, complaining after only an hour's work she felt like a "boiled owl". For their constitutionals, they wore pith helmets and carried umbrellas lined with waxed paper but suffered badly. Another young lady from England, who had claimed to have "the constitution of a crocodile", was soon worn down. There were black rings around her eyes and she could not talk on almost any subject without beginning to cry. It was still better, said Nellie, than being "steamed alive" down in Kucheng.

That evening Mr Thomas had changed for dinner into a lightweight linen suit: he was sweating heavily as he climbed the small incline from the native house in the village where he was staying up to the two houses. He brought with him, wrapped in a leaf, a small handful of wild strawberries. Far away he could hear the gongs and clappers from the opera stage. The path was dark, but he knew the way, winding up the side of the hill with some scrubby bushes and undergrowth on the left. When he reached the first of the two bungalows near the top he rapped on the door where five women missionaries of the Zenana Missionary Society were staying.

"Good evening, young ladies, may I escort you to dinner?" he said, bobbing his head in a slight bow.

"We would feel ever so much safer if you did, Mr Thomas," said Hettie from Ireland, and ran off laughing to fetch the others.

They walked the few steps to the next house, where Nellie and Topsy were staying with the Stewarts, and stepped directly onto the verandah. Ah Cheng, in a white jacket, handed round glasses of cold water mixed with syrup. Then they went into dinner: Mr Thomas took in Topsy, and the English lady with rings round her eyes linked arms with Nellie.

"Let us pray," said Mr Stewart. "Lord, may we be thankful for what we are about to eat, and may we be given the strength to continue our labours. We know that Satan rages but we know better still that God reigns. Lord, save our Chinese brothers and sisters in darkness and may we learn to do Thy work better. Amen."

They sat down and began to eat: it was a simple meal. Tomorrow was Herbert's birthday and the best food was being saved for the breakfast table. Mr Thomas had only joined them from his outpost in the next valley three days before. It was his first year in China and Mr Stewart encouraged him kindly to tell something of his tale.

He had just qualified as a surveyor in London, when one Sunday he walked by the China Inland Mission on Stoke Newington Green. He saw the placard: "Jesus needs you, by Dr J. Hudson Taylor, lately in China: All welcome. Refreshments will be served." After a magic lantern show, titled "From God's battle-front", Hudson outlined his grand plan of campaign. If one thousand men and women volunteered for service, and each one preached to six thousand Chinese every year, every Chinese family would hear God's word by the end of the century.

Thomas was inspired and inscribed his name on the register that same evening. Six months later he was on his way with passage paid. "I answered God's call," he finished, "and I have felt better for it ever since. My health is also much improved. The fog in north London troubled my chest dreadfully in the winter."

∽

That evening while Topsy played Happy Families with Mr Thomas and the Stewart children, Nellie wrote home to her mother in Melbourne. "My darling Petsy," she began, as she had started every letter since the sisters had left their comfortable red-brick home two years before. "We came up to Huasang yesterday in chairs. It was a very nice trip up, quite cool till about ten o'clock and then not so bad, as we had got a little higher. One old scamp of a coolie tried to make the children walk. He argued fearfully but in the end I got my way.

"We had to walk when we got to the last stairs up the mountain. They are called *liang* and are especially terrible. When I got to the top I sank expiring into my chair. The coolies were sympathetic but inexorable.

"The Stewarts are staying in the Church Missionary Society House — mud and wood shanty would be a better name for it.

There is a verandah along the front and two fair-sized rooms behind, and then little rooms at the back.

"Did I tell you that Mr Stewart is a grandson of the Duke of Wellington? He does not like it to be mentioned.

"This time we are staying with the Stewarts but usually we stay next door in the Kuniong's precincts — you remember, the Kuniongs are the Misses. There is a nice-sized room with folding doors always kept open, and bedrooms six in number. Each has a little comfortable bed, table, chest of drawers and a bamboo chair. There are five other Kuniong there now.

"We had to leave Kucheng not only to escape the heat but because of the Vegetables: hundreds are there under pretence of seeing the theatre. The Vegetables have the upper hand with the Mandarin, and they like people to know it. But I am sure you will not have a particle of fear for us. Pray instead for those poor darkened souls in bondage to the devil.

"Dear Petsy, let me cheer you up with something more amusing. Mr Thomas would dearly like to become Topsy's beau: he is short and not hugely good-looking but in these parts que voulez-vous. But every time we look at him we remember the tale they tell about him in Foochow.

"It is said that when he came from England, he proposed to a mission lady after they had passed through the Suez Canal. Because he was so shy, he did it in writing. And at the end of the letter he asked her, if her answer was unfavourable, to help him in approaching another young lady on board!!!"

༄

After three hands of Happy Families, the children were sent to bed and Mr Stewart said he would accompany the new arrival back to the village.

"I wished to warn you to take particular care," he said as soon as they went outside. "I know for a fact that some of the local villagers support the Vegetarians: you should be on your guard at night: sleep with a stick at your side."

"Surely," asked Mr Thomas, "those who claim to be Vegetarians will not kill human beings if they will not even eat from the animal kingdom?"

"I fear that is too simple a view. The diet is a discipline which binds the society's members together when they have taken a secret oath. They are opposed to opium smoking as well as to eating flesh — and blame us foreigners, not without reason, for bringing in the noxious drug."

Mr Stewart hesitated, and then went on. "There are more particular reasons too for their hostility here around Kucheng. Last year there was a dispute in a village between the Vegetarians and a man who hung the Ten Commandments in his house. The tale is too intricate to explain to you now, but I took the case up and four of the Vegetarian leaders were arrested. Their followers then threatened the magistrate and the four were released. Since then they have become more arrogant: I have already reported the facts to the British consul in Foochow, but he is a weak reed and will do nothing."

By this time they had reached the little village: the two men paused for a moment at the sound of a distant shout in the valley, then bid each other goodnight.

&

Mr Stewart was right: the Tsaihui — or Vegetarians — had attracted a good measure of local support. For several weeks placards with the words "Officials oppress and the people rebel" had appeared in Kucheng town without being taken down: at the least, it showed that the "rebels" had friends among the gentry. Some soldiers had been sent from Foochow, but they stayed within the city limits and no one was arrested. Someone else came from Foochow — the fortune teller Cheng Chiu-chiu, a man of the people but able to write poetry who let his finger-nails grow long. Later there came also a message from the White Lotus secret society saying that the time had come for action.

On the night of July 31, 1895, more than a hundred people "dared to join" the Tsaihui at the opera stage overlooking the valley, hangers-on and regular braves mixed up together. Most were poor peasants, but there were also some coolies, charcoal burners, noodle makers, and one man dressed as a Buddhist priest.

Many had had their fortune told by Cheng: he always gave the same advice. They suffered from an ill fate which could only be averted if the foreigners were killed. "Have they not already poisoned you with opium, stolen your babies, brought foreign goods into the shops and taken your livelihood away? Now is the time to kill, to burn and plunder — but make sure that you bring back all the goods to be shared out equally." The band took a solemn oath: "If I am faithless, let me be burned alive or drowned or pulled apart by wild horses."

Late in the evening they marched for Huasang, behind a flag bearing the characters "The dragon will conquer the foreigners' god." Timid militiamen in a village on the way, peeping from their wooden fort, counted nearly two hundred on the move — but many of those marching had second thoughts and slipped back to town.

When they came near Huasang they doused their torches and entered the village where their friends had prepared boiled water. Cheng rinsed his mouth, spat out, and repeated his order. Without any attempt at concealment, they ran raggedly up the hill, led by Cheng who waved a red flag.

∽

The two Stewart girls, Kathleen and Mildred, had got up early to pick flowers for Herbert's birthday from a little mound behind the houses. "Look, Milly," Kathleen called out. "There are ever so many dang-dang men coming up the hill." The dang-dang men were the local porters who carried bamboo poles. Milly, a year older, had sharper eyes: "Those are spears in their hands, Kathie," she cried. "Quick, we must run back to Mama."

૭૭

Mr Thomas, sleeping in his "native house", had heard shouting which he thought at first was the children at play. Yet it sounded too loud for that, and he remembered Stewart's advice. For some minutes he shut his eyes, hoping that the worrisome sound would disappear. There was more shouting: he got up and carefully dressed.

૭૭

Nellie and Topsy were woken by three men with trident spears who tipped their beds over and dragged them out. Nellie was stabbed immediately and collapsed at the door. Topsy was marched outside and surrounded by several more men.

"Walk! Walk!" they shouted at her. "Tell us where you have hidden gold!"

"We have no gold," she replied: "There is money in the bedroom. Go and take it." Angry, one of the braves dug a spear into her. She was marched to and fro and asked more questions. At every answer, she was stabbed again.

૭૭

Most of the band had rushed past the lower house in their excitement: a servant there burst into the two rooms where the five Kuniong were sleeping. "Quick, the Vegetarians have come and are beating people," he cried. "Quickly leave and hide on the hill." He tried to drag them out, but the Kuniong shut their doors upon him for privacy while they put on their day clothes.

Minutes were lost while they dressed: some of the band returned and caught the five Kuniong climbing out of the back windows. They were immediately surrounded and ropes produced to bind them.

"May we fetch our umbrellas? The sun will be too hot," said one of the Kuniong — probably the English girl with dark eyes.

"We can give you money: we have done you no wrong — do not kill us," said another Kuniong.

There was a pause. Some of the villagers had followed and were watching: one old man stepped forward. "Take their money and let them live, otherwise you will make great trouble for yourselves and for us," he urged.

The men hesitated, and looked back at the upper house which some of their comrades had started to loot. At this moment Cheng returned still waving his red flag: "You have your orders: kill everyone!" He struck the first blow, almost severing the English girl's head.

◦◦

Kathleen and Milly hid in a bedroom, were discovered and whacked about but survived. So did little Evan. Herbert was badly wounded: he would die later. So would the baby, stabbed in one eye. His nurse was killed on the spot. No one knows how the Stewart parents died: their bodies were burnt when the house was set on fire.

◦◦

Mr Thomas had finally dressed and stepped outside: the village was deserted except for several mules in the shade of the sloping thatch. The sound of shouting had grown louder: he knew something was very wrong and walked slowly uphill, wondering at his own calm. A villager whom he did not recognise ran towards him and pulled him to one side with a shout: "They are killing people!" He continued more cautiously, working his way through the bushes to within twenty or thirty yards of the houses.

◦◦

"Here I could see everything and appeared not to be seen at all," he would record later in his written account of the tragedy. By that account, he saw very little and to come out of his hiding would have meant "certain death". A retreat horn was sounded, the main house was fired, and the Vegetarians withdrew crying out repeatedly "Now all the foreigners are killed". Afterwards all was action: finding the wounded, stemming the blood with old calico and cold water rags, sending for the magistrate from Kucheng, organising the bearers to carry the dead and living to the Min River, there to board a steam launch for Foochow.

In his statement, Mr Thomas showed only one brief emotion. "Had they (the Kuniongs) been able to escape into the brushwood round, there seems little doubt they might have been saved. The great misfortune was that only two were dressed." Who knows what more might he have written in his private diary. An admission of doubt that this terrible deed was permitted by "Him without Whom not even a sparrow falls to the ground?" Or perhaps a confession of weakness?

∽

A week later an Indignation Meeting was held in Shanghai by the China Association: the Astor Hall was packed. Those who attended must truly be in earnest, said the North-China Herald, "who will give up the Gardens, the cool breeze, and the Band, when the day's work is done, to sit crowded in a hot hall, and listen to speeches from men whom they meet every day."

There were fierce speeches denouncing this latest Outrage by Chinese which must, said every speaker, have been instigated by the fertile brains of anti-foreign Mandarins. But the greater wrath was directed at the home governments and especially the one in London. In the past they had failed to take effective action to impress on China the gravity and heinousness of its crimes. The officials were laughing in their sleeves: this time there must be no more humbugging, but Prompt and Vigorous Action.

Protests were made and various Vegetarians were eventually executed. One matter still had to be cleared up. "Refined and delicate ladies have been brutally massacred in cold blood," the

Rev. Hykes had told the Astor Hall in a thunderous speech, "and God only knows what horrors preceded their murder." Later it was concluded that the reports about torture and worse indignity were "without foundation". When Kathleen saw Topsy being prodded with spears, she must have been mistaken. The others too died without being mutilated: that was a comfort indeed.

ల౨

Mr Thomas married another young lady from the Zenana Missionary Society a few months later: within three years he had died of a fever.

Note

This is a semi-fictional reconstruction of the Kucheng massacre on August 1, 1895, later seen as the first precursor of the Boxer Rebellion. For the missionary material, I have relied heavily on the letters home by Nellie and Topsy Saunders, edited by D. M. Berry and published as *The Sister Martyrs of Ku Cheng* (London: James Nisbet & Co., n.d.). The origins of the Tsaihui (Caihui) or Vegetarians and their reasons for staging the Kucheng massacre have been carefully researched by Mary Backus Rankin in "The Ku-t'ien Incident (1895): Christians versus the Ts'ai-Hui", *Papers on China: XV* (1961), pp. 30–61 (Harvard University, East Asian Research Center).

Kucheng is modern Gutian, a three hour bus ride from Foochow (Fuzhou) in Fukien (Fujian) Province. I visited there briefly in 1998, and walked past a new reservoir to a temple in the valley, with an outjutting opera stage. From there I looked up at the encircling hills where the missionaries used to retreat to Huasang (Huashan). The mission buildings and the city wall of Kucheng have disappeared: there were not yet taxis in the streets, but there were new smart restaurants and hair salons.

The failure of the missionaries to understand Chinese resentments at their presence is reflected in almost everything they wrote and said. So is their goodwill, their self sacrifice, and their obstinacy. The only name I have changed, and whose character I have imagined, is that of the young missionary, Mr Thomas in my account, who watched from the hillside. It would be unfair to invest him by his real name with my own speculations. His bare narrative was published in the North-China Herald and we can only guess at what more or less he may have seen or done. Today, as a century ago, everyone who visits or works in China remains a watcher of some kind, even with the best of intentions.

COLIN HUEHNS

Six Settings of the Nine Songs by Qu Yuan

As an undergraduate at Cambridge University reading Music, searching for texts to set to music for my portfolio of compositions for my Final Year submission, stumbling on David Hawkes' translations of Qu Yuan's *Nine Songs* was a godsend. Here at last was poetry which fulfilled all my requirements. First of all, from a practical angle, it was manageable in terms of size — each poem was about a page or so in length; also, and importantly, it was likely to be relatively unfamiliar and interesting to my teachers and friends and therefore not laden with expectations as to how I would set the words. But, more interestingly, it possessed innate poetic metre which, somehow, eluded specific explanation; in other words, it was most certainly "musical" but the music which it presupposed was now lost in the mists of time, and I was, by inference, free to mould my own musical expression which embodied the spirit of the words as I perceived it to be. But, most crucial, the language of the poems attracted me — at the same time both crystal clear but also opaque, at once both deeply moving and profoundly expressive. Expressive of what? It was possible to explore the meaning of the poetry, but difficult, as David Hawkes' copious and invaluable notes often explained, to be absolutely certain of understanding the poems correctly; but this was precisely why I was attracted: "With walls of iris, of purple shells the chamber; Perfumed pepper shall make the hall ..." (iv. *The Lady of the Xiang*: 21–22). Here was a magical and fantastic world. I was entranced and intoxicated.

At that stage, my involvement with Oriental culture had been minimal. I did not speak Chinese, though I had attempted to start learning on several occasions. I had been to China twice already for long summer holidays, touring as far afield as Yunnan, Tibet and Xinjiang, but was the first to admit that my understanding of Chinese culture was, at best, superficial. However, like many others, it was through reading translations of Chinese history and literature — of which David Hawkes' *Songs of the South* stands in the forefront — that I was able to begin to deepen and broaden my understanding of this lovely and dangerous world about which I knew so little but wanted to know so much.

As a musician — at that time with aspirations to be a violinist and composer — I was most interested in attaining some sort of aesthetic appreciation of Oriental art and music. How and why was a drop of rain on a flower in a Chinese watercolour so achingly lovely, the fade of a single note plucked on the *qin* so complete, why were the Lady of the Xiang's eyes, "dark with longing" (lines 1–2), so beguiling — a song setting I dedicated, with a young man's exuberant enthusiasm, to my girlfriend of the time — when the drop or the fading note or the eyes were at the same time so deceptively simple? With all the complexity of Baroque counterpoint, Romantic symphonies and Modernist experimentation at my fingertips, why were these images so much more potent to me, and why did I want to explore their potential so much more thoroughly? My experience of Baroque counter-point or Romantic chromaticisms was one of musical expectations either realised or thwarted, cadences either achieved or inter-rupted, or, alternatively, these musical procedures as mocked by the Modernists. I felt exhausted by this manipulation of my emotions, and, what is more, I was fed up with the mocking; deeply, deeply fed up. Like most of my friends, I could manipulate a four-part fugue with reasonable fluency, even put together pastiche Mahler or Schoenberg or whatever, but, somehow — and perhaps unlike them — I did not care, because, somehow, I felt that I had lost sight of the beauty in the raindrop, in the fading note and in the eyes "dark with longing". I yearned to rediscover that loveliness.

To me, it came back to a question of musical and poetic language. Not being able to speak Chinese, who was I to comment on whether the translations captured the spirit of the original texts? But it was as if, for me, they had become the *urtext* versions. I was prepared to trust that the translator had done his job — I liked his work far too much to take any other view — and this allowed me to experience the poetry afresh.

After some thought, I decided that the secret lay in the "curves" of each poetic line. I read the *Nine Songs*, with no expectations as to how the poetry would progress and develop. Instead I had to follow their expressive flow, interpreting and experiencing, but rarely predicting where the "curves" would lead. As when the Lady of the Xiang's lover gazes out wildly over the white sedge (line 5), suddenly here was action, movement, consequence, a poetic curve more rolling, progressive and vital than the more gently sensuous curves which had preceded it (lines 1–4): "The Child of God, descending the northern bank, Turns on me her eyes that are dark with longing. Gently the wind of autumn whispers; On the waves of the Dong-ting lake the leaves are falling." Then (line 6): "… a tryst is made to meet my love this evening" — clearly something more complete and luscious is about to be realised. Then, inexplicably: "But why should the birds gather in the duckweed? And what are the nets doing in the tree-tops"; simply the first of a series of sumptuous images — beautifully curved brushstrokes — which interlace and interweave through the rest of the poem. Leading where? I did not know, or, perhaps, even care.

And so my setting. Melodic curves to mould the words into song, harmonic curves to give depth and subtlety, rhythm to control the ebb and flow, and timbre to cushion the softnesses. A high flute accompanies the solo male voice with rippling curves as we ponder those "eyes … dark with longing"; then pulsating chords underpin the mood and movement of the lover's expectation of making his tryst with his partner; then rippling harp pulsations drive the music through "walls of iris, of purple shells ... Perfumed pepper ..." However, no conclusion seems to be reached, and we are left with an unanswered statement in the last line: "I wish I could play here a little longer." The flute and pizzicato double bass take us wistfully down the scale. I too longed not to leave.

In all, I set only six of the *Nine Songs* to music. Even so, the whole cycle still lasts approximately half an hour. The ones I chose were: *The Great Unity, God of the Eastern Sky*; *The Lord within the Clouds*; *The River Earl*; *The Lady of the Xiang*; *Hymn to the Fallen*; and *Honouring the Dead*. I included four solo singers — two ladies (soprano and mezzo-soprano) and two gentlemen (tenor and baritone) — accompanied by an orchestra of fourteen: flute, oboe (doubling cor anglais), clarinet (doubling bass clarinet), bassoon (doubling contrabassoon), harp, three percussionists, two violins, two violas, cello and double bass. The first and sixth songs employ all four soloists singing together, mainly in octaves and unisons; the second through to fifth are each solos for the four singers in turn: tenor, mezzo-soprano, baritone and soprano.

Time passed, the work received its première at the West Road Concert Hall in Cambridge in 1988 and was subsequently performed in St. James Church, Piccadilly, in London. But from then until now, it has gathered dust on my shelf, though I still remembered its curves and often sang them to myself, recalling the melodies and the words which inspired them. Invigorated, over the years, my experience of Oriental art and music has increased. I have travelled widely in East and Central Asia and lived in China for several years, learning to play the instruments of the Chinese *erhu* and Mongolian horsehead fiddle families. I now teach these instruments in London and give regular broadcasts and recitals on them and have also made several recordings. At one such recital in Oxford, I had the pleasure of meeting David Hawkes for the first time. I am fluent in Mandarin Chinese and could probably even read the *Nine Songs* in the original Chinese, though somehow have never wanted to, not wanting to change —

or maybe spoil — my experience of these poems through David Hawkes' translations. I try to remember the curves that I imbibed from them whenever I play my *erhu* — or violin, for that matter — whenever I write a scholarly paper on the history of Chinese musical instruments, and their clarity and lucidity but opaqueness whenever I speak or write in Chinese, or even English. I remember the melodies both in the words and in the music.

∽

The Lady of the Xiang

Translated by David Hawkes
Set to music by Colin Huehns

This is the version of the poem published in the revised Penguin edition of *The Songs of the South* (1985, pp. 108–9). We have enclosed in square brackets the four lines not included in the setting. (The composer has also very slightly modified the wording in one or two other places.) This is also the poem translated by Brian Holton as "Guidwyfe o the Xiang".

The original score is reproduced by kind permission of the composer. — *Editors*

The Child of God, descending the northern bank,
Turns on me her eyes that are dark with longing.
Gently the wind of autumn whispers;
On the waves of the Dong-ting lake the leaves are falling.

Over the white sedge I gaze out wildly;
For a tryst is made to meet my love this evening.
But why should the birds gather in the duckweed?
And what are the nets doing in the tree-tops?

The Yuan has its angelicas, the Li has its orchids:
I think of my lady, but dare not tell it,
As with trembling heart I gaze on the distance
Over the swiftly moving waters.

What are the deer doing in the courtyard?
Or the water-dragons outside the waters?
In the morning I drive my steeds by the river;
In the evening I cross to the western shore.
I can hear my beloved calling to me:
I will ride aloft and race beside her.
I will build her a house within the water
Roofed all over with lotus leaves;

With walls of iris, of purple shells the chamber;
Perfumed pepper shall make the hall.
With beams of cassia, orchid rafters,
Lily-tree lintel, a bower of peonies,
With woven fig-leaves for the hangings
And melilotus to make a screen;
[Weights of white jade to hold the mats with,
Stone-orchids strewn to make the floor sweet;
A room of lotus thatched with the white flag
Shall all be bound up with stalks of asarum.]
A thousand sweet flowers shall fill the courtyard,
And rarest perfumes shall fill the gates.
In hosts from their home on Doubting Mountain
Like clouds in number the spirits come thronging.

I'll throw my thumb-ring into the river,
Leave my girdle-gem in the bay of the Li.
Sweet pollia I've plucked in the little islet
To send to my far-away Beloved.
Oh, rarely, rarely the time is given!
I wish I could play here a little longer.

THE LADY OF THE XIANG (XIANG FU-REN)   TO Harriet

Andante (♩ = 84)

Flute
Clarinet
Harp
Baritone Soloist
Violins
Violas
'Cello
Double Bass

(21)

11
Baritone Soloist
(half-spoken)
A tempo
Fallen.
(pp)
over the white sedge I gaze out wildly; For a tryst is made tomorrow for this evening
But why should the birds gather in the duck..weed? And what are the nets doing in the tree-tops?
mp espr
22
Violins
Violas
Cello
Bass
sonore
sempre
22
Clarinet
Baritone Soloist
The Yuan has its an..gelicas, the Li has its or..chids; I think of my lady but dare not tell it, As with trembling heart I gaze on the distance Ov...er the swiftly moving
dim
Violins
Violas
Cello
Bass

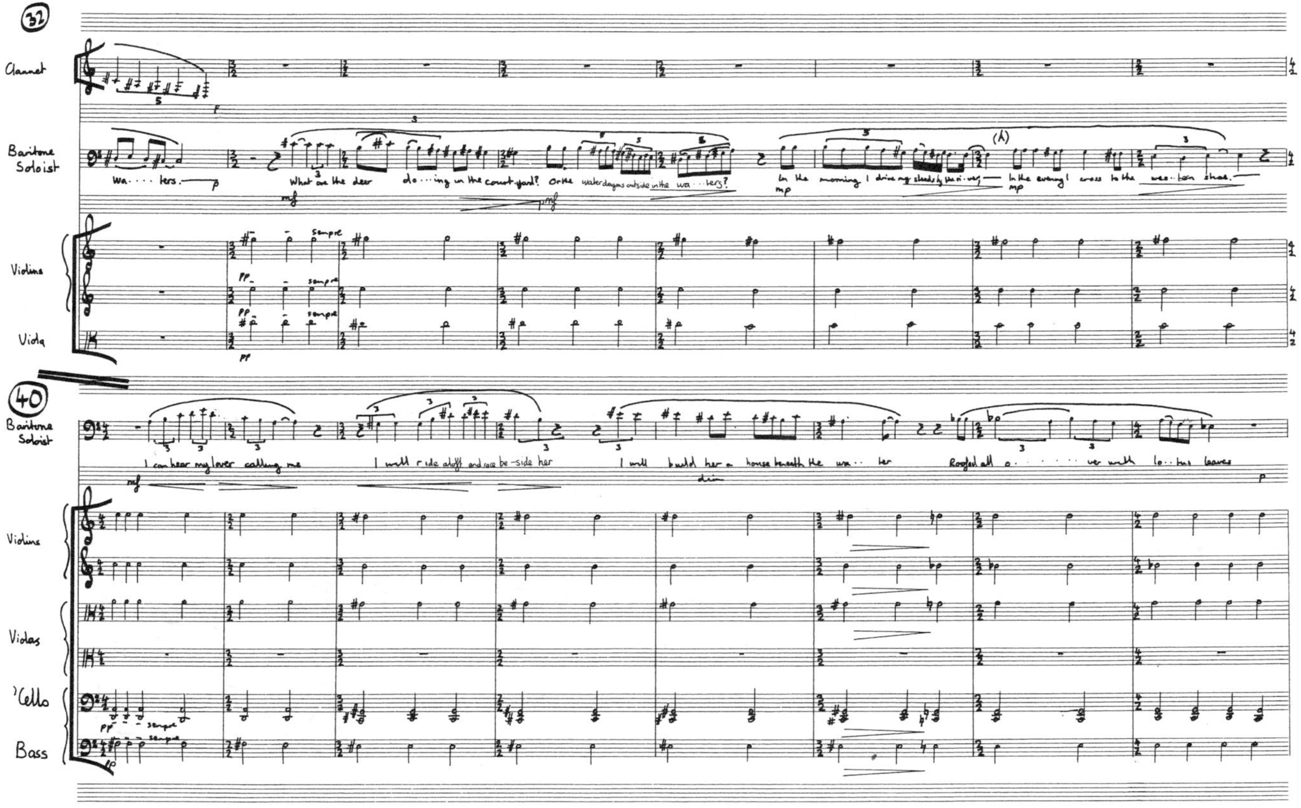

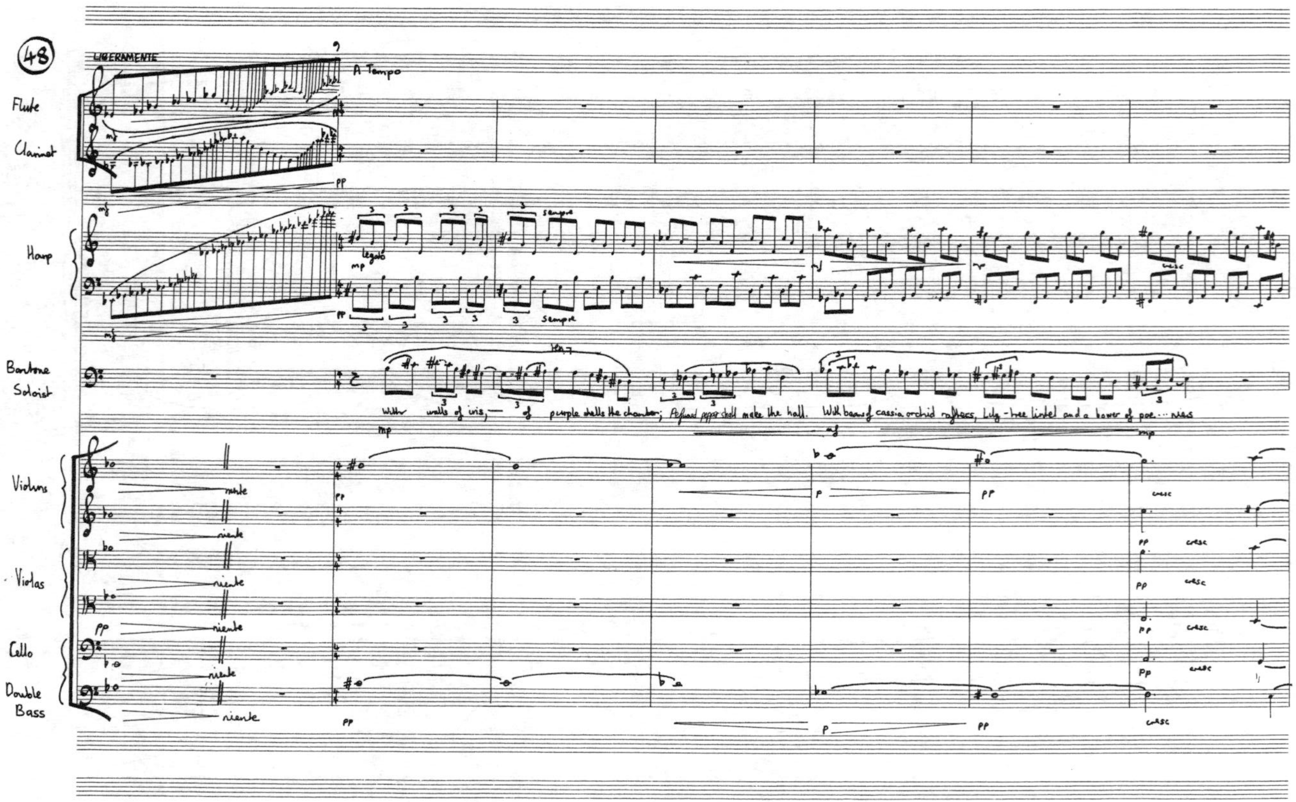
48
LIBERAMENTE
A Tempo
Flute
Clarinet
Harp
legato
sempre
Baritone Soloist
With walls of iris, — of purple shells the chamber; Perfumed pepper shall make the hall. With beams of cassia orchid rafters, Lily-tree lintel and a bower of poe... nies
Violins
Violas
Cello
Double Bass
niente
cresc

55

Harp

Baritone Soloist

Violins

Violas

'Cello

Double Bass

18 STAVE

26
62
Flute
Clarinet
Harp
Baritone
Violins
Violas
Cellos
Double Bass
molto leg.
pp
gliss.
pp sub.
top of the harp
Sur la touche
I'll Hmmmy Hmmb-ring into the ri-ver,
Leave my girdle gem by the bay flee li—
Sweet pollin I've plucked in the little islet
mp
mf
Gradually getting slower at an even deceleration
dim.
Pizz.
10:6
7:6
4:3
pp sub.
p

71
Poco rall. al fine
Flute
Harp
Baritone Soloist
To send to my far-away Be-lov-ed.
Oh, rarely, rarely — the hour is given! I wish I could play here a little longer.
Violins
Violas
Cello
Double Bass
(pizz.)

DANIEL HUWS

Twm Siôn Cati

A Denbighshire friend in a letter to Edward Lhuyd, about 1700, wrote: "The latest news from our parts is that the rapperies, about 24 in number, who came out of the woods and mountains to infest these parts all this last summer … and stole abundance of oatbread, salt butter and some money are now (Nov. 5th) happily retired to their winter quarters." Much of Wales is mountainous and used to be largely wooded, good country for rapperies, or brigands. Sir John Wynn of Gwydir in his *History of the Gwydir Family* gives a vivid account of the lawlessness of parts of north Wales in the early sixteenth century. Later in that century a celebrated band still flourished in the upper Mawddwy valley, *Gwylliaid Cochion Mawddwy*, "the Red Brigands of Mawddwy". These were more or less extirpated. In 1555 they had overstepped the mark, ambushing and killing Lewis Owen, an unpopular and severe sheriff, in the last month of his year of office. George Owen, in a draft of his work *The Dialogue of the Government of Wales*, written in 1594, identifies Cwmystwyth in Cardiganshire, not far from Tregaron, as the chief resort of thieves and outlaws in Wales: "Many theeves that lyved as outlawes and some not outlawed in deede made their abode and … they lyved by openn robbyinge." The reasons, he suggests, were that it was near the meeting point of three jurisdictions, and that there was lack of "diligence" by the local sheriff and justices: "I am sory to speake I have harde that diuerse of these gentlemenn do not loose by those kinde of spoilers and that it is very comon that those theeves and owtelawes doe yeerely compounde and agree with those sheriffes as sone as they come into office." Welsh poets of an earlier age had been ready to show sympathy with the outlawed remnants of Owain Glyndŵr's supporters and with other later outlaws. A famous poem by Tudur Penllyn celebrates the late-fifteenth-century outlaw Dafydd ap Siencyn and his way of life. But despite their celebration in poetry, there is no narrative celebration of the exploits of outlaws. There is no Welsh *Water Margin*. But this is not so much avoidance of a rich subject as exemplification of a strange feature of Welsh literature: extended written narrative largely disappears from about 1400 until the appearance of the first novels in Welsh in the late nineteenth century.

Many friends of David and Jean Hawkes will remember Bryncaregog, their house remote in the hills of south-west Wales. Bryncaregog lies towards the western edge of a large scantly inhabited tract of mountain. To the north are the headwaters of the Tywi and the Teifi, and beyond them Pumlumon and the headwaters of the Severn, Wye and Rheidol. Edward Thomas, staying in Tregaron, walked in these hills in 1910 and describes them in a letter to Helen.

> These mountain farms have a chapel smaller than themselves for each group of a dozen or so. They are just like one-roomed cottages with a fire place at one end for God to sit by on winter nights.
> People, usually women and children, were haymaking in the little green fields among the rushy brown hillsides. Only one man passed me riding a pony and leading another. I could see him at some of the rises miles ahead. They ride the ponies as if sitting on a gate — I mean without any of the pomp of English horseriding; and they wear trousers and usually bowler hats.

Much has changed since 1910. Many of the rises have been obscured by great plantations of conifers. But farmers and shepherds still use ponies when rounding up their sheep.

A stream called Afon Pysgotwr Fawr rises near Bryncaregog

and flows eastwards. Two miles downstream — by which point
the metalled road has turned into a cart track — is a farm, Bryn
Ambor, scene of a notorious murder in the early 1980s when the
owner, living alone, was shot dead with his own shotgun by an
English stranger who had taken to living in the hills, a young man
reputed locally to have been the farmer's unacknowledged son.
Two miles further downstream Pysgotwr Fawr joins the Doethïe
(by this point marking the old boundary between Cardiganshire
and Carmarthenshire) which in turn a mile further on runs
into the River Tywi. Rising from the eastern bank of the Tywi at
this point is a well-formed conical hill standing on the valley
floor, wooded, still, on all its lower slopes, with native oak. The
hill is called Dinas, a word which in place-names signifies a
prehistoric fortified site. High on its steep western slope, looking
towards Bryncaregog, overlooking the old drovers' road beside
the river, is a cave, a small cave, more a huge cleft than a cave,
entered through a narrow gap between two massive tall
monoliths, a cave which has been known for at least two hundred
years as the Cave of Twm Siôn Cati. Nearby is a large farm called
Ystrad-ffin.

S. R. Meyrick in *The History and Antiquities of the County of
Cardigan* published in 1808 mentions "Twm Sion Catty" who was
"esteemed as an eminent antiquary and poet" but was "better
known from the tricks attributed to him as a robber, many of
which are still retained in the memory of the people in
Cardiganshire and Carmarthenshire"; he inserts some of the
stories. This was the first appearance in serious printed literature
of a character obviously by this date well known in local legend.
In 1822 W. F. Deacon, an Englishman, published a sketch, *Twm
John Catty, the Welsh Robin Hood*, and in 1823 a play, *The Welsh
Rob Roy*. Deacon provoked a response from T. J. Llewelyn
Prichard, a struggling actor, who in 1828 published *The Adventures and Vagaries of Twm Shon Catti*, a book in which Prichard
claims to offer a true Welsh account of his hero, in contrast to the
misrepresentations of the Englishman. It was printed for the
author in Aberystwyth and turned out to be an extraordinary

success, welcomed even as "the first Welsh novel". Expanded editions, pirated editions, translations into Welsh, and a host of reprints appeared (the latest from Llannerch Press in 1991). Prichard's sources were an eighteenth-century chapbook and local tradition. His book established Twm's enduring fame and led to his name becoming one familiar to all Welsh children. Oral tradition about Twm was still very much alive when George Borrow, near Tregaron, got talking to a former drover and recorded some of the stories in his *Wild Wales*. In these and other stories, although robberies do figure, Twm's dominant characteristic is that of a trickster. Twm was brought to a new audience in the trilogy of T. Llew Jones, *Y Ffordd Beryglys* (1963), *Ymysg Lladron* (1965) and *Dial o'r Diwedd* (1968) which have become a children's classic. Throughout the tradition, a cave features. Prichard gives a detailed description. The cave is the cave on Dinas.

The Welsh devotion to genealogy used to be a standing joke among the English — the joke has lost much of its force in the face of the universal concern with family history. But the conversation beginning "Where are you from?", the need to try to place a person, to find mutual acquaintance if not kinship, is still almost inescapable in Welsh Wales. Its roots can, if one chooses, be traced back to the law of Hywel Dda under which rights of inheritance and the obligations of *galanas* (to provide compensation for the misdeeds of kinsmen) depended upon knowledge of degrees of kinship. There are references to pedigree books by Gerald of Wales in the twelfth century, and from the later Middle Ages many books of pedigrees of the *bonedd* (the well-born, the gentry) survive, books compiled by bards and heralds and antiquaries. About the end of the fifteenth century a fashion for decorated pedigree rolls crept into Wales. Such rolls, written on parchment, twenty or thirty or forty feet long, decorated with painted coats of arms, sometimes accompanied by a brief historical running commentary, could trace the ancestors of a family back to Welsh royal lines (these, mostly authentic), to the kings of Britain (mostly fictitious creations of Geoffrey of

Monmouth), to Brutus and Aeneas and Japhet and Noah and Adam.

In the reign of Queen Elizabeth decorated pedigree rolls suddenly became common among Welsh gentry. In England, such rolls were issued by the College of Arms, certified by heralds. In Wales, the earliest large-scale purveyor was no herald of official standing; he was Thomas Jones of Fountain Gate (Porth-y-ffynnon), Tregaron, gentleman. At least fifteen original rolls issued by him survive, while over twenty more are known from later copies. The survivors date from 1572 to 1608. In a roll dated 1608 Thomas Jones describes himself as "principal herald for all Wales" but no evidence of any formal connection to the College of Arms is known. Thomas Jones's rolls are well designed, well written and prettily painted. Over the years, he used a number of scribes. One of the craftsmen employed by him, active in the years 1590–1, is known by name: Richard Adams, "paynter of Ludlow, servant to Mr Thomas Jones". Ludlow was the seat of the court of the Council of Wales and the Marches, the town to which above all others the gentry of Wales were most regularly obliged to go. Nowhere could have been better to gather commissions for pedigree rolls than Ludlow when the court was sitting. Welsh bards had for centuries earned a living by singing the praise of patrons; Thomas Jones, with a perceptiveness worthy of the 1990s, hit on a new mode of exploiting "heritage".

The identity of Thomas Jones of Fountain Gate has never been in question. He is Twm Siôn Cati. What has not been resolved is the relationship between Twm Siôn Cati, brigand, and Thomas Jones, gentleman. Meyrick, in 1808, setting Twm, "an eminent antiquary and poet", in the printed record for the first time, was obliged to conclude: "How far the stories told of him are authentic I cannot tell, but I think them not at all in character with his other pursuits." Meyrick had personal grounds for putting forward this opinion: many of his friends were eminent antiquaries. Twentieth century works of historical reference, the *Dictionary of Welsh Biography*, for instance, offer a sanitized Twm Siôn Cati: a gentleman of good family, albeit a bastard, who turned his antiquarian learning to the admirable cause of providing his fellow gentry with copies of their family trees. Stories of a youth marred perhaps by a few "sportive escapades" had been blown up out of proportion by local legend and apocryphal tales (tales that were attached in the first place to "others of the same name"). The truth in so far as it is recoverable looks more interesting and more complex.

There are grounds for believing that Twm Siôn Cati was more than a youthful tearaway who matured boringly into a pillar of society and respectable antiquary. There is, for a start, the legend, so long as one is prepared to credit it with a modicum of basis in fact, and with some psychological validity; there are the surviving poems attributed to him and about him; and there is the quality of his friends. It is one of the friends, John Dee, who sets Twm's life on good historical footing by recording his date of birth, Lammas Day or the Feast of St Lawrence (the note is ambiguous, but in either case, Sun in Leo), 1532. From the surviving fragments of Dee's diary (Dee was a distant cousin of Twm, both sharing descent from Hywel Moethe, as did another cousin, Lord Burghley, who, according to Twm, acknowledged their kinship) we know that Dee's friendship with Twm began not later than 1579. Dee's interest in dates of birth was of course astrological.

Twm was the bastard son of Catrin (or Cati) an illegitimate daughter of Maredudd ab Ieuan ap Robert, great-grandfather of Sir John Wynn of Gwydir. Twm's father was Siôn ap Dafydd ap Madog ap Hywel Moethe of Porth-y-ffynnon, Tregaron. Twm is sometimes referred to also by the ancestral name Moethe (Moetheu), a name by which his own illegitimate son John was known. By 1559, when Twm is first known to appear in a legal document, he is already Thomas Jones alias Twm Siôn Cati. Of any formal education we know nothing. There must however have been some bardic education: an interest in poetry and genealogy had been implanted early, before 1564: Gruffudd Hiraethog, the north Wales bard who died in 1564, in one of his manuscripts cites a pedigree drawn by Thomas Jones of Tregaron.

The suspect felon and the poet-genealogist overlapped. Some early seventeenth-century manuscript collections of pedigrees are attributed to Thomas Jones; they are not however in his hand and must be derivative. Nor, it appears, are any of the pedigree rolls which he produced.

Poetry even today has a more prominent social role in Welsh-speaking society than it does in England. David, when he lived at Bryncaregog, was given a copy of a Welsh poem which had been written to celebrate the building of the house. The completion of a new house (these days, in Wales, seldom, alas, a matter of celebration to the local community) used to be something which called for a poem, as a marriage or a birth or a death still might. So too, even today, might memorable untoward happenings, whether in high life or low. Twm Siôn Cati was a poet and kept the company of poets. He was sufficiently well schooled in the bardic metres to be able to compose *awdl*, *cywydd* and *englyn*, the three favoured forms of classical Welsh poetry. A manuscript bardic grammar (Bangor MS 2) is in part derived from one which belonged to him. In *Cambrobritannicae Cymraecaeve Linguae Institutiones* by Siôn Dafydd Rhys, an ambitious work which includes the first attempt to explain in print the rules of bardic poetry, published in 1592, "Tomas Sion, alias Moetheu" is extra-vagantly praised for his expertise (the expertise probably related more to genealogy than to poetry). The few surviving poems by Twm suggest that satire and bawdry were his forte, and the poetic repartee often associated with *englynion*. Poets thus linked to him include Siôn Tudur, Siôn Mawddwy, Dafydd Benwyn and Sils ap Siôn. A *cywydd* by Sils ap Siôn describes grandiloquently the war, a war fiercer than that brought by Menelaus upon Paris, that arose when Dafydd Benwyn stole Twm's mistress, Eli Bach.

Twm's first appearance in the record in 1559 is by way of a pardon, one of the hundreds granted in the great amnesty of Elizabeth's first year, granted to Thomas Johns alias Cattye, "nuper de Tregaron", gentleman (the name is repeated in three slightly variant forms, suggesting that the pardon covers three earlier indictments) for "omnia escapia et cautiones". One interpretation

of this has been as a pardon for "political misdemeanors". In
Wales, criminal jurisdiction similar to that of English assizes was
exercised by the Crown side of the Court of Great Sessions, a court
set up after the Act of Union, sitting twice yearly in each county.
The records of this court have survived remarkably fully for many
counties. They are still largely uncalendared and unindexed. But
a chance find of a reference in a Glamorgan plea roll for 1561
shows Twm appearing, two years after his pardon, upon suspicion
of felony. The likelihood is that a combing of the Great Sessions
records would reveal more of Twm's felonious years; and that
"political misdemeanors" can be ruled out.

In a manuscript written by John Brooke of Dinas Mawddwy
about 1590 (NLW MS 872) are three *englynion* exchanged
between Twm and one Morus ap Rhys ap Hywel Goeg. In the
first, Twm welcomes Morus and the *gwylliaid*, the brigands, to
town. Morus answers:

> *Tomas aer Melwas a wyr moli   cedyrn*
>   *ceidwad Aberhodni*
> *llyma fyd da pan feut ti*
> *ar heolydd yn rheoli*

(Tomas heir of Melwas who knows how to praise the powerful,
keeper of Aberhodni [Brecon], what a fine world, you who were
ruler of the highways)

Twm then replies:

> *Cadw'r gyfraith faith yr wyf i   yn gadarn*
>   *a gadael y perthi*
> *nid wyf i ffôl yn rheoli*
> *mewn glas dail mal y gwelaist ti.*

(I keep the far-reaching law firmly and have left the woods. I am
not foolishly ruling in green leaves as you once saw)

The facts implicit in these *englynion* — that Twm had abandoned
his old ways, had flattered the powerful and was now "keeper" of
Brecon (Aberhonddu) — and their tone of complicit familiarity,

and their date, well within Twm's lifetime, go far to confirm what the stories tell: that Twm having been an outlaw decided to go straight and lived and held office in Brecon. A Thomas Jones was bailiff of Brecon (there was no office of mayor) in 1569. This is the likely year of the *englynion*. But one *englyn* implies more: "Tomas heir of Melwas". Melwas in Welsh legend (like the later Lancelot) stole Arthur's wife. Twm had found status by conquest of the wife of someone important. One Brecon family with which Twm became familiar was that of Sir John Price (d. 1555). Sir John, a native of Brecon, had been one of Henry VIII's visitors of monasteries and acquired the lease of the Priory after the Dissolution; he was of scholarly bent, made an important collection of manuscripts and in 1546 published the first book in Welsh. Twm drew up a family tree for Gregory, one of the Price sons, explaining how the idea had come to him: "I of late perused a booke of your father's wherin conteigned the petigries of kings, princes, and lords." The probability is that at this time Twm came to know Joan, one of the daughters of Sir John, whom we shall meet again. A rooted mode of life is suggested by Twm's purchase of land in 1572 near Fountain Gate, his father's home. He is described in the deed as "of Caron": he had returned home, or had his eye on doing so.

In 1550, at about the time that Twm Siôn Cati may have been discovering the attraction of a lawless life in the Welsh hills, John Dee, at the age of twenty-three, already famous, lectured on Euclid at the University of Paris, the first ever to do so, to overflowing theatres. During the 1550s Dee became known to his countrymen as a brilliant mathematician, as philosopher, geographer, antiquary, welcome in Queen Elizabeth's court — he did not attend often enough for her liking — where he was, indeed, her astrologer, or, in her own words, her "Philosopher". Around 1579, when he first refers to Twm, he had engaged the interest of the Queen and her advisers in the idea of a British Empire, an empire which would include the lands settled, as Dee convinced the world, by Madog and his Welsh followers in the twelfth century, north America. His library at Mortlake, before it was plundered, was the largest private library in England; had his advice been taken, a royal library, a precursor of the British Library, would have been established. But Dee's restless mind was equally interested in matters which lay beyond mathematics and science and history, matters which met with little sympathy in Reformation England: hermetic philosophy, magic, conversation with angels. These interests came to predominate. He fell in thrall to Edward Kelley, his skryer, or medium, a man who made a fool and a cuckold of him. Old patrons died, the young looked on him as a crank. In 1596 he was granted the wardenship of Christ's College, Manchester. With his third wife and their many young children he left London for Manchester. Siberia.

On 10 August 1596 John Dee recorded in his diary that he was visited in Manchester by Thomas Jones, who then "rode back towards Wales again — thirteen days — to meet the cattle coming." Twm was now an old man. In 1597 the poet Siôn Mawddwy wrote a light-hearted *cywydd* on behalf of Twm Siôn Cati begging for him the gift of a horse from George Owen of Henllys (the historian of Pembrokeshire). Twm is portrayed as an old man, bald and white-bearded; no lively stallion is called for, the poorest plodding jade would do. The aged figure who left Manchester to meet the cattle still had twelve years to live, one more than Dee. For neither were they to be peaceful ones.

"To meet the cattle coming." Had Twm's main business all along been that of a cattle-dealer, a *porthmon*? The *porthmon* was for centuries, indeed, until the coming of the railway, a key figure in Welsh life. He collected the cattle and drove them to the rich markets of England (where they would be fattened before being sold). He knew the world. For other travellers, he provided the safety of a convoy. In a bankless age he was entrusted with large sums of money. He often became rich. And had Twm's apprenticeship been as a rustler? An *englyn* attributed to him in a manuscript written soon after his death boasts of being able to drive cattle from Cornwall to Arwystli (in mid-Wales), to housebreak and distribute largesse.

In 1601 Twm submitted a long Bill of Complaint to the court

of Star Chamber. It gives us an unexpected glimpse of the wild life of Tregaron at that time (even today Tregaron has a reputation of its own). Twm was at the time steward of the lordship of Caron. His Bill recounts a long-standing feud between him and Morgan David, the vicar of Tregaron, and accuses the vicar, and his men, of a series of brutal acts. Twm, by his own account — the vicar no doubt had another story — had tried to protect parishioners from the vicar's rapaciousness. The vicar and his men had caused £40 worth of damage to Twm's corn in one summer (an indication of the extent of Twm's land, if of nothing else) and had bastinadoed his servant, John Moythe (in fact, Twm's illegitimate son), kicking him into a ditch and putting his arm out of joint. In 1598 the vicar and his henchmen had even tried to hang John Moythe: the print of the rope remained on his neck for six months. The following year Twm himself was attacked by men and women armed with swords, staves, pitchforks and pikes and all but killed, and later that year was wounded by the glaive of Morgan David. Lastly, when Twm was holding his court leet, he was saved in the nick of time after the vicar had approached him with a concealed dagger. As so often with court records, nothing more is known of the case.

Twm's will, made in May 1608, proved in May 1609, survives. It too carries echoes of the turbulent life. He mentions his son-in-law, Griffith David, and his base son, John Moythe (who was left some cattle and sheep and a feather bed). Nothing is known of the mother of either his daughter or John. All land, jewels, plate, gold, silver and the residue of his goods were left to his "loving wife" Joan (his goods were valued in an inventory at £139). The strange thing is that his marriage to Joan had taken place only a few months before he made his will, when he was aged seventy-five. And Joan married Twm within weeks of being widowed.

Legend and historical record agree that Joan was daughter of Sir John Price and wife of Thomas Williams of Ystrad-ffin (the house near the cave). They also agree that another of her husbands was Sir George Devereux. In legend, Twm was her true love, a man without means, and he won her hand, after outwitting her, only after the death of the other two. In this regard, the historical record differs. Thomas Williams of Ystrad-ffin had five sons, all illegitimate, but no child by Joan. But he left Joan a fortune in his will, £200 a year in rents and goods worth £3000. Nevertheless the executors brought a case against her for having, with the help of her new husband, Twm, altered the will in her own favour for the sake of £200 worth of jewelry. By May 1609, within a year of making his own will, Twm was dead. By February of the following year Joan was wife of Sir George Devereux. Sir George had forfeited his property to the Crown on the attainder of his nephew, the Earl of Essex. By 1611, with the help of his wife's wealth, he had sufficiently recovered his status to be sheriff of Carmarthenshire. Were these wills and sudden marriages (even perhaps a sudden death) simply the acts of people with eyes on material ends? One might have thought so had it not been for one odd fact. When John Dee in his notebook recorded Twm's date of birth he noted on the same page the date of birth of Joan, 14 November 1542 — she was ten years younger than Twm, a mere sixty-five when they married. But Dee's note had been made earlier. To his mind, although her husband was still alive, Twm and Joan were a couple. Their acquaintance if not their dalliance must surely have gone back to the 1560s when Twm was in Brecon. There remains scope for a story along the lines of the legendary one.

To discover more, at least in the imagination, perhaps we should return to 1596 and the meeting in Manchester, the aged drover going out of his way to visit his distant cousin. The mathematical genius and magus turned crackpot, now in northern exile, the hero of the Welsh wild west embroiled in sordid feuding; two fading stars, sharing pride in their Welshness and their descent not only from Hywel Moethe but from Hywel Dda himself. Their rambling conversation, casting back over two utterly different but equally extraordinary lives, is one of the great unwritten Imaginary Conversations, or, on stage, a great unwritten two-hander.

Sources

Much of the historical evidence is presented in J. F. Jones, "Thomas Jones of Tregaron alias Twm Shon Catti (1530–1609)", *Transactions of the Carmarthenshire Antiquarian Society and Field Club* (1939), 71–87; D. H. Evans, "Twm Siôn Cati", in *Coleg Dewi a'r Fro*, ed. D. P. Davies (1984); and D. C. Rees, *The History of Tregaron* (1936). Evans prints some of Twm's poetry. On the pedigree rolls, see M. P. Siddons, *The Development of Welsh Heraldry*, 3 vols. (1991) and *Welsh Pedigree Rolls* (1996). On Dee and Twm, see R. J. Roberts, "John Dee and the Matter of Britain", *Transactions of the Honourable Society of Cymmrodorion* 1991, 129–43. Unpublished sources, in the National Library of Wales, are Great Sessions 22/31 and Gogerddan Deeds 614 and 670. The Edward Thomas letter is in NLW MS 22915C.

The David Hawkes Collection at the National Library of Wales

The Library was very fortunate to receive in 1983 this important collection of Chinese and Japanese printed literature as a donation from Dr Hawkes, who was living at that time in nearby Llanddewibrefi. This was the "working library" of a professor and as such it reflects the personal interests of Dr Hawkes, containing as it does books on many aspects of Chinese culture, together with a group of works concerned with Japanese studies.

The collection comprises in all some 1,710 titles in about 4,400 volumes, with Chinese ancient literature forming the bulk of the collection. There are a number of copies signed and annotated by notable sinologists in the collection, the most significant of these being a Po-na edition of the twenty-four dynastic histories that used to belong to Arthur Waley and still contains his pencilled notes. Many of Dr Hawkes's own translations and studies, including a copy of his original D.Phil thesis of 1955, are in the collection.

In 1989 it became possible for the collection to be catalogued because the Library was fortunate in being able to arrange for Mr Wu Jianzhong to undertake the project as part of his training whilst studying for a research degree at Aberystwyth. Dr Hawkes gave generously of his own time and expertise to help with the project, and several of the staff look back with pleasure on a happy period of co-operation during this time. Mr Wu Jianzhong is now Director of Shanghai Library, the largest public library in China.

The National Library of Wales is pleased to associate itself with this publication and wishes to congratulate Dr Hawkes, a true friend and benefactor, on his eightieth birthday. Pen-blwydd hapus.

Huw Ceiriog Jones,
Llyfrgell Genedlaethol Cymru/The National Library of Wales,
Aberystwyth,
Ceredigion,
Cymru/Wales.

JOSEPH S. M. LAU

Mixed Doubles

Flirting with Chinese Couplets and Riddles in English Translation

According to the account given by Liang Yusheng 梁羽生 in the new edition of his *Golden Treasury of Chinese Couplets* 名聯觀 止,[1] it was the scholar Chen Yinke 陳寅恪 (1890–1969) who set the Chinese questions for the Tsing Hua University entrance examinations in 1932.[2] One of the questions was extremely short. In fact it amounted to precisely three characters: Sun Xingzhe 孫 行者. The students were simply told that this "household name" (one of the several names of Monkey, or Sun Wukong, in the novel *The Journey to the West*) formed the first line of a Chinese couplet, and that they were to complete the couplet by filling in the second line (obeying — this was understood — the strict rules for parallelism in such composition).

In the same account we are told that over half of the students who sat the examination handed in blank papers and scored zero for this particular question. However, among the submissions there was one that must have caused a stir. The candidate in question paired Sun Xingzhe 孫行者 with Hu Shizhi 胡適之. Now Hu Shizhi 胡適之 is of course another Chinese household name. And he was especially in the limelight at the time, as one of the leading intellectual figures of the May Fourth Movement. In fact, in 1932, Hu was Dean of the College of Arts at Peking University. For a student to single him out in this way in an entrance examination, and to compare him with Monkey, could be seen as both brilliant and daring. But does the couplet so created actually work? In Liang's opinion, though the pairing is certainly an ingenious one, by the strict standards of couplet composition, the candidate only got the thing half right. What went wrong?

It may be useful at this stage to provide the Western reader with one or two general guiding ideas concerning the phenom- enon already referred to as the Chinese couplet, a miniature literary form which Liang traces back a thousand years, to the period of the Five Dynasties. One of the most helpful authorities in this respect is the American Congregationalist missionary, Arthur Smith, who wrote at some length on the subject in his classic work *Proverbs and Common Sayings from the Chinese*.[3] He states: "The theory of the Chinese *duizi* [or *duilian*] is expressed in the name. [The Chinese words mean literally 'opposites'.] It is the opposition of characters. Its essence is thesis and antithesis — antithesis between different tones and different meanings, resemblances in the relations between the characters in one clause and those in another clause. While children are yet in their most ductile intellectual condition, and as soon as they begin to appreciate the flavour of characters, they are taught to set one against another. The construction of antithetical sentences affords a fertile field for Chinese ingenuity, a field to which we have nothing in English even remotely correspondent ..."

To return to the 1932 Tsing Hua University entrance examina- tion: according to Liang, the given names Xingzhe 行者 and Shizhi 適之 can be considered a correctly constructed antithetical pair; but the pairing of Hu 胡 and Sun 孫 works only if these two words are to be understood purely as surnames. And the words have a wider range of usage than this. In other words, the proposed match fails to recognize the elasticity of these two characters, in that they can be more than nomenclatorial identifications.

Is there an alternative answer to the examination question? Liang himself hastened to propose Zu Chongzhi 祖沖之 (429–500), the noted mathematician of the Six Dynasties, famous for his calculations of the value of π, which were — according to Joseph Needham — one thousand years ahead of those of his European counterparts.[4] Liang's argument is as follows. The word Sun 孫 in Sun Xingzhe 孫行者 also has the ordinary meaning "descendant" and is more than just a surname; therefore the word Zu 祖 in Zu Chongzhi 祖沖之 makes a more fitting *duilian* antithesis. Why? Because Zu 祖 also has the ordinary meaning "forefather", and is therefore also more than a surname. Liang of course has a point.

Suppose (despite the Rev. Smith's warning that there is "nothing remotely correspondent") we try playing the Chinese couplet game in English? What then? Impossible, I hear you cry. But as the Queen remarked to Alice, "sometimes I've believed as many as six impossible things before breakfast."

Let us take it as given that the word *xingzhe* 行者 means "a junior unshaven monk performing menial tasks at a Buddhist temple", a "cleric" or "pilgrim", and that *shizhi* 適之 means "going somewhere". Add the surname Hu 胡 (Who?), and we have this embryonic English couplet for our possible amusement:

Sun the Pilgrim,
Who's going somewhere.

I don't suppose anyone without access to these two lines in the original Chinese will be amused in the slightest. Possibly bemused … Oh well, let's keep trying. For the moment let's ignore the fact that Sun Xingzhe 孫行者 and Hu Shizhi 胡適之 are proper names at all, and see what happens.

As noted above, the word *sun* 孫 means "descendant". *Hu* 胡, on the other hand, can mean many things: but for our purpose we will stick to its most elementary usage: "Why?" So, stage two of our transmogrified couplet runs:

Descendant the Pilgrim:
Why is who going somewhere?

Hm … It is not difficult to see that in translation *sun* 孫 (descendant) and *hu* 胡 (why) don't "agree" with one another, don't form an antithesis (which was precisely Liang's point). On the other hand, *sun* 孫 (descendant) and *zu* 祖 (forefather) form a perfect pair. They form as natural a couple as rain and cloud.

Now let's look at the latter part of the name of Liang's preferred candidate, the mathematician Zu Chongzhi 祖沖之, and see how he comes out in the wash. The first word *chong* 沖 means (among other things) to "flush", and *zhi* 之 in this context means simply "it". Thus, Zu Chongzhi 祖沖之 turns into "Forefather flushes it". Now combine the two names, Sun Xingzhe 孫行者 and Zu Chongzhi 祖沖之, into an English couplet, and we have:

Descendant the Pilgrim;
Forefather flushes it.

Not much better than the previous "Why is who going somewhere?" attempt. A Mixed Doubles line-up like this new "forefather flushing" one is simply preposterous, I hear you cry. Utter nonsense, isn't it? And efforts to make it read more smoothly do not greatly improve things:

Down goes the Pilgrim;
Grandad flushes it.

Well, I suppose that's what happens once you start flirting with Chinese couplets in translation. Anyway:

A little nonsense now and then,
Is relished by the wisest men ...

Lest anyone should think that all Chinese couplets are as hopelessly barren and recalcitrant as this one, let's move on to another example which looks on the face of it more amenable to translation:

有酒不妨邀月飲
無錢那得食雲吞

If we don't insist on retaining the parallelism between 月飲 and 雲吞, this couplet should be a translator's delight. A skeletal telegram-translation could run like this:

Have wine why not
     invite moon drink;
Lack money how can
     eat cloud swallow.

"Cloud swallow" 雲吞 is of course the Cantonese *wonton* 餛飩, or "meat dumpling". "Moon drink" and "cloud swallow" are in seamless counterpoint or antithesis. Things seem to be going excellently! What is so remarkable about "cloud swallow" *yuntun* 雲吞 is the way the character *tun* 吞 cuts both ways. As a component of a bisyllabic compound, it blends with *yun* 雲 to give the colourful name of a delicious Cantonese dish. By itself, as a verb, *tun* 吞 fits in beautifully as a "respondent" or "partner" to "drink" *yin* 飲. Our translation may make more sense if we "flesh out the skeleton" a little, and replace "eat cloud swallow" with "eat meat dumplings". Thus:

> With wine, why not invite
> the moon for a drink?
> When broke, who can afford
> to eat meat dumplings?

This is certainly an improvement in terms of intelligibility. But alas, what Liang so rightly calls that "quintessentially Chinese flavour of this miniature literary form" has vanished without trace.

Some couplets acquire their distinctive flavour through a certain ingenious "cross-breeding" of words, what we could call "verbal coupling". This is the literary legerdemain of the Chinese couplet-game taken to an extreme. Take this example:

席上魚羊，鮮乎鮮矣
窗前女子，好者好之

Before we attend to the actual mechanics of the "verbal coupling" involved in these two lines, a little anecdote about the genesis of this couplet is in order. As the story goes, a certain humble Qing-dynasty scholar by the name of Wang Ruyang 汪儒揚 had earned a reputation for his skills in the art of writing couplets. He caught the attention of the prime minister's elder daughter, so much so that she decided to play match-maker for her own sister. Accordingly, she wrote a glowing letter of introduction singing his virtues and asked him to deliver it personally to her father.

Wang was courteously received by the prime minister, who treated him to a feast of fish and mutton. Between drinks, the old man decided to see for himself if the famous couplet practitioner could live up to his reputation. As he searched for an opening line, his eyes fell on the dishes on the table. The sight of the fish and mutton inspired him to chant:

> Fish and mutton on the table,
> Fresh and rare.

By the very act of translation into English, the entire process of "verbal coupling" in this line has disappeared. On the surface of the Chinese original, *yu* 魚 is fish and *yang* 羊 is mutton: the words bear no obvious relation to each other. But when they are spliced together, to form a single Chinese character, they conspire to hammer out the new word *xian* 鮮. The adjective *xian* 鮮 has two meanings in the present fleshy/fishy context: fresh and rare.

Our couplet practitioner's challenge was indeed a tough one. To respond in kind, he had to come up with a line of his own incorporating a character born of a similar "verbal coupling". Happily, just as he was racking his brains for an answer, a number of young ladies happened to pass by outside the window, chatting and giggling among themselves. He was struck by what he saw and immediately intoned the line: "窗前女子，好者好之."

Wang's answer is a miraculous example of the art of couplet composition. The elements for the cross-breeding are provided by the two words *nü* 女 (woman) and *zi* 子 (here a simple suffix). Spliced together, they make up the character *hao* 好, which means "good" or "lovely" (as an adjective), and to "like" or "love" (as a verb). In plain English:

> Women by the window,
> Lovely and much to be desired.

It must now be abundantly clear that any attempt on the part of the translator to reproduce the extraordinary linguistic acrobatics of the Chinese couplet is doomed to be an exercise in futility. If this is the case, then why do I even bother, I hear you say? Frankly, it is precisely this kind of exercise in futility that tickles me. I derive immense pleasure from engaging in this sort of nonsense. "Descendant the Pilgrim/Why is who going somewhere?" Playing with words is fun. Nonsense helps to relieve the interminable boredom of academic life. "What a great relief is nonsense to a man who has been working hard!"

Fortunately, though the flavour and vigour of the Chinese couplet can seldom be captured in translation, the essential information it contains is sometimes retrievable. Let us return for a moment to the prime minister and the young scholar:

> Rare and fresh indeed are the
>> Fish and mutton on the table;
> Beauteous and loveable are the
>> Women by the window.

Could this perhaps pass for a strange sort of English love poem? For the bizarre ravings of some besotted gourmet–littérateur? Or at the very least for a piece of throw-away amorous doggerel? In the end, perhaps all such judgements are in the eyes of the beholder.

No less inviting a word-game for the exhausted and nonsense-inclined translator–scholar is offered by the *dengmi* 燈謎, or Chinese Lantern Riddle. The riddle is an ancient and universal literary form, and the Chinese have been inveterate lovers of riddles down the ages. The Lantern Riddle is thus described by our authority the Rev. Smith: "The Empire is hung with lanterns on the evening of the Feast of that name at the fifteenth of the first moon, and the lanterns are papered with Riddles, for the correct solution of which such prizes as a few cash, or a handful of water-melon seeds are offered."[5] The most famous example in Chinese literature is surely in chapter 22 of *The Story of the Stone*, when the Imperial Concubine Jia Yuanchun comes on a brief visit to her family.[6]

There used to be a café in Hong Kong, in the 1950s and 60s, on Des Voeux Road Central, that was often fondly (and informally) referred to, in typical *dengmi* fashion, as "Boundless Wind and Moon", i.e. 風月無邊 or 無邊風月.

How does this one work? Take away the "bounds" or "rims" from "wind" *feng* 風, and you have 虫, a "corrupt" written form for *chong* 虫, which is the abbreviated form of "worm" or "bug" 蟲. Remove the surrounding "bounds" from "moon" *yue* 月, and you have "two" *er* 二. The official "registered" name of this particular café was in fact Bugs Two Eating Place 虫二餐室. On the basis of his ability to use this intriguingly elegant name for his business, we can only surmise that the proprietor must have been one of the last of the dying breed of decadent Chinese literati, a weird throwback to the old world. Wind and Moon are the two characters that best conjure up that old and (alas) vanished Chinese world of sensual pleasure, of sentimental charm and romance. What else can Boundless Wind and Moon be if not a euphemism for Days of Wine and Roses? A place for shared sentiment and sensuous assignations …

The most popular vehicle for a Chinese riddle is verse. Verily:

蟲入鳳中飛去鳥
七人頭上一把草
大雨落在橫山上
半邊朋友不見了

Now let's see how this four-line game is to be played. Let's take it line by line.

First, line one: literally, "An insect enters the phoenix, the bird flies away." You are gazing at a Chinese phoenix *feng* 鳳. Watch how a fully-fledged character meaning insect 蟲 manages to shrink (Alice again?), become the tiniest and slimmest of bugs 虫, and wriggle its way into the nest of the phoenix! When once the bug has finally made its forced entry, and when subsequently the wind 風 blows, what can the poor bird 鳥 in residence do then, poor thing, but fly away?

Now, for the second line, you need to inform your imagination with a certain knowledge of the "radical" 部首 system inherent in the structural composition of Chinese written characters. This will help to unravel the "riddle" embedded in this line. Literally, "A bundle of grass on the heads of seven men." "*What?!*" I hear you cry. Be patient. First, let's take a look at these "seven men" and see what they are up to. When *ren* "man" 人 is used as a side-radical, it looks like someone standing on one foot: 亻. Now dash off the character for *qi* "seven" 七 in a hurry, i.e. in a rough or "grassy" manner, and you have something between a "seven" 七 and a "dagger" 匕, something that should look like 乚. A "fusion" or "splicing" of the man on one foot 亻 and the dagger-like object 匕 produces *hua* 化, all ready for a dressing of the top-radical "grass". When all three elements are put together, flowers begin to bloom.

The third line: literally, "Heavy rain falls on the tilted mountain." Simple. A "tilted mountain" *shan* looks like this: 彐. When *yu* 雨 rain (the top-radical for precipitation) falls on 彐, it is transformed into snow *xue* 雪.

The last line is equally "user-friendly": "Half a friend disappears." A friend is "two moons" *peng* 朋. When half a friend is gone, only one moon *yue* 月 stays to keep you company.

The four-line riddle can thus be neatly decoded: 風花雪月, Wind–Flowers–Snow–and–Moon, *la dolce vita, dolce far niente, la vie en rose,* call it what you will.

Our trusted friend the Rev. Smith gave us his version of this four-line conundrum over a hundred years ago:

> The Insect enters the Phoenix nest,
>> The Bird from thence has flown;
> Seven Mortals fixed till on their heads
>> The dark Green Grass has grown.
> A copious Rain is falling there
>> Where a Mountain stands on end;
> But the strangest sight of all is this,
>> To see only half a friend![7]

Let me be foolhardy enough to volunteer my own translation, with which to end this escapade, this "windy-flowers snowy-moon" piece of nonsense:

When the bug invades the phoenix,
    The bird takes flight;
Atop the heads of seven men
    Sits a bundle of grass.
When heavy rain falls on
    The tilted mountain,
Half a friend disappears
    Without trace.

If you fail to make head or tail of this riddle-poem in translation, then I think I can safely say that my literary flirtations have been an out-and-out success. Game, set and match to me and my hard-worked partner at the net, my co-conspirator and translator.

Translated by John Minford

Notes

1. The two-volume 名聯觀止 was published in Shanghai by Shanghai Guji Press in 1993, and in Hong Kong by Cosmos Books in 2000. Liang is well known for his Martial Arts novels.
2. Chen, "that very learned and courageous man", was appointed to the Oxford University Chair of Chinese in 1938, but was "tragically prevented by blindness from taking up his appointment when he came to England after the war in 1946." See David Hawkes, "Chinese: Classical, Modern and Humane", an Inaugural Lecture delivered before the University of Oxford on 25 May 1961, reprinted in *Classical, Modern and Humane: Essays in Chinese Literature* (Hong Kong, 1989).
3. Revised edition Shanghai, 1914. Smith was born in Vernon, Connecticut, in 1845. He was active as a missionary in Shandong from 1872 to 1905, when he retired to Tongzhou, to "devote himself to his literary endeavours".
4. See Needham, *Science and Civilisation in China* (Cambridge, 1959), Vol. 3, p. 101.
5. See Smith, *Chinese Proverbs*, p. 164, note.
6. See *Stone*, vol. 1, pp. 443–451.
7. See Smith, *Chinese Proverbs*, p. 176.

TAO TAO LIU

Hu Shi and The Story of the Stone

With his 1921 pioneer study,[1] Hu Shi (1891–1962) completely changed the thinking about the novel *Hongloumeng* 紅樓夢, or, to use its original title, *The Story of the Stone* 石頭記. He then continued writing about the novel for the next twenty years as new materials surfaced. The result was that comments on the novel from the Qing Dynasty, previously called Red Studies 紅學, became known as Old Red Studies 舊紅學. Hu Shi could thus claim to have kick-started New Red Studies 新紅學, which still endures to this day. Actually, Hu Shi did not particularly like *The Story of the Stone,* and privately thought it inferior to *The Scholars* 儒林外史. He held that Wu Jingzi, the author of *The Scholars*, was far more original and "in advance of his time" than Cao Xueqin, whose ideas he found rather "banal" (平凡).[2] In a letter to Su Xuelin he wrote, "My feeling is that the *Hongloumeng* is not as good as *The Scholars*. In terms of literary technique, it is not as good as *Lives of Shanghai Singing Girls* 海上花列傳 or *The Travels of Lao Can* 老殘遊記".[3]

The Story of the Stone was only one of the traditional Chinese novels that Hu Shi made the subject of his scholarly studies. But it was this essay of his that was the most successful, and which virtually launched a whole new genre of study. However, because he had his eyes fixed on a slightly different and broader agenda at the time, that of promoting vernacular 白話 literature and "Re-ordering the Chinese Literary Heritage" 整理國故, he almost appeared to be surprised by the effect of his work on *The Story of the Stone*.

Promoting the use of the vernacular as the written language of literature formed one of the cornerstones of the movement for new literature, of which Hu Shi was an acknowledged leader. His seminal article in *New Youth* entitled "Towards a tentative proposal for literary reform" in 1917 opened up the theoretical bases for writing in the vernacular rather than in Classical Chinese. He harangued everyone on the importance of using and writing in present day living vernacular *baihua*. He called this "Literature in the language of the nation, and the national language of literature", which sounds better in the original Chinese as 國語的文學, 文學的國語.[4] His argument was that Classical Chinese had been a dead language for two thousand years and that all the worthwhile literature had been written in the vernacular. He gave as examples the Yuefu ballads, the poetry of Tao Yuanming, the lyrics of Li Yu (the Last Emperor of the Later Tang) — a rather arbitrary list that he dealt with at greater length and expanded in his *History of Vernacular Literature*.[5] All of these literary works were composed in the living language, the language that their creators heard and spoke, a language which had evolved over the years. Classical Chinese, by contrast, was a dead language preserved artificially by the demands of the Civil Service Examinations, as he states at the beginning of his *History of Vernacular Literature*; and a dead language cannot produce living literature. He wanted to oust it, to do away with this state of affairs, by putting forward vernacular works that expressed true feelings, "real literature" as opposed to "dead". As the literati of the past used the models of Classical Chinese to learn to write in Classical Chinese, so the twentieth-century Chinese must look to other models to write in the vernacular. The choice was clear: either one started to take a serious look at vernacular works, or one remained trapped in the model pieces of past masters of Classical Chinese.[6]

The Story of the Stone was one of many novels that he selected from the vernacular repertoire that had hitherto been regarded by the literati as the "petty vehicle" 小道, universally read but never considered seriously. His scholarly research was conducted with the intent of raising the literary status of vernacular literature, by using all the tools of textual study that had been previously reserved for the Classical canon. In addition to the well-known works in the vernacular, he also wanted to broaden the horizon of readers by introducing less-known vernacular works, including some written in regional dialects. His admiration for and interest in the late-Qing novel *Lives of Shanghai Singing Girls* stemmed from the fact that it was a unique novel written in the Suzhou or Wu dialect.[7] Hu Shi praised it as a masterpiece, and as the first novel written in the Wu dialect. He gave examples from the novel of dialogue which vividly expressed the emotions of the characters. He wanted to promote the use of local dialect in fiction because he felt that dialect alone was able to reflect in a vivid way the genuine speech and emotions of real people in China. It may surprise us that he was able to mention this now little-read novel in the same breath as *The Story of the Stone*, but his intention was quite consistent and logical, in that he was promoting literature in the vernacular, and that included local dialects. Although literature written in dialects other than national or standard Chinese, 國語 (itself based on the northern dialect), gradually died away, not all the educated or all the officials of the land spoke standard Chinese with ease at that time.[8] Standard Chinese itself was descended from Mandarin 官話, which had been the spoken language of bureaucracy in late Imperial China. But the strength of local dialects especially in Hu Shi's time should not be underestimated. Hu Shi himself spoke Mandarin with an Anhui accent. He had been brought up as a child in Anhui Province, speaking Anhui dialect. He knew Shanghai dialect from having been educated in that city. He only began using standard Chinese when he attended school in Shanghai.

The other cornerstone of the New Literature Movement was to Re-order the Chinese Literary Heritage. This became quite a controversial issue because it was considered by some people to be counter to efforts to create a new literature. It was seen as a waste of time and energy to study works from the past, when they could be creating new ones. This was refuted by Hu Shi and his

followers. Zheng Zhenduo organised a composite article in the 小
説月報, in 1923, "On the Re-ordering of Chinese Traditional
Literature and Modern Literature".[9] In the introductory section
Zheng argued that it was important to re-assess the works that the
Chinese already knew to be amongst the best of their literary
heritage, works that were universally read and loved, but had
never been taken seriously. By ignoring the traditional dichotomy
between the vulgar 俗 and the elite 雅 they could create a new
canon of Chinese literature that better expressed the identity of the
new Chinese nation, as opposed to the old Imperial order. Zheng
hoped that in this process the gold would be separated from the
dross. Far from being a distraction from the creation of a new
literature for the new republic, the fruits of this re-assessment
would be a necessary re-affirmation of the ability of living Chinese
culture to create literature. It would draw attention to examples
from the past that could be used as models for the present and
future.

Gu Jiegang, Hu Shi's pupil and close associate, was one of the
contributors. He argued that re-ordering Chinese literature was
like re-drawing a map. We must know where we are, and where
we are going; but to understand where we are, we not only need
to have a map of the present, we also need to be able to compare
it with a map of the past. Wang Boxiang, another contributor,
compared the activity of re-ordering Chinese literature with that of
translating and introducing foreign literature, which was very
much in vogue at the time. It was as though the past was itself
"another country", as L. P. Hartley once put it, and works from the
past, just like literature from another country, needed a new
ordering and a new interpretation. All the contributors, whilst
disagreeing with each other on certain aspects, agreed that they
should explore and scrutinise Chinese literary works from a wider
perspective, from all levels of society and from all corners of the
land, just as they were exploring and scrutinising works from
abroad. There was also no mistaking their iconoclastic intention to
subject Chinese literature of the past to a severe critique.[10]

For Hu Shi, there was, in addition to all this, something of a personal crusade, to introduce what he called the "scientific method of study" 治學方法 into Chinese scholarship. Apart from being a personal commitment, it was also part of the general belief of the intellectuals of the early decades of the twentieth century that it was Chinese culture, and its too-readily held belief in unsubstantiated ideas and superstitions, that lay at the root of the "China problem" (the blame was moved to other causes in the 1930s). It was therefore Chinese culture itself that must be changed. One way to achieve this was to educate people in the scientific method; witness how many of these men themselves started their studies abroad in the sciences — for example, Lu Xun in medicine and Hu Shi in agricultural science. Hu Shi reiterated that all research should have the same approach, whether it was being conducted in the sciences or the arts, whether the subject studied was "astronomy, geology, physics or chemistry". The researcher identified a problem, looked for evidence, and came to a conclusion on the basis of the evidence. He considered his studies on the *Stone* to be good examples of this scientific method. His motto (for which he was heavily attacked by the Communist Party in the 1950s as a "liberal individualist") was "Think boldly and find proof carefully."[11] In his "Travels in Mount Lu", he gave two reasons for pusuing his studies on the *Stone*: the negative one was to refute the speculations of the writers of the Old Red Studies school, and the positive one was to teach a method of scholarship, "to teach men to accept only after doubt, to accept only after investigation, and to accept only after full evidence has been produced."[12]

> I feel that when we study *The Story of the Stone*, we can only deal with two aspects, one is the matter of authorship and the other is the matter of the editions.

By "the matter of authorship" he meant the historical study of the novel's author and his background. He had proved to his satisfaction that the author was Cao Xueqin, whose family life he believed formed the subject of the novel. He claimed that there was in the novel a large element of autobiography, thereby overturning the speculative theories of the Old Red Studies of the novel, according to which it was an allegory about various personalities in the Qing court during Kangxi's time. By "the matter of editions", he meant textual research, in which he was well trained, with its scrutiny of texts and use of earliest editions. In this he was in fact following the best practice of Qing scholars. He may have trumpeted his understanding of the value of concrete evidence from his exposure to the philosophical school of Pragmatism during his studies in America, but his work was equally within the Chinese scholastic tradition. The value of his contribution was to apply these scholarly methods to vernacular fiction, and also to produce for publication and dissemination a well-researched and accurate text, with modern punctuation, for all readers to enjoy. In dealing with such literary works, his own inclination was to stick to empirical, evidence-based methods. He felt that comments about the quality of the literary work or its meaning were best left to the literary critics. Such considerations belonged in the subjective realm of opinions.

> Young friends, do not think that these studies of fiction are intended to exhort you to read fiction. These are all examples of a method of scholarship. In these studies I want readers to get something of the spirit of science, something of the scientific attitude and something of the scientific method … The scientific attitude puts aside opinions, it puts away emotions; it knows only facts and marches only with proof.[13]

He had demonstrated that Gao E had edited and probably written the last forty chapters of the *Stone*, but it was not his desire to express a literary, let alone a moral, judgement. By contrast, his pupil Yu Pingbo was impassioned in his dislike of Gao E. Hu Shi seems by nature to have been a detached man in a scholarly way, a man ready to accept pluralism. This is shown in the opinions of all who knew him personally, in the many accounts that have appeared in both China and Taiwan since the 1980s. He accepted with equanimity the fact that other scholars disagreed with him, and even lent (via Sun Kaidi) Zhou Ruchang, who as a young

researcher disagreed with his findings, his precious 1754 manuscript copy of the novel.[14] This was because he respected Zhou's
work. He was also often willing to play the peace-maker, as when
he rescued Gu Jiegang when his relationship with Lu Xun got into
deep water in Xiamen. Hu Shi's encounters with Lu Xun were not
easy, even though his letters and works mentioned Lu Xun and his
brother with respect. Lu Xun's description of Hu Shi as a devious
man has not done the latter any favours, and may not have been
true.[15]

When Zhou Ruchang wrote the piece in 1995 about Hu Shi, he
still seemed unable to avoid giving the impression that somehow
Hu Shi did not deserve to be considered the instigator of New Red
Studies. In Zhou's view, Hu did not appreciate the true deeper
value of the novel and all it stood for. Perhaps Zhou was right.
Few of us would really agree with Hu Shi, even privately, in
putting *The Scholars* above the *Stone*, let alone *The Travels of Lao
Can* or *Lives of Shanghai Singing Girls*. We should acknowledge
objectively that Hu Shi never really wished to promote the *Stone*
over and above other fictional works. He never envisaged (and
would certainly never have approved of) the future direction of
studies of the novel — as in the Maoist era, when it was turned
into a critique of the Chinese class system. He was first and
foremost a scholar intent on the scrutiny of manuscripts, printed
texts and authorship problems. One may disagree about his re-
ordering of the Chinese literary heritage and his ranking of
individual works in the new canon. But few would deny that Hu
Shi's pioneer work on the *Stone* and the Chinese Literary Heritage
helped create the new landscape of Chinese literature, a landscape
that is still in existence.

Notes

1. 〈紅樓夢考證〉in《胡適文存》, vol. 1 (3), 亞東圖書館, 上海, 1921, pp. 185–
   249.
2. 〈談〈據儒林外史〉推贊吳敬梓〉, originally in《臺北圖書館學會會報》, 14,
   1962, reprinted in《胡適紅樓夢研究論述全編》, 上海古籍出版社, 上海, 1988,
   p. 257.

3. ibid. p. 280.

4. 〈建設的文學革命論〉,《胡適文存》, vol. 1 (1), 亞東圖書館, 上海, 1921, p. 73.

5. 《白話文學史》, preface dated 1928, reprinted Hong Kong 1959, pp. 1–6.

6. Nevertheless text remained supreme, and emphasis was on the text of vernacular works, rather than on the performance; although scholars did grapple with the oral tradition, the difficulties at that time of dealing with performed works need to be borne in mind.

7. 〈海上花列傳序〉, preface to an edition of the novel by the 亞東圖書館, 上海, preface dated 1926, in《胡適文存》, vol. 3 (6), 亞東圖書館, 上海, 1930, pp. 728–739.

8. Although the adoption of Mandarin as the basis of modern written *baihua* was rapidly accepted because of the customary usage of Mandarin, this could nevertheless be said to put restrictions on writers who were not natives of the North. If one looks at a biographical dictionary of 20th-century Chinese writers, one quickly sees that very few of them were native speakers of the northern dialect, and even fewer (probably Lao She was the only one) native-speakers of the Peking dialect. Writers like Lu Xun from Zhejiang wrote in a style that was heavily impregnated with the vocabulary and syntax of Classical Chinese, as well as foreign words and syntax. His written style was far from genuine spoken Chinese, possibly because he was never really totally at home in the northern dialect. Moreover, Hu Shi himself spoke of the difficulties of writing completely in the vernacular, as he himself had been steeped in Classical Chinese composition (整理國故與〈打鬼〉, ibid. pp. 207–212). He was like a woman with bound feet whose feet had now been unbound. This problem must have been compounded for many writers of the period by the fact that 國語 was based on the northern dialect, and so was not a natural or native medium of speech for them.

9. 〈整理國故與新文學〉,《小說月報》, 1923, vol. 14, no. 1, pp. 1–12.

10. "The bush fire that we started has already burnt the whole earth. Whether good or bad, this is now a reality that it is no use regretting…. One can only square one's shoulders and take the responsibility for both good deeds and bad." From Hu's letter to 錢玄同, quoted in 周質平,《胡適與魯迅》, 時報出版社公司, 臺北, 1988, pp. 27–28.

11. 〈大膽的假設,小心的求證〉, in 〈治學的方法與材料〉,《胡適文存》, vol. 3, 亞東圖書館, 上海, 1930, p. 188.

12. 〈廬山遊記〉, ibid. p. 273.

13. 〈介紹我自己的思想〉,《胡適文選》, 亞東圖書館, 上海, 1930, p. 24.

14. 周汝昌, 〈我與胡適先生〉,《胡適研究叢刊》, 1, 北京大學出版社, 北京, 1995, pp. 222–231.

15. "When *New Youth* published an issue, there would be a meeting of the editorial board to decide on the articles for the next issue. At the time the

people who most attracted my attention were Chen Duxiu and Hu Shizhi. If we make a comparison with an arsenal, Mr Chen's would be the one with a huge banner outside it with large writing on it saying, 'Beware of Weapons Within'. But the door would be standing open, and whilst there were a few guns and swords, they could be seen at one glance, so that there was no need to be on your guard. Mr Hu's would be an arsenal with a tightly shut door, and a very small paper notice on it, saying, 'Relax, no weapons inside'. This was actually true, but some people — at least those like me — would take a few minutes to think about it. Bannong was a person with no arsenal at all, so whilst I admired Chen and Hu, I loved Bannong." From 〈憶劉半農君〉, in《魯迅全集》, 人民文學出版社, 北京, vol. 6, pp. 71–72, quoted in 周質平,《胡適與魯迅》, 時報出版社公司, 臺北, 1988, pp. 19–20.

Pine, Crane, Long Life
Fang Zhaoling

桜鶴延年

庚辰 方召麐

MICHAEL LOEWE

He Bo Count of the River, Feng Yi and Li Bing

Nearly fifty years ago David Hawkes opened the eyes of the western reader to a view of Chinese culture that was hitherto virtually unknown, except by Arthur Waley. He told of the calls made to the supernatural spirits of mountain, valley and river, of the appeals addressed to invoke the help of the shaman and the poems that had arisen in the romantic, exuberant culture of the land of Chu. Fifty years is a long time in the development of Chinese studies, particularly those that we have just witnessed, bringing with them new types and examples of literature, traces of religious beliefs long suppressed and the untold riches in material form that supplement *The Songs of the South* and may help to solve some of their problems. That the young scholar was able, fifty years ago, to interpret so many of the mysteries to which those poems allude, and that he did so without the scholarly aids that now weigh down our shelves, can never cease to draw our deepest admiration. The few lines that follow are contributed as a tribute to David and as thanks for his pioneering work to which we are all indebted. They draw from a medley of myth and history, calling on a tale of how human sacrifice was once suppressed, relating how a hero brought the mighty waters under control and in one case showing how the worship of a destructive deity was transferred to the homage paid to the shrine of a human hero responsible for relieving mankind of some of their tribulations.

ॐ

He Bo 河伯, variously rendered River God, Count of the River, God of the Yellow River or the River Earl, is the title and subject of a poem in the *Chu ci* that may perhaps bear several interpretations.[1] Probably it is best taken as a song uttered in ecstasy by one of his brides. In time He Bo seems to have been identified with another figure, known as Feng Yi 馮夷 or Bing Yi 冰夷. The rites associated with these two and the myths in which they figure perhaps derive from the two ever present and contradictory dangers to which China's farmers were exposed; that of the destruction of their livelihood by flood; and that of the failure of the rain needed so desperately to nurture their crops to their maturity.

Feng Yi is described as a figure with a human face who rides on two dragons;[2] according to some, his pair of dragons once harnessed, he mounts the clouds.[3] He leaves no trace of his passing in his travels, and he may journey to the very gate of Heaven.[4] We may recall the strong beliefs that prevailed in China that rain falls in abundance when the dragon rides upon the clouds, and the ritual attempts made with the use of clay dragons, or the dragon dance,[5] to bring about this desired event. Feng Yi may perhaps be seen as the Master of the Rain.

He Bo, Count of the Yellow River, is known as a powerful spirit who must be propitiated by sacrifice, as will be described below. In 109 BC, Han Wudi is said to have sacrificed a grey horse and a jade ring to appease the god, who is addressed in the poem that was compiled for the occasion.[6] That his powers were by no means always beneficent is clear from an allusion seen in another part of *The Songs of the South*; God once gave orders to save the peoples of the earth from suffering.[7] In the course of obedience to this command, God's messenger Yi Yi 夷羿 saw fit to shoot at a dragon so as to discharge his duties; the dragon was in fact a creature into whom He Bo had been transformed.

We may ask in what ways these two figures were associated. Feng Yi, we may read, having once attained the *Dao*, was submerged within the Great River; or he was drowned there while bathing; or he was drowned when crossing the river.[8] Elsewhere we find that He Bo had a wife named Feng Yi;[9] or that Heaven changed Feng Yi so that he became He Bo; or when Feng Yi crossed the river and drowned, Heaven nominated him, or her, to be He Bo.[10] From a late source we hear of a mountain in Taiyuan, to which the local inhabitants set fire in times of drought, beseeching the while for the rain to fall. It was said that the spirit of the mountain had married He Bo's daughter; so when He Bo saw the flames he would send down the rain to save her.[11]

These varied tales derive from different sources that were compiled at different times. Can we perhaps discern from these and from what follows below an original set of two beliefs, one in Feng Yi, Dispenser of the gentle rain from Heaven, and one in He Bo, Controller of the mighty waters of the river? There followed beliefs and activities to appease He Bo by means of sacrifice; Feng Yi was once the victim of such a sacrifice; and with the identification of the two figures as one, He Bo was eventually credited with the power of bringing down the rain.

In this way we may perhaps speculate, before looking at an anecdote about He Bo that was included in the additions that Chu Shaosun 褚少孫 (?104–?30 BC) made to the *Shiji*.[12]

In the time of the Duke of Wei 魏 later called "The Cultured" [reigned 445 to 396 BC], Ximen Bao 西門豹 was the magistrate of Ye 鄴 county [in the modern province of Henan]. On his way to take up his appointment there, he fell in with an old man and asked him what were the main types of suffering and distress that the inhabitants had to endure. "Oh," said the old man, "they are obliged to provide brides for the Count of the River, and that is why they are impoverished." When Ximen Bao asked for the facts he was given the following account.

"Every year the elders and the clerks of the local offices levy a general tax on the inhabitants, to raise sums that are counted by the million. They use a fraction of this, some two hundred to three hundred thousand cash, to make provision for a bride for the Count of the River; they share out the rest of the proceeds with the prayer-makers and the shamans and they all take it off home. When the appropriate time comes, the shamans make the rounds of the

families to see what beautiful girls they may have, and pronounce
that one of them is fit to be the bride of the Count of the River.
Immediately they escort her away; she is bathed and a trousseau of
silk fineries is specially made for her. For the period of vigil that she
is to undergo they prepare a special lodge on the river's bank,
draped in golden and crimson hangings. Once the bride-to-be is
inside, she is supplied with beef, wine and other delicacies, sufficient
to last her for ten days or more.

"Then the girl is decked out with her powder and her fineries, as
a bride who is being made ready to lie upon a wedding couch. They
have her take her place on top and she is set to float downstream.
At first she does indeed float, but after going for some twenty or
thirty leagues she sinks. Any family that has a fine girl among its
members is only too frightened that the shamans and prayer-makers
will choose her to be the bride for the Count of the River. So very
often they make off with her, so that they can lie hidden a long way
off. This is the reason why parts of the city have become more and
more empty without any inhabitants and why it is getting to be
impoverished. All this has been going on for a very long time.

"There is a common saying of the people that if no bride is made
for the Count the waters will rush in and overwhelm everything and
all the inhabitants will be drowned."

Ximen Bao answered: "When the time comes to find a bride for
the Count I would like the elders, the shamans, the prayer-makers,
all parents and old men to bring their daughters to the river's bank.
Will they please come and let me know, and I shall go along with
my daughter too."

Everyone agreed with this suggestion and when the time came
Ximen Bao went to meet them at the riverside. All the elders,
officials, local magnates, fathers and old men of the villages were
there, so that altogether there was a crowd that was two or three
thousand strong, if you included all those who went there to watch.
The shamaness, an old woman of over seventy, was accompanied by
some girl attendants, all dressed in silken singlets and standing in
their places behind the shamaness. "Call the Count's bride," Ximen
Bao cried out. "Let us see how beautiful or ugly she is." So the girl
was brought out from the draped tent. Ximen Bao took a look at her

and, turning to the elders, shamans and prayer-makers, "This girl isn't pretty enough," he said, "I have to trouble the chief shamaness to go and notify the Count of the River that we are going to find a really beautiful girl, and that we will bring her along very soon." Then he had his men take hold of the shamaness and bundle her into the river. A little later, "What a long time she's being," he said. "Her pupils had better go and hurry her up." So he had one of her attendants thrown into the river. A little later, "What a long time her attendant is being," he said. "We had better send somebody else to see that she gets a move on"; and he had another attendant cast into the river. Altogether he had three thrown in, and then, "These attendants are all girls," he said. "They can't have given the message clearly enough; so I have to trouble the elders to do so"; and he had them thrown into the depths.

Then Ximen Bao spruced himself up and bent his body into a posture of reverence. For a long time he stood facing the river, with all the elders and officials who were at his side looking on in terror. So he turned round: "What on earth shall we do," he said, "as none of the shamans or the elders have come back? I think that we shall have to send one of those clerks or those bigwigs to go and hurry the others up."

Everyone who was there fell down with their faces on the ground, striking them until the blood flowed, and they looked ashen, pale like the dead. "Very well," said Ximen Bao, "we'll wait a moment," and after a while he told the clerks to rise to their feet. "It looks to me that the Count of the River is going to keep his guests for quite a long time to come," he said, "so you had all better get back to your homes."

The officials and people of Ye were terrified out of their wits, and from that day on they never dared to mention the idea of providing a bride for the Count of the River.

Chu Shaosun also credits Ximen Bao, as an historical figure, with the skills needed to complete some highly effective hydraulic works, by which some of the waters of the Yellow River, or the Zhang 漳 River, were diverted into the twelve channels that he dug and which served the inhabitants as a source of irrigation.[13] This in turn calls to mind what is known of another historical

figure who lived somewhat after Ximen Bao, and for whom fact
and fiction, history and myth once again form a medley. Once
again there is a river god who must be appeased, human sacrifice
gives way to offerings of animals; the god is defeated in a staged
battle; and Li Bing 李冰, hero of the day, merits and receives due
worship.

Li Bing is described as the Governor of Shu (Sichuan) during
the last decades of the Qin kingdom, before the unification.[14] At
the time the god of the Yangzi River demanded two girls each year
as the price for withholding the floods. Li Bing dutifully prepared
to float his own daughter downstream, but before doing so he
challenged the god of the river to a battle. This took the form of
a fight between two teams of oxen or water buffalo, won by Li
Bing and ending with the god's death.[15] The tale implies the
transformation of both parties into animals and it is said to have
given rise to the theatrical drama of the ox fight staged regularly
in the spring and winter.[16] If floods did break out, they would
not pass beyond the shrine dedicated to Li Bing, who is said to
have had five stone buffalo carved with which to confront the
waters.[17]

Alternatively Li Bing set up sites for the sacrifice of animals to
this dangerous spirit and commissioners of the Han empire were
later sent to perform these rites.[18] Or else the tale is transferred to
the Min 岷 River and Li Bing's spirit has assumed supernatural
powers. After a terrible storm and flood one night it was found
that miraculously the dykes that held the waters had been moved
some considerable distance; all the banners hanging in the shrine
erected to Li Bing were wet.[19] According to one account Li Bing
had had his son Erlang 二郎 make the five stone buffalo, together
with three statues of human beings; possibly credit for allaying the
floods passed from Li Bing to Erlang.[20]

A late tale of strange events includes mention of Li Bing and
Erlang and Buddhist influences.[21]

> Once upon a time there was a young man who came from Guanxian
> 灌縣 and did everything that duty demanded to look after his

parents. His was a poor household and he used to mow the fields as a means of earning enough to keep his mother provided. Now Heaven was greatly moved by his devotion to his duty and saw to it that the crop which he was mowing was very abundant; so much so that whenever he cut it down, it sprang into life again the very next day.

The young man thought that this was very strange; and when he dug down into the ground he found a large pearl and hid it in his rice caddy. The next day, when he opened his rice caddy to have a look he found that the rice had already filled it up to the brim. Then he put the pearl into his money box, and he found that the coins had filled that right up to the top in the same way.

That was how the family grew rich, to the astonishment of the neighbours who tried to find out the reason why; and in trying to have a look at the pearl they jostled round him so as to seize hold of it. This put the young man into the greatest of difficulties, so he promptly put the pearl into his mouth. Once it had made its way down into his stomach, the young man was seized by a violent thirst. In his longing to drink he emptied the whole of a large tub of water; but as he still had not found enough to drink he went away to do so straight from the river. When his mother followed after him she saw that he had been transformed into a dragon, all except for one foot which had not been changed. So she went to catch hold of it, crying out in great alarm, "What a terrible dragon you are!"

The next thing that happened was that the waves rose up and formed an eddy and the dragon made off following the course of the river. But he was forever turning his head round to have a look at his mother, and whenever he did so a large set of rapids was immediately produced; and that is why to this day we have the name of the "Twenty-four Gaze-lady Rapids". But the dragon felt very sore that in the past his neighbours had banded together to harass him, so he raised a great flood by way of revenge for the wrongs that he had suffered.

Some time later Li Bing tried to bring this dragon under control; and he fought a battle with him, with the help of his son Erlang. Unable to win, the dragon assumed human form and escaped. But there was a person called Wang Po 王婆; in fact he was a

Bodhisattva in the guise of a young man. To help Li Bing to capture that terrible dragon he set up a wayside stall to sell noodles. When the dragon felt hungry he would go and eat them, but the noodles were transformed into iron chains and the dragon was fastened to the top of an iron pillar fixed in the depths of the waters; and that's why even now there is a shrine which is named "The temple where the dragon was brought to heel".

In historical terms, Li Bing is credited with the project for separating the dangerous waters of the Min 岷 River (modern Sichuan) into several channels, thereby relieving the neighbourhood from the press of floods. This project, reconstructed and renovated in recent times, is still in use, as may be seen today at Dujiang yan 都江堰, in the very Guanxian that is mentioned in the story. A stone statue, identified as that of Li Bing, was found close by in 1974.[22]

Irrigational and other projects are under way in central China today; and these involve the deliberate flooding of large areas of land and village, whose inhabitants are to be moved to safety. As has been shown in recent years, it is from these areas that archaeologists have drawn some of the most important evidence that throws light on the art, literature and religious practice of the land of Chu. Much that may well be of great value but still awaits their spades will soon lie submerged beneath the mighty waters that are being relentlessly unleashed by man rather than at the hands of an unappeased spirit of the river. Dare we hope that another hero, such as Ximen Bao or Li Bing, may arise to show his strength and save these treasures from destruction? And if so may we hope that David will once more assume the task of interpreting their messages?

Notes

1. *Chu ci* 2 ("Jiu ge"), 18a–19b (*Chu ci bu zhu, Si bu bei yao* ed.); David Hawkes, *Ch'u Tz'u: The Songs of the South* (Oxford: Clarendon Press, 1959), p. 42; second edition (Harmondsworth: Penguin Books, 1985), pp. 113–5; see also Arthur Waley, *The Nine Songs* (London: George Allen and Unwin Ltd., 1955), pp. 47–52.

2. *Shan hai jing* 12 ("Hai nei bei jing"), Yuan Ke 袁珂 *Shan hai jing jiao zhu* (Shanghai: Guji chubanshe, 1980), p. 316.

3. *Shui jing zhu* (*Si bu bei yao* ed.), 1.3b (citing *Kuo di tu* 括地圖).

4. *Huainanzi* 1.3b–4b (Liu Wendian, *Huainan Honglie jijie*).

5. Loewe, "The Cult of the Dragon and the Invocation for Rain", in *Divination, Mythology and Monarchy in Han China*, Cambridge: Cambridge University Press, 1994, Chapter 7.

6. *Shiji* 29, p. 1413; Chavannes, *Mémoires Historiques*, vol. III, pp. 533–4; *Han shu* 29, p. 1682.

7. *Chu ci* 3 ("Tian wen"), 11b; *The Songs of the South* first edition p. 50, second edition p. 129.

8. *Huainanzi* 11 ("Qi su"), 14a; *Zhuangzi* (Guo Qingfan 郭慶藩, *Zhuangzi jishi*, rpt. Taipei: Huazheng shuju, 1991) ("Da zong shi"), pp. 247, 249 note 12; *Sou shen ji* 4, p. 27 (*Cong shu ji cheng* ed.).

9. *Long yu he tu* 龍魚河圖, as cited *Hou Han shu ji jie* 59.17a.

10. *Sou shen ji* 4, p. 27; see also Yuan Ke, *Shan hai jing jiao zhu* 7 ("Hai nei bei jing"), p. 317 note for a lost citation from the *Baopuzi*.

11. Duan Chengshi 段成式 (c. 800–863), *You yang za zu* 酉陽雜俎 14, p. 106 (*Cong shu ji cheng* ed.).

12. *Shiji* 126, p. 3211.

13. *Shiji* 126, p. 3213; for attribution of some of this project to Shi Qi 史起, see *Lü shi chun qiu* (Chen Qiyou 陳奇猷, *Lü shi chun qiu jiaoshi*, Taipei: Huazheng shuju, 1988) vol. II, p. 990; *Han shu* 29, p. 1677; *Shiji* 126, p. 3213 note 1; Zuo Si 左思 (Taichong 太沖; c. 250–c. 305), "Wei du fu" 魏都賦 in *Wen xuan* (punctuated edition, 2 vols., Taipei: Wunan tushu chuban youxian gongsi, 1991) 6, p. 158; David R. Knechtges, *Wen xuan, or Selections of Refined Literature*, vol. I, p. 448. For a report that these waterways were put in order in AD 115, see *Hou Han shu* 5, p. 222.

14. As with the tales of He Bo, the sources for Li Bing's accomplishments vary widely in time and space, and may include some anachronisms. Probably the earliest references are to be found in *Feng su tong yi* (Wang Liqi 王利器, *Feng su tong yi jiaozhu*, Beijing: Zhonghua shuju, 1981), Fragments (Xin Qin 新秦), p. 583, and *Hua yang guo zhi* 3.3a (*Si bu bei yao* ed.).

15. *Feng su tong yi*, as cited in note 14.

16. *Tai ping guang ji* (Beijing: Renmin chubanshe, 1959) 291, p. 2316.

17. *Quan shang gu San dai Qin Han San guo Liu chao wen* (Hebei Jiaoyu chubanshe, 1997), "Han wen" 53, pp. 737–8; *Mao ting ke hua* 茅亭客話 1.3b (*Jin dai bi shu* 津逮祕書).

18. *Huayang guo zhi* 3.4a; for the popular sacrifice of a very large number of sheep, see Fan Shihu 范石湖, *Li dui shi xu* 離堆詩序, as cited by Cao Xuequan 曹學佺 (1574–1647) in *Shu zhong ming sheng ji* 蜀中名勝記 6, p. 82 (*Cong shu ji cheng* ed.).

19. *Shu zhong ming sheng ji* 6, p. 82, citing *Gu jin ji ji* 古今集記; Du Guangting 杜光庭 (850–933), *Lu yi ji* 錄異記 4.4a (*Jin dai bi shu*).

20. *Shu zhong ming sheng ji* 6, p. 82.

21. *Shuo wen yue kan* 說文月刊 3:9 (1943), p. 82, Lin Mingjun 林名均, "Sichuan zhi shui zhe yu shui shen" 四川治水者與水神; the tale included in this article was related to its author when he visited Guanxian in 1929.

22. *Shiji* 29, p. 1407; Chavannes, *Mémoires historiques*, vol. III, p. 523; *Han shu* 29, p. 1677; Needham, *Science and Civilisation in China*, vol. 4, Part III, pp. 288–96; *Wenwu* 1974.7, pp. 27, 29.

DONALD MITCHELL

"Der Trunk des Abschieds"

An Afterword on Mahler's *Das Lied von der Erde*

Dear David,

It so happens that at the very time I was thinking about how best I might celebrate your birthday, I was myself engaged in preparing my old Songs and Symphonies of Life and Death, *the third volume of my Mahler series, for its first, and long overdue, publication in paperback. As a result I was constantly turning over its pages in search of things in need of revision and was reminded of how generous you were in aiding me in my investigations into the original Chinese texts which were the models for the verses of Hans Bethge that Mahler chose to use in* Das Lied von der Erde. *As I wrote in my acknowledgements I should have got nowhere without you. In addition our valued association brought me into touch with John Minford and to a warm friendship, memories of which remain with me to this day.*

I have never been so foolish as to think that anyone could ever write the last word on Das Lied, *least of all myself. On the contrary if I have learned anything from my musical studies over what is now a long lifetime, it is that the greatest of works, however familiar they may be, have the capacity, quite without forewarning, to surprise one with a sudden revelation. I freely confess that there was an aspect of the crucial third recitative in* Das Lied *that I had passively observed every time I heard it — the absence of the big flute obbligato that is so conspicuous a feature of the first and second recitatives. But I had never asked myself* why *it is that the*

*flute is silent — absent — when the narrator embarks on the
crucial last recitative; and in coming up with, I believe, an answer,
I found a clarification of the whole extraordinary spiritual drama
"Der Abschied" enacts which had certainly till now eluded me.
These last months I have been working all this out and I hope that
just a few pages from the complete text may appear in your*
Festschrift, *accompanied, as they are, by much admiration and
gratitude for your outstanding contributions to knowledge and
scholarship. This short excerpt from my complete text I have
entitled, "Der Trunk des Abschieds': an Afterword on Mahler's* Das
Lied von der Erde*", and in this guise it is specifically dedicated to
you. Happy Birthday!*

ೂ

Mahler, as I have so often remarked, was an inveterate, ceaseless
traveller through numberless varieties of landscapes and human
experience, through time, through musical history itself. So it
came as no great surprise to me, years ago, when I realized that
it was his knowledge of Bach's Passions and cantatas that helps us
to comprehend the peculiar form of "Der Abschied", the sixth and
final movement of *Das Lied von der Erde*, Mahler's symphony for
tenor, alto and orchestra, composed in 1908. With that knowledge
in mind we can, I suggest, begin to understand that it is in fact an
innovatory solo cantata that brings the work to its conclusion, a
cantata, if you like, which we might justifiably regard as Mahler's
own Passion, his solitary exercise (if the word may be forgiven) in
this form.

In this context, the recitatives, three of them, so astonishing in
their impact, so totally *unexpected*, speak for themselves. Each, be
it noted, defines a different stage in the protagonist's — the
soloist's — journey. I use that word advisedly because it is now,
with the onset of "Der Abschied" that we realize that a journey is
what we ourselves are to undertake, along with the protagonist.
And the vehicle for that journey will be the great funeral lament
in C minor, which begins to assemble itself in fragmentary form in

the brief orchestral prelude to "Der Abschied" which precedes the
first recitative.

There is much that might be said about the recitatives alone.
However, I must content myself with remarking briefly on how
Mahler chooses to compose them, for example that in the first two
the singer-narrator is accompanied by an elaborate obbligato for
the flute, improvisatory in character (though not in notation) and
thereby reflecting in its deliberate irregularity the irregular sound,
rhythms and patterns of Nature. This first recitative, indeed,
marvellously depicts the world at sunset and prepares us for the
sight of the rising moon and a world asleep. By the time we reach
the second recitative the narrator, still accompanied by the flute,
has been transformed into the protagonist whose journey we are
now to share. Responses to, and descriptions of, Nature give way
to exclamations of an altogether profounder identity with the
earth. In the "aria" that succeeds this recitative, its vocal climax is
reached to words that summon up an image of spiritual
intoxication generated by the earth's capacity ever to renew its
beauty: "O Schönheit, o ewigen Liebens, Lebens, trunk'ne Welt!"
[O beauty! O eternal-love-and-life-intoxicated world!] Now it is the
world that is the source of intoxication. This can in no way have
been an accidental allusion. The first and fifth songs in *Das Lied*,
which frame what is virtually the first part of the work, are both
of them drinking songs, "Das Trinklied vom Jammer der Erde", a
statement of protest and despair, and "Der Trunkene im Frühling",
which rounds off the five-movement sequence, a song rooted in
rejection and nihilism. The titles of the songs are self-explanatory;
indeed the title of the fifth song unites the two principal images
which service *Das Lied* throughout: symbolic acts of drinking and
the advent and presence of Spring.

Likewise, it is no accident that the liberating ecstasy of this
passage clearly anticipates the character of the coda which brings
the movement to a close. (Or, rather, it doesn't, because as the
youthful Benjamin Britten perceived in 1937 the final moment,
that final chord of the added sixth, which combines the twin
tonalities of the work, C and A, is "printed on the atmosphere",

"goes on for ever".) As we shall see, this calculated recall at this critical point of imagery central to the concept of *Das Lied*, takes on added significance, especially in the light of the path that the narrative is now about to pursue. (To the ultimate act of drinking I shall return below.)

I have already touched on the narrative concept that under-pins *Das Lied* and suggested that with the onset of "Der Abschied" we find ourselves not only *somewhere else* (both sonically and in location) but *going somewhere else*. It is for that last reason, I believe, that after the second recitative (and ensuing "aria") Mahler interpolates an interlude in C minor for the orchestra alone, in which all the fragmentary "march" elements we have been aware of from the start of the movement are developed, cohere, into an impassioned, extended lament. This is not, however, a stationary moment of ritual but on the contrary an unequivocal *rite of passage*. When we arrive — accompanied by climactic *sforzando* strokes on the tam-tam, the very sonority that has initiated the movement *pianissimo* in its first bars — we have indubitably *passed over, passed to the other side*. (Mahler himself in his short score designates the strokes on the tam-tam that mark the beginning of the funeral march, "Grabgelaüte" [funeral bells].)

But what in fact is the clear evidence for believing that in *Das Lied*, in its finale, at its most critical point, we have made the crossing to the other side? I believe this rests with features of the third and *last* recitative which again, to my mind, have received insufficient scrutiny and assessment from scholars and performers. I refer first to the conspicuous absence of the flute obbligato that has previously characterized the first and second recitatives. I commented, it is true, on this absence in my earlier work on *Das Lied*, noting that now in recitative three, it is none other than a distantly tolling obbligato, this time for the tam-tam — the very sonority symbolic of death! — that accompanies the voice. But what I failed to do was to draw the obligatory conclusion that the abandonment of the flute *had* to be so. There was no longer any possibility for the protagonist to overhear the sounds of Nature or discern their irregularities; he is now somewhere quite else, in that silent no-man's-land, awaiting — or awaiting to confront — his final destiny. He is *beyond life*. The silencing of the flute, and the strokes of the tam-tam, tell us that. Furthermore, the momentum of the orchestral lament carries over into the contour and rhythm of the recitative's opening phrase, "Er stieg vom Pferd ..." (After all, it is only logical that the traveller, whoever he may be, should dismount to the music by which he has arrived.) There is also a purely practical consideration that I am certain Mahler would have had in mind at this critical moment in the narrative, to be as little distracted as was musically possible from the voice and — above all — *words*.

I think it was the late Christopher Palmer who was the first to suggest that it is "symbolically, [Mahler's] old enemy, death, who arrives on horseback" and hands the waiting friend the drink, the draught, the elixir — call it what you will — that will enable him to experience, to become part of, the bliss that attends man's recognition of the life that death in fact bestows: our "immortality" is embodied in the process by which the earth perpetually renews itself, and thereby its inhabitants. Small wonder that it was precisely here, for the coda, the work's dénouement, no less, that Mahler had to ditch Bethge and find his own words to match the culminating freedom of the music, for which we have been prepared by earlier stages in the movement's evolution:

Die liebe Erde allüberall
Blüht auf im Lenz und grünt aufs neu!
Allüberall und ewig blauen licht die Fernen,
Ewig ... ewig!

[The dear earth everywhere
Blossoms in spring and grows green again!
Everywhere and forever the distance shines
        bright and blue!
Forever ... forever ...]

Intriguing though the question is of the identity of the participants in the final dialogue, it is not really the issue that for me is of prime importance. It is, rather, that in the special context of the third recitative, the moment we have reached in the narrative, Mahler turns yet again — and for the last time — to the image of an act of drinking (emphasis mine):

> *Er stieg vom Pferd* und reichte im den Trunk des Abschieds dar.

> [He alighted from his horse and handed him the drink of farewell.]

Thus it is, though the significance of it has long gone unappreciated, that the image of drinking that has been central to the symphony's first part *resurfaces* in "Der Abschied": we witness the consumption of the elixir that leads directly to the final intoxication and ecstasy — "Die liebe Erde" — by which we must now suppose the protagonist is himself consumed. All sense of a unique personal identity is gone but like the last chord, to quote Britten's words yet again, we must imagine him continuing to exist for ever, "printed on the atmosphere". Here, again for the first time, the image of Spring is released in the guise of the earth's perpetual renewal, wherein is incorporated mankind's immortality. It is that final enlightenment that constitutes the last image of "intoxication", one this time which erases any distinction between death and an eternity of liberation from life. Ewig ... ewig ...

Should we not re-title the symphony? *Das* Trink*lied von der Erde*, I believe, would remind us of the image about which the whole work is built and, in Mahler's final articulation of it, finds its consummation.

IAN McMORRAN

Ming Loyalism and Historical Fiction

Notes on Some Examples from Ming–Qing Literature

In the immediate aftermath of the catastrophic events that culminated in the proclamation of a Manchu dynasty in Peking in 1644, Chinese literati loyal to the Ming house were confronted with desperate choices. Suicide was the ultimate gesture of fealty made by those who, convinced that the dynasty was irretrievably doomed, decided to share in their ruler's fate. Others, equally prepared to die for the Ming cause, flung themselves more optimistically into the resistance movements that were subsequently organized around a succession of imperial princes in the South. Many others opted for some form of passive resistance and withdrew from public life altogether: some chose monastic seclusion as Buddhist monks, while an indeterminate number simply avoided any form of official administrative or political involvement under the new dynasty.

Later, as the Manchu rulers strengthened their control over the country, and Chinese collaboration became widespread, active resistance either disappeared completely or at best survived underground — if one is to believe the rhetoric of the Triads and other secret societies — as long as the Qing dynasty itself. By the early 1700s the "fight" had largely gone out of Ming loyalism, leaving little more than a lingering nostalgia for a lost dynasty and the rich cultural effervescence that had since been replaced by a stricter, puritanical regime. But Ming loyalism still found other ways of expressing itself, and it is scarcely surprising that the literati should have turned to literature as an outlet for their sentiments.

Among the forms of relatively passive loyalty to the Ming that satisfied both the moral imperative and the psychological need to pay homage to the late dynasty, was the writing of its History. It was moreover a time-honoured precept — and one to which the Ming founder had himself expressly subscribed[1] — that whereas a State might be destroyed, its History should be preserved. And each new dynasty, including the Ming, had always, as a matter of course, compiled the official History of its predecessor. Consequently, the new Manchu rulers tried simultaneously to assert their legitimacy and direct Ming loyalist sentiment into an observably harmless channel by encouraging leading Chinese literati to take part in the Ming History project. However, participation in compiling this official History, under strict supervision, required a degree of caution and compromise that many loyalists could not stomach. While work on the official Ming History dragged on throughout the seventeenth century, a considerable number of private histories and independent, personal accounts, particularly of events in the recent past, were written. Many, though far from all, of these have survived, but their authors frequently became victims of Manchu inquisitorial repression. The fate that overtook those who took part in Zhuang Tinglong's independent history of the Ming in the 1660s was an early example of what was to follow.

It was against this kind of background that the *Shuihu houzhuan* 水滸後傳 (first published in 1664),[2] *Nüxian waishi* 女仙外史 (first officially published in 1711), *Qingzhong pu* 清忠譜 and *Qian zhong lu* 千忠錄, which have all been interpreted as inspired to some extent by Ming loyalism, were composed. There may be some doubts about the authorship of the *Qian zhong lu*, attributed to Li Yu 李玉 (?1596–?1676) who certainly wrote the *Qingzhong pu*, but Li, Chen Chen 陳忱 (?1614–?1666), author of the *Shuihu houzhuan,* and Lü Xiong 呂熊 (?1633–?1714), author of the *Nüxian waishi,* all lived during the long period of inquisitorial literary repression ushered in by the Ming History Case at the beginning of the 1660s.

In terms of both form and content, there are considerable

differences between these works, which in any case constitute only a small selection from the literature of this period, but they are all pieces of historical fiction that seem to convey a serious message, either incidentally or as their very *raison d'être*. The inquisitorial climate made it necessary to conceal or to some extent mask any such message in so far as it could be construed as subversive. Yet, despite the resulting ambiguity, it is clear that they amount to something more than mere wishful thinking or an optimistic gloss on grim historical realities.

The *Shuihu houzhuan*, a forty-chapter novel, was presented as a sequel to the famous *Shuihu zhuan*, and deals with the adventures of a group of thirty-two surviving members of the band of Song-dynasty rebels, who eventually establish their own utopian kingdom in exile in Siam. Commentators generally agree that, as elsewhere in Ming–Qing subversive writing, one should, in reading this novel, substitute Ming for Song, and the obvious parallel between Siam and the Burma of the refugee Yongli Court (1646–1662) seems a further indication that one should do so.

The *Qian zhong lu* is a *chuanqi* play that gives a dramatic account of the survival and escape of the second Ming emperor, Jianwen, after Yongle usurped the throne in 1402. As such, it incorporates the legend that Jianwen, effectively "abdicated" upon the fall of Nanking, became a monk, remained in hiding for years in a mountain temple, and, having outlived his wicked uncle, eventually returned to the capital where he was welcomed back and cared for in an imperial palace for the rest of his life.

Li Yu, in his *Qingzhong pu*, pays tribute to Donglin resistance to the dictatorship of the eunuch Wei Zhongxian during the Tianqi period (1621–1627). This tragic *chuanqi* drama focuses on actual events surrounding the arrest of the Donglin stalwart and uncompromising critic of Wei Zhongxian, Zhou Shunchang 周順昌 in Suzhou, in 1626. When imperial guardsmen arrived in the town with orders from Wei to arrest Zhou, this provoked a series of riots, the townspeople, along with a number of literati, rallying to the support of Zhou. Li's twenty-five-act (折) play gives an extremely sympathetic account of the role played by Zhou and the leader of the popular resistance to the imperial guards, Yan Peiwei 顏佩韋. Zhou subsequently died in prison in Peking, while Yan Peiwei, along with four other Suzhou citizens was eventually executed. It also goes on to portray the revenge of the people of Suzhou, who, after the fall of Wei Zhongxian, destroy the altars he had caused to be set up in his own honour, and render due sacrifice at the tombs of the five popular martyrs. The final note is one of optimism, with imperial order restored and the populace happy.

Lü Xiong's *Nüxian waishi* is different again, blending history, legend and the supernatural in a novel of one hundred chapters. Lü takes the legend that the Jianwen emperor survived the burning of Nanking in 1402 and escaped to become a monk, and links it to the historical revolt, led by the mysterious woman Tang Sai'er 唐賽兒, which actually took place in Shandong in 1420. There is a strong supernatural element running throughout the novel, several of the characters being immortals in human form. Tang Sai'er herself is portrayed as an incarnation of the moon goddess, Chang'e 嫦娥, while the usurper, Yongle, is the incarnation of a baleful star, Tianlang, "the wolf of the heavens". The story unfolds simultaneously on two levels, the quasi-historical and the supernatural. The mystery surrounding the historical Tang Sai'er to some extent facilitated the author's task: in fact, after the insurrection which she led had been put down, Tang was never found, despite all the efforts of the imperial authorities, who arrested and interrogated vast numbers of Buddhist nuns. Inevitably, legends grew up around such a charismatic personality. The author also takes considerable liberties with history: the original revolt, which was probably largely inspired by the Buddhist White Lotus sect, was certainly unconnected with the usurpation of the throne by the third emperor almost twenty years earlier, but in the novel it is transformed into a movement uniting ordinary people, loyal officials and generals in armed support of the second emperor. Ironically, in the light of the actual history of the early Ming, the author takes appropriate "revenge" on the third emperor. The latter had expunged the second emperor from the dynastic record and prolonged the reign of the founder by four posthumous years to cover the gap thus created. In the novel, it is the second emperor's reign that is prolonged until its twenty-sixth year, while that of Yongle is consigned to the limbo of illegitimacy!

It seems clear that underlying the *Shuihu houzhuan* was a desire on the part of Chen Chen to "transmit loyalism", as Ellen Widmer puts it, in her study of his novel, "mutedly but widely".[3] But this raises the more general problem of the difficulty, and indeed danger, of such undertakings. To publish anything in the way of loyalist literature that could be understood as anti-Manchu by its Chinese readers could be equally well understood as such by Manchus or by Chinese collaborators (and the latter would not hesitate to denounce the authors, as happened in the notorious Ming History Case). Consequently, those who expressed themselves unequivocally, as did Wang Fuzhi, for example, throughout his voluminous writings, were obliged to keep their work secret, hoping that it would be published at some future time — hence Wang's frequently expressed hope that future generations would be able to grasp his message, and interpret his "dreams".[4]

For those who published their writings during their own lifetime the dilemma was acute. Between the outright explicit and the subtly implicit, various kinds of subterfuge were adopted, but there remained the problem of knowing at what point the writer's loyalty to the previous dynasty would be interpreted as opposition to the new order. In between lay an ambiguous no-man's land where a certain romantic nostalgia for the past might be considered acceptable as long as it remained passive and uncritical of the present. After all, the Manchus had, on taking Peking, at first presented themselves as righteous avengers of the last emperor, (who had, in fact, not been overthrown by them, but by peasant rebels), and they subsequently paid at least lip-service to honouring the late dynasty in so far as this was compatible with their own legitimacy. It would seem that it was into such an interstice that *Nüxian waishi, Qian zhong lu, Qingzhong pu* and *Shuihu houzhuan* all fitted, to a greater or lesser degree.

In dealing with Zhu Di's usurpation of the throne, and loyally defending the Jianwen emperor, the authors of *Nüxian waishi* and *Qian zhong lu* were ostensibly concerned solely with Ming dynasty history, even if they re-wrote it. And it must be said that Li Yu also takes some liberties with history in his *Qingzhong pu*, making, for example, Zhou Shunchang see the fresh corpses of the Donglin martyrs Yang Lian, Zuo Guangdou and Wei Dazhong while awaiting his own trial in prison in Peking, although they had in fact died about eight months previously. All these authors directed their criticisms towards indigenous Ming villains, the rebellious emperor Yongle and the wicked eunuch Wei Zhong-xian, both of whom usurped imperial authority. Nevertheless, it required only a short imaginative step on the part of the reader to pass from native to foreign usurpation, from one northern aggressor to another. One may also surmise that the supernatural framework of the *Nüxian waishi* made possible a natural defence against any inquisitorial attack: it was "only a fairy tale"!

Similarly, the reader of *Shuihu houzhuan* has only to substitute "Ming" for "Song" and "Burma" for "Siam" to read it in a contemporary seventeenth-century context. Ellen Widmer interprets its banal "happy ending" with its series of marriages as a device to protect the author from reprisals. Nevertheless, with this novel, as with that of Lü Xiong, one is left wondering to what extent there exists an element of sheer escapism and wish-fulfilment on the part of the author.

In fact, when considering such works, it is often difficult to decide whether their authors are primarily, or only incidentally, expressing their loyalty to the old and opposition to the new dynasty. Is a given piece of writing a vehicle for Ming loyalism, or merely reflecting contemporary attitudes in the course of a narrative that is itself intrinsically neither pro-Ming nor anti-Manchu?[5] How far is its author indulging in his own romantic fantasies, or attempting, inspired by the tradition of moralising historical criticism, to set the historical record straight? The difficulty is only compounded by a writer's choice of ambiguity.

At least, in the case of the *Qingzhong pu*, the author appears to be paying unambiguous homage to the Donglin martyrs' resistance to the dictatorship of the eunuch Wei Zhongxian. And, while one may, along with modern critics, note the importance that the author attaches to the role played by ordinary Suzhou citizens in supporting them against the agents of Wei Zhongxian and the central government, it would seem to require quite a stretch of the imagination to link all this to the Qing administration's own persecution of the Jiangnan region in general and of its literati in particular. Indeed, condemnation of eunuch wickedness and factional strife were themes upon which the Manchu administration harped, particularly during the Regency after 1661, and in this respect, Li Yu may be said to have been preaching to the converted.

On the other hand, the Donglin literati had seen themselves and were regarded by their successors — including scholar activists like Huang Zongxi and Wang Fuzhi — as belonging to a line of loyal critics of administrative malpractice and upholders of true Confucian values who had throughout history been prepared to sacrifice themselves in defending their ideals. In this respect, many scholar–officials of the late Ming period must have felt a strong bond of sympathy with both Fang Xiaoru and the other Confucian advisors in the entourage of the Jianwen emperor (who had clearly set out to reign as a good Confucian monarch) and with the activists in the Donglin movement and its later offshoots. They were all on the same side, as it were. Throughout the Ming dynasty there had existed a certain malaise, a feeling that an injustice had been done to the second emperor and his counsellors. From time to time memorials were initiated, in an attempt to rehabilitate them, but no action was ever taken. After all, any action in favour of the Jianwen emperor inevitably had implications not only for Yongle's legitimacy but also for that of his successors.

In paying homage to the unfortunate Jianwen emperor — the declared intention behind the composition of the *Nüxian waishi* — Lü Xiong was certainly in tune with those of his contemporaries who still could not accept the injustice of the third emperor's usurpation of imperial power. In 1645 the short-lived Hongguang imperial court in Nanking had finally conferred on the second emperor the posthumous title *Rang huangdi* 讓皇帝 ("the emperor who abdicated"), thus apparently lending credence to the legend of his survival, and had also honoured Fang Xiaoru and others who had remained loyal to the second emperor and suffered martyrdom as a result. Qian Qianyi, in a preface (dated 1658) to Zhao Shizhe 趙士哲's *Jianwen nianpu* (a chronology of the emperor's life that extends it to 1440), also expresses his admiration for Jianwen's character. And as Wang Chongwu, who made an exhaustive study of the Jianwen legend, remarks: "Ming loyalists in the early Qing period such as Li Qing 李清 (1602–1683) and Zhang Yi 張怡 (1608–1695) stoutly believed that the fall of the dynasty was the ultimate working-out of Huidi (i.e. Jianwen)'s revenge."[6]

Should one then consider the above as a surreptitious form of alternative history, setting the record straight? To what extent is this historical fiction, or escapist fiction with political, utopian overtones? Perhaps one should simply regard it as, at least in part — these works are in any case not homogeneous — a tribute to the figures portrayed in them. Historical tribute was, after all, a transcendent form of recognition that conferred a certain immortality and everlasting honour on a select few.

In addition, it would seem that the dividing lines between history and fiction in a traditional Chinese context have not always been quite as clear-cut as one might at first suppose, particularly where legends are concerned. Official history, even that of its great Han exemplar, the *Shiji*, which earned praise in its own time as a *shilu* (實錄) (a veritable record/an account of the real), has not always confined itself to verifiable fact, or excluded all that was legend. For example, the *Shiji*, quite apart from its treatment of the five emperors and other ancient legends, is far from reliable when dealing with the history of the more recent Warring States period. Back in the 1920s, Maspero identified a flagrant example of its historical inaccuracy in the biography of Su Qin 蘇秦, which he considered to be based on a *"roman politique"* of the third century B.C. (a literary *genre* to which he also assigned the *Guanzi* 管子 and the *Yanzi chunqiu* 晏子春秋).[7] Moreover, whatever Sima Qian's literary debts to earlier traditions may have been, he has always been admired for the style in which he presents the material of his biographies, and one has only to consider the detail of his scene-setting descriptions and vivid dialogues to recognise the extent to which a literary imagination was at work. For example, the final poetic exchange between the King of Chu and his beloved concubine was originally supposed to have taken place in the privacy of Xiang Yu's tent. Sima Qian's source for what must have been largely a product of the literary imagination of its first chronicler was the *Chu Han chunqiu*.[8] Sima Qian reproduces Xiang Yu's words, but the concubine's equally famous reply was restored by Feng Menglong in his *Qing shi*. Sima Qian's biographies seem to constitute a natural bridge between history and fiction, and if they are still read today it is surely for their literary qualities.

Given the enormous prestige enjoyed by the historical discipline throughout the Chinese cultural tradition, even a very minor attempt to re-examine its parameters and interface with those of fiction might well appear to be at best a trivial pursuit — not to say a sacrilegious one, in so far as history has always been an expression of orthodoxy. After all, students are weaned on such examples of the historian's absolute devotion to his duty to the principle of accurate recording as appear in the *Zuozhuan* account of the Qi annalists' determination to register a regicide, even at the cost of their own lives.[9] And, although historians had also a duty to pass moral judgment (*baobian* 褒貶) and the right to ensure appropriate concealment (*hui* 諱), they may, in general, be said to have conformed to the Confucian axiom "述而不作". This would seem to be diametrically opposed to fiction as we understand it today.

Unfortunately, the English term fiction does not correspond exactly to what the Chinese traditionally referred to as *xiaoshuo* 小說, originally a dismissive description of miscellaneous writings that, according to the bibliographical sections in the official histories, included at one time or another such works as the *Shanhai jing* and the *Cha jing.*

Lu Xun, in his exploration of the evolution of the notion of *xiaoshuo*, and its relation to historical writing,[10] notes that from the Song onwards — specifically, from Ouyang Xiu's contribution to the bibliographical section in the *Xin Tangshu* — works on divine retribution and accounts of the supernatural that had previously been included in the section on historical works were considered as fiction and ceased to be classed as history. (He also notes that, at the same time, such works as the *Cha jing* 茶經 and *Jie zi shiyi* 誡子拾遺 were relegated to the category of *xiaoshuo* — which was consequently extremely heterogeneous!) In the sixteenth century, in an effort to define the *genre* more precisely, the bibliophile Hu Yinglin 胡應麟 (1551–1602) subdivided *xiao-shuo* into six categories: *zhiguai* 志怪, *chuanqi* 傳奇, *zalu* 雜錄, *congtan* 叢談, *bianding* 辨訂 and *zhengui* 箴規; but it was Ji Yun 紀昀 (1724–1805) who reduced it to three categories, which, as Lu Xun points out, really corresponded to two of Hu's categories — those of *zalu* and *zhiguai* — and excluded that of *chuanqi* (to which Hu had assigned such writings as the tales of Feiyan 飛燕, Cui Yingying 崔鶯鶯 and Huo Xiaoyu 霍小玉). Ji Yun justified his systematization, which for the first time consigned the *Shanhai jing* 山海經 to the realm of *xiaoshuo*, by asserting that such writings were "nebulous and unsubstantiated" (恍忽無征), and that if they were taken as true history the essence of history would be adulterated and its rules broken (以為信史而錄之則史體雜史人例破矣). Lu Xun concludes his account by affirming that historical legends (非依托之史) were subsequently classed under the *xiaoshuo* category as *zhiguai*, while "history was allowed to contain little in the way of legendary accounts" (史部遂不容多含傳説之書).

While this is an accurate description of the state of affairs in more recent times, the situation in earlier periods was rather more complex. It is not surprising that the legendary and fictional sometimes found their way into history, given the fact that writers of short stories like the Tang author Li Gongzuo, for example, tended in their search for verisimilitude, to blur the distinctions between fiction and history by presenting their tales as true historical accounts. Their stories regularly begin, after the style of historical biographies, by situating the main character quite precisely, in terms of local and family origins as well as chronologically. Perhaps this explains how Li's tale of a young widow's revenge, *Xie Xiao'e zhuan* 謝小娥傳, despite its supernatural element — the ghosts of the murdered father and husband of the heroine appear to her in a dream in order to reveal the names of the bandits who had killed them — became incorporated in the biographies of heroic women in the *Xin Tangshu*.[11] As an example of filial vengeance it was possibly held to be too good not to be true!

Similarly, Sima Guang, in his *Zizhi tongjian*, perpetuated what was to become a celebrated example of female virtue, by including Ouyang Xiu's account of a virtuous widow who cut off her own arm because she considered that it had been defiled by an innkeeper who touched it when refusing her — and her husband's corpse — accommodation. But, as the commentator to the history feels obliged to point out, Ouyang Xiu's source was a "piece of Five Dynasties fiction" in the first place.[12]

Indeed, one is sometimes tempted to create a Chinese neologism along the lines of "*shihuan* 史幻", analogous to *kehuan* 科幻, to describe the category that includes *yanyi* 演義, and *waishi* 外史, and has been rendered in English by "romance". The four works discussed above might all be said to fall into this category. Such historical fiction, feeding on legends, tends like legend itself to expand almost spontaneously, embellishing history and turning the black-and-white of sober historical chronicles into a "technicolour" version in which the human — and at times the superhuman and supernatural — dimension is privileged. If Chinese historical writing may properly be described as "an attempt to reimagine the past while recovering it",[13] the spirit behind these Ming–Qing works is not so very far removed from that of the founding father of Chinese history, Sima Qian.

Notes

1. *Ming taizu shilu, Hongwu* 37, 1a–b, Taibei, 1962.
2. Ellen Widmer, *The Margins of Utopia,* Cambridge (Mass.), 1987, p. 39.
3. *ibid.,* p. 48.
4. Ian McMorran, *The Passionate Realist,* Hong Kong, 1992, pp. 161–163.
5. In this respect see the perspicacious remarks made by the authors of *Redefining History* in discussing Pu Songling's work: Chun-shu Chang & Shelley Hsueh-lun Chang, *Redefining History,* Ann Arbor, 1998, pp. 136–141.
6. F. W. Mote's biography of the second emperor in Goodrich, L.C. & Fang Chaoying (eds.), *Dictionary of Ming Biography,* N.Y. & London, 1976, p. 404, quoting Wang.
7. H. Maspero, *Etudes historiques,* Paris, 1967, pp. 53–62.
8. Sima Qian, *Shiji,* Peking, Zhonghua shuju, 1963, pp. 333–334.
9. James Legge, *The Chinese Classics,* London, 1872, Vol. V, Part II, pp. 509–514, concerning the assassination of Zhuang, ruler of Qi in 548 B.C. (Xiang Gong year 25).
10. Lu Xun, *Zhongguo xiaoshuo shilüe,* Peking, 1996, pp. 1–6.
11. Ouyang Xiu, *Xin Tangshu,* Peking, Zhonghua shuju, 1975, pp. 5827–5828.
12. Sima Guang, *Zizhi tongjian,* Hong Kong, Zhonghua shuju, 1971, pp. 9510–9511.
13. cf. Chun-shu Chang, op. cit., p. 76.

Part 3

Translations

Flourishing as a Pine Tree,
For Professor Hawkes on his
Eightieth Birthday

Jao Tsung-i

如松之盛

霍克斯教授八十大壽
壬午送壹寫贈

DUNCAN CAMPBELL

The Gardens of His Youth

Extracts from Zhang Dai's *Dream Memories of Taoan*

Translator's Introduction

Fall'n the great house once so secure in wealth,
Each scattered member shifting for himself;
A half a life-time's anxious schemes
Proved no more than the stuff of dreams.
Like a great building's tottering crash,
Like flickering lampwick burned to ash,
Your scene of happiness concludes in grief:
For worldly bliss is always insecure and brief.

> — David Hawkes, trans., *The Story of the Stone*
> (Penguin, 1973), Vol. 1, p. 143

Quitting the place that one loves means that we are condemned to inhabit our loss forever.

> — James Cowan, *A Mapmaker's Dream: The Meditations of*
> *Fra Mauro, Cartographer to the Court of Venice*
> (Vintage, 1996), p. 27

By Zhang Dai's (1597–?1689)[1] own account, the contrast between the two halves of his life could not have been more extreme. Born into the very lap of late-Ming luxury and extravagance, the collapse of the Ming dynasty in 1644 left him totally bereft, his "state fallen, his family destroyed".[2] Dissuaded from committing suicide by his wish to complete his monumental history of the Ming, he chose to live on, surrounded by the detritus of his former life. All that remained to him were his memories and his lingering desire both to recall these to mind and to record them:

> When from my pillow I hear the crow of the cock as the night air begins to withdraw, I am led to think back over my life; all the various splendours and frivolous beauties that it beheld seem empty as they pass before my eyes and the past fifty years become but a dream. And now that the yellow millet is cooked and my carriage has returned from the anthill, how am I to endure this pain? Recalling the distant past, I recorded my memories as and when they occurred to me, intending them as an offering to be presented to the Buddha, accompanied by a confession for each and every one of them. I have not sought to arrange them according to month or year and thus my record differs from that of a chronological biography; nor have I sorted them into various categories and thus my record is also dissimilar to the usual forest of anecdotes. Whenever I happened by chance upon a memory it was for that moment as if I were again journeying along a former path or encountering once again a friend of old.[3]

If in Zhang Dai's *Dream Memories*, the dream is a way of understanding his life, it becomes also the vehicle for his specific memories and it is to the gardens once owned by his family and wherein he had spent much of his youth that his mind often returns. Translated below are Zhang Dai's elegiac accounts of eight such gardens, all of them once found in or around his birthplace of Shanyin, along with a record of an imaginary garden, a dream within a dream. His memories, he tells us, are snatched at on the very cusp of his awakening from the greatest of all dreams. As such, they both capture the essential ambiguity of memory (its twinned pain and pleasure) and represent the irreducible core of his authentic self (his "single speck of attachment to fame"), a core "so hard and so firm that, like the *sari* spoken of by the Buddhists, it will survive the flames of the fires of the kalpa".[4]

Zhang Dai's evocation of the gardens of his youth embodies something of the contemporary obsession with both gardens and dreams; his book may also be said to presage aspects of the greatest Chinese treatment of these two themes in the eighteenth-century masterpiece *The Story of the Stone.*

෬

Mushroom Skin Pavilion

Mushroom Skin Pavilion[5] was little more than a single rustic-looking pavilion. And yet, once it had been completed, the capabilities of the hill upon which it stood had been fully realised. Not one of the pavilions that my family subsequently built there could equal it; neither could the towers, the belvederes, nor the studios that followed. In brief then, one could say that every tower later added to the pavilion served merely to detract from it, as did each additional wall. When my great-great-grandfather Zhang Tianfu finished construction of the pavilion he added not a single rafter or a single tile beyond it, and even within the pavilion itself he gave it no railings or doorways. Herein lay his conception of the pavilion.

The trees he planted out with his own hands around the pavilion grew thick of girth; their pure shade and the light mist that clung to them cast a vast shroud which made it seem as if one was enveloped by an autumnal river. The stone terrace that stood in front of the pavilion gathered to itself all the manifest beauties of the pavilion and laid first claim over them. To stand high upon the terrace and gaze into the distance afforded one an uninterrupted prospect. Reverence Pavilion Mountain and the various other peaks squatted below the foothill; the valley brook circled around, its water appearing to flow from some point above the pine leaves. Below the terrace, winding away to the right, a zigzag flight of steps described three turns, and ancient pines stood hunchbacked. On the summit a single tree hung low, inverted like a small canopy, its smaller branches twisted and gnarled and propped up with poles, whirling in the wind like a feather screen with bent handles. Before the *Guichou* year [1613], the pavilion had been given neither a wall nor a terrace, and the beauty of the pines was displayed to even greater effect.

Pebble Garden

Pebble Garden[6] floated like a basin upon the water, capturing its power but appearing so serene that it was as if it were not surrounded by water. There where the Hall of the Flower of Longevity stood, the garden was bounded by an embankment, by Little Eyebrow Hill, by Heavenly Questions Terrace, by Bamboo Path, long and zigzagged and surrounded by water. The inner chambers were cut off from the rest of the garden by the Study of the Clouds of Dawn, by Intoxicating Sip, by a long gallery, by a small zigzag bridge, by East Hedge, hidden and secluded and also surrounded by water. Overlooking the pond, the garden was split in two by Fragrance of the Sea-Perch Pavilion, by Flowering Prunus Cell, quiet and distant, again surrounded by water. Following along the course of the wall, it was protected by the Adytum of Pure Six, by the Hermitage Without Leaks, by Vegetable Garden, by the neighbouring households, intimate and tranquil, this being where the power of the water was finally played out.

The countenance of the water derived from that of Master Pang's Pond. Whereas others rejected the pond, I for my part esteemed it greatly and long wished to build a garden there, casting not a single glance in the direction of any other site, my emotions swayed only by that place and pledging myself to it alone, there where Dragon Hill undulated, to be reached only after one took three turns, quite beyond the regard of the water. People praised Pebble Garden for its ability to make full use of water and it did indeed seem to capture the power of the water.

Whilst my grandfather Zhang Rulin was still alive, the garden became the very byword for luxurious splendour. On one occasion two old men were taking a turn around the garden when one of them turned to the other to exclaim: "This is indeed a veritable paradise the equal of Penglai or Langyuan!" To this, the other uttered the riposte: "Those places were nowhere as splendid as this!"

Prunus Bookroom

When the old buildings behind Calyx Ledge Tower fell into ruin, I had a four-*chi*-deep foundation rammed, and upon this I constructed a large one-roomed study. Off to the side of the study I extended an alcove that resembled a gauze screen, and there I placed my couch. The study was surrounded by open space and, having built a platform along the base of the back wall, I proceeded to plant three large tree peonies in a bed of watermelon mulch. Soon the flowers grew higher than the wall and, within the space of a year, they had produced more than three hundred blooms. Two Western Palace crab-apple trees stood in front of the platform, and when in blossom they resembled a deep fall of fragrant snow. The four front walls were high, and opposite these I established a stone terrace upon which I placed a peak or two of Great Lake Rock. The gnarled trunk of the West Brook prunus and one or two Yunnanese camellia trees stood seductively beside the rocks. Beneath the prunus, I planted a blue crown passion-flower and soon it had entwined itself around the trunks like tassels. The bamboo shed visible beyond my window was covered in rambling rose. Below the steps, kingfisher grass grew dense, in the midst of which, here and there, were dispersed a crab-apple tree or two. Beyond the clear front and back windows, the rambling rose and the crab-apple trees gradually began to cast their shadow. Here I would sit or lie, not allowing any but the most refined and honoured of guests to join me. Out of admiration for Ni the Eccentric's "Belvedere of Pure Intimacy", I named my study "Yunlin's Secret Belvedere".[7]

Without Doubleness Studio

The tall paulownia trees of Without Doubleness Studio[8] stretched three *zhang* into the sky, casting about them a tapestry of blue-green shade. To the west of the garden wall, where the ground opened out slightly, the shade was supplemented by that of the wintersweet, but it was nonetheless only on overcast days that the sun's rays did not penetrate here. The wall outside the back window was higher than the window-sill, and there several square bamboos soughed away in the breeze, calling to mind a horizontal scroll by the Yuan dynasty Master Sheng Mou entitled: "The sounds of autumn ring in one's ears."[9] The down-cast shafts of sunlight, when seen dancing within the gaps in the shade, glistened like glass or mica, and sitting there made one feel oneself transported to the Land of Purity. Books lined all four walls, overflowing the shelves and scattered upon the couches; tripods, vases, goblets and jars were everywhere to hand. To the left I placed a stone couch and a bamboo side-table, screening the area off with a gauze curtain to keep the mosquitoes and the flies away. As the dark shade began to penetrate the gauze it would turn my face a brilliant jade-green.

During the long days of summer, the scent of the Fujianese orchids, the jasmine and the fragrant grasses would insinuate itself within the folds of my gown. Around the time of the Double Ninth Festival, the chrysanthemums would be shifted to stand beneath the north window, the pots arranged in five rows of differing heights. So brilliant was the hue of the flowers in the crystal-clear rays of the sun that it was as if they had been immersed in an autumnal river. In winter, the paulownia trees lost their leaves and the wintersweet would burst into flower, a warm sun would bathe the windows and the warmth of the fire-red brazier would be supplemented by that provided by felt rugs; narcissi had been planted amidst the white Mount Kun pebbles and arrayed at the foot of the steps. In spring, mountain orchids would cover the base of the surrounding walls, and beyond the sill a half *mu* of white peonies would burst into blossom, many of them specimens of unusual varieties. There it was that I would doff my gown and stretch out my legs, never going out my door except on most pressing business as the seasons turned from hot to cold. Thinking back upon it now, it was as if the studio belonged to a different world.

Garden of the Mirror of Heaven

Beside the Bathing Ducks Hall of the Garden of the Mirror of Heaven[10] the tall scholar trees and dense bamboos cast a shade that seemed woven of a thousand layers. Sitting facing Orchid Pond, the garden appeared to float upon a vast expanse of rippling waves, and both the water and the trees were bright and clear of hue, with fish and birds and water mellow, all as if one had ascended into the firmament. It was here that I studied, with the deep green vista at my disposal whichever way I turned my head. Whenever within my secluded window I opened up my books, the characters on the pages would turn a brilliant jade-green.

Each year as the spring grew old the bamboo shoots from Broken Pond village would be bound to pass by here on their way into town. A swift little boat would fly into sight, pausing only long enough for the pedlars to throw a bundle of their largest shoots into the pond as they passed, shouting out to those of us in the garden: "The bamboo shoots are here — come and drag them out!", before flying off again amidst the sound of beating oars. My gardener would then proceed to make his way out upon the pond to collect the bundle.

Shaped like ivory trunks, the shoots were as white as snow, as delicate as the root of the lotus, as sweet as the juice of the sugarcane. When boiled, the taste was quite beyond description, and yet I am mortified by shame when I think of such things now.

Suspended in the Branch Tips Pavilion

In my sixth year I accompanied my late father here to Suspended in the Branch Tips Pavilion to study. As I remember it, the pavilion stood beneath a steep cliff face, propped up by timber poles and rocks and with no earth foundation whatsoever; the flying kiosk and the empty hall were as closely connected as the teeth of a comb. Dense shrubbery and tall trees covered the cliff face above the pavilion, interrupted here and there by the eaves and brickwork of other pavilions. The name of the pavilion was taken from that line of the Tang poet Du Shenyan that goes: "And in the tips of the branches was suspended a Jade Hall."[11] Suspended in the camphor trees by means of thick cords, the prospect it afforded one was sublime.

Later on, my second uncle built a hut beneath the cliff as well, and believing what he had been told by the Geomancers to the effect that the pavilion interfered with the dragon veins of the mountain, he taxed his mind for ways to buy it from us. Overnight, the pavilion was dismantled and moved elsewhere and the spot soon reverted to dense vegetation.

Such were the pleasures afforded me by this place in my childhood that in my dreams I often find myself searching for it again.

The Fish Pond of Savouring the Mountains Hall

Twenty years ago I lived most of my time in the Land of Accumulated Fragrance,[12] and if I happened to go into town during the day, I would always make a point of returning there in the evening. A solitary pine squatted beside Savouring the Mountains Hall, its branches all akimbo and some of them dipping their tips into the water in a most unconstrained manner, the pond here being a full three *mu* in circumference. Lotus blossoms crowded the bank, their seed-pods numbered in the hundreds and thousands and all quite delightful in their fresh beauty. Wine brewed with the raindrops collected from the lotus leaves after a recent shower proved a most fragrant potion.

The fish pond outside the gate extended for three hundred *mu* and was planted mostly in water-chestnut and water-lily. The small water-chestnuts resembled ginger shoots and one could pick and eat them; in texture they proved as soft as lotus seeds, in smell, as fragrant as the Fujianese orchid, their taste incomparable. In late autumn, once the tangerines had been ripened by the frost, one could pick the fruit, but only those that had turned a bright orange and then only one by one and very carefully. During the third month of winter I would come here to view the fish; more than a thousand fishing skiffs would line up upon the pond as neat and closely knit as the scales on the fish themselves. Those using hand-held nets would snare them, those using larger nets would pull them in, those with fishing prongs would spear them, those with smaller nets would spread them out, those using bamboo traps would enmesh them and those using hanging traps would pull them in, churning up the soil from the bottom of the pond and turning it into a seething broth of mud. The fish caught in the nets would struggle frantically to free themselves; those lucky enough to have escaped would pant with exhaustion, the smallest fry and the finest scale exposed to view. The skiffs would gather to divide up the catch, the total weighing in at over three hundred *jin*, before setting off home laden with red-eyed and white-bellied fish. I would arrange to meet up with my brothers here to spend the entire day cooking fresh fish and drinking our fill.

Belvedere of the Mountain Top Flower

The Belvedere of the Mountain Top Flower[13] stood within the Pine Gully and below Mushroom Skin Pavilion, set among layered cliffs and ancient trees, poking up above the tips of the forest and surrounded, in autumn, by red leaves. In the eddy that formed as the gully stream forked beneath the slope, the rock foundation of the mountain was sharp and angular, as if set in opposition to the water. The belvedere was given neither door-sills nor lattice windows, nor was a tower or platform built there, the intention being to signal the fact that the conception of the belvedere was as yet not fully realised.

My great-uncle Zhang Wuxue returned from Guangling with a belly-full of ideas for gardens and pavilions and sought to try them out here by building terraces, and pavilions and galleries, by erecting a plank bridge, by having a tower placed directly opposite, by siting beside it halls and belvederes, by entwining the hill with a undulating line of prunus trees. And yet, his efforts in this respect appeared altogether too stiff and solid and crowded, giving only a constricted expression of his original conception, like an ink slab placed within a stone grotto. Standing upon the other side of the river and gazing over at the hill, at the belvedere, at the rock foundation and at the pines that stood in Pine Gully, perversely, the "true face of Mount Lu" could only be obtained from beyond the hill itself.

My uncle requested that I supply him with a couplet. To capture the small details of the place, I came up with the following lines:

> *Hidden within the folds of Mi Fei's Sleeve,*
> *At home in a fan painting of Wheel River Estate.*

Brook Pavilion of the Auspicious Plants

The Brook Pavilion of the Auspicious Plants was sited upon one of the branch foothills of Dragon Hill and stood no taller than the buildings that surrounded it. Prognosticating that fantastic rocks would certainly lie beneath the surface here, my cousin Zhang E proceeded himself to wield the hoe and hump away basketfuls of earth, insisting on uncovering the rocks before his own stonemasons had time to do so. The earth was carted away and the rocks broken up, down to a depth of more than three *zhang*, at which point the foundation was pounded flat and a building constructed. If today a building went up, tomorrow it would be dismantled, only to be reconstructed the day after, and then, the next day, dismantled yet again. This was done seventeen times before finally the Brook Pavilion was completed. But there was in fact no brook here, so the pavilion was given a brook. When the brook was found to be somewhat inadequate, a pool was formed, a gully created, several hundred hands being assembled each day to complete this task, before my cousin made the decision that he may as well have a pond excavated, that the pond may as well be widened by a *mu*, may as well be given a depth of eight *chi*. But the site was without water, and so the pond was filled up bucketful after bucketful, and a table-like stone was left standing in the middle, around which the water eddied as if around a floating mountain peak, and the whole garden began to acquire a most exquisite look. And then my cousin decided that the mountain rocks, having been only recently exposed, lacked the requisite cast of age and hoariness, so he had them coated in horse dung and planted in moss and lichen. When the moss did not immediately grow, he summoned painters to colour them with the blue and green pigments of azurite and malachite. On yet another day, having stood there looking all about him, my cousin suddenly declared that the stone table ought not to be without a Heaven's Eye pine or two coiled upon it and so at great expense he purchased five or six such pines and had holes bored in the rock for the trees to be planted. When the rock could not stand the impact of the metal rods, it split apart; neither rock nor covered in trees, it was now no longer even a table. Enraged by this development, my cousin ordered men to continue work all night, in the attempt to shape it into the form of a mountain inkslab. But when work had been completed, the rock was missing a corner, so my cousin had another huge rock carted here to make up the deficiency. By nature impetuous, my cousin would not wait until the trees grew large but rather would have them replaced by larger trees, and when these transplanted trees died, he would search out for even larger trees to replace them with. This would go on endlessly, with live trees replaced by ones that would die, these dead trees in turn replaced, and in this way his trees could not but die, but would never die immediately.

By now, the Brook Pavilion was a good four *zhang* lower than had been its original foundation and so my cousin had earth moved and a large hill built up to the east of it and had buildings of a full *mu* in area constructed, but these too were all prone to the vicissitudes of constant change. Once a building had been completed, he would sit looking at it for a long while, but by the next day it would in all probability have disappeared. In this way, although the Brook Pavilion was itself a tiny structure, the expenditure lavished upon it was truly enormous.

My cousin happened to be reading a novel one day when he came across the following tale:

On a dream tour of Hell one day, Yao Chong found himself in a huge workshop wherein a thousand forges blazed and several thousand evil ghosts laboured, and where the molten metal flowed urgently. Upon inquiry, he was informed: "We are forging the Prince of Yan's ill-gotten gains." Later, he reached a place where the forges stood idle, attended only by one or two exhausted ghosts listlessly working the bellows. When Yao Chong asked where he was, their reply was: "This is the treasury of the Master." When Yao Chong awoke from his dream, he sighed to himself: "Even the wealth of a Prince of Yan is only held at the pleasure of Heaven."

Much taken with this story, my cousin decided to take the sobriquet "Guest of the Prince of Yan".

My second uncle had accumulated a fortune of some forty to fifty thousand *taels*, but all this flowed away rapidly through my cousin's hands. In the *Jiashen* year [1644], when my uncle died in office in Huaian, my cousin hastened there to attend his funeral, returning with more than twenty thousand *taels* worth of accumulated salary, along with the various baubles and bolts of silk that my uncle had saved and collected. Within three months, all this too had gone. Contemporaries likened him to Yu Hong and his "Four Exhaustions".[14] As to the living quarters attached to the Brook Pavilion, not a day would go by without these being erected, renovated or sold, in an endless tumult of activity. My friend Xia Erjin would while away his days cutting out cloth to make lanterns in the shapes of flowers, and everyone called him a "Bankrupt Emperor Yang of the Sui". My cousin, for his part, they labelled an "Impoverished First Emperor of Qin". It is enough to bring a wry smile to one's lips.

Langhuan Paradise

Taoan's dreams are predestined, and often in his dreams he finds himself within a stone hermitage, set amidst "chasms inside chasms, caverns in crags".[15] In front of this hermitage, a torrent rages and a brook swirls, the cascading water producing a snow-like foam, with fantastically shaped ancient pines growing amidst eccentric aged rocks and with famous flowers interspersed here and there. Here in the midst of it all he sits, in his dreams, with serving boys plying him with tea and fruit, and surrounded on all sides by shelves laden with books. Whenever he happens to open up a volume, he finds that the text is written largely in the tadpole, bird trace or thunder script of antiquity, and yet in his dreams it is as if he can understand even the most troublesome and abstruse of passages. When living in idleness with nothing to occupy his time, he finds himself dreaming of this place as the evenings gather in around him. Meditating upon it when he awakens, he resolved to seek out a marvellous site that could be made to resemble that of his dreams.

Out beyond the suburbs stands a small hill, its rock structure sharp and angular. It is covered in dense bamboo that inclines itself towards the interior of the garden. It is here that I wish to build my hermitage, its hall oriented on an east-west axis and with studies leading off from both the front and the back. Behind the hall I will construct a flat stone surface upon which I will plant a Yellow Mountain pine or two, with gorges formed of fantastic rock to separate them. I will plant also two Sal trees in front of the hall to provide some shade. To the left, I will add an empty chamber facing the foothills that spread out in perfect order before me, split asunder as if by the blows of a sword. Here the plaque will read: "A Single Hill". To the left will crouch a three-roomed hermitage belvedere, overlooking a large pond; the autumnal water will be clear and chill and in the depths of the willows I will read. The plaque here will read: "A Solitary Stream".

Setting off around the hill in a northerly direction will bring one to vihara and small huts, ill-built and low-hung and hugging the contours of the hill, to ancient trees and layered cliffs, to a small stream, to a dense grove of exquisite bamboo. There where the hill ends will be found an excellent cavern and there a tomb will be built for one still living, to await Taoan's transubstantiation, its inscription reading: "Alas, here lies the tomb of Master Zhang Taoan of the Ming." To the left of the tomb, upon a single *mu* of fallow ground, a thatched hermitage will be erected wherein sacrifices may be made to the Buddha and to an image of Taoan himself, and monks will be invited to live here to maintain the place. The large pond will be more than ten *mu* in size and beyond the pond a small river will meander three or four times but prove wide enough to allow boats to enter the pond. The banks of the river, on both sides, will be steep and there fruit trees will be planted; sweet tangerines, prunus, pears and dates, hemmed in by a fence of thorny limebush. A pavilion will be sited on the summit of the hill and the twenty *mu* of fertile fields that border the hill to the west will be planted out in rice of both the glutinous and the non-glutinous varieties.[16] The gate will look out over the wide river, and a small tower will soar above it, from upon which one will be able to gaze at Brazier Peak and Pavilion Mountain. Beneath the tower will stand a gate with a plaque that reads: "Langhuan Paradise". Following along the river on foot to the north one will come upon a stone bridge, rustic and ancient of appearance and covered in shrubbery. Here one may sit, enjoy the breeze and gaze up at the moon.

Notes

1. For short biographies of Zhang Dai, see A.W. Hummel, ed., *Eminent Chinese of the Ch'ing Period, 1644–1912* (Washington: Government Printing Office, 1943), pp. 53–54 and W.H. Nienhauser, ed., *The Indiana Companion to Traditional Chinese Literature* (Bloomington: Indiana University Press, 1986), pp. 220–21. Wai-yee Li, *Enchantment and Disenchantment: Love and Illusion in Chinese Literature* (Princeton, N.J.: Princeton University Press, 1993), pp. 47–50, 169, offers a suggestive discussion of the contrast in mood between Zhang Dai's *Taoan mengyi* [Dream Memories of Taoan] and that of *The Story of the Stone*; see also her "The Collector, the Connoisseur, and Late-Ming Sensibility", *T'oung Pao* (1995), 81(4/5): 269–302 for a more general discussion of Zhang Dai.
2. This expression occurs in both Zhang Dai's "Ziwei muzhiming" [Inscription for My Own Tomb] (Yun Gao, ed., *Langhuan wenji* [Changsha: Yuelu shushe, 1985], p. 199) and in the "Zi xu" [Author's Preface] to his *Dream Memories of Taoan* (Xia Xianchun & Cheng Weirong, eds., *Taoan mengyi: Xihu Mengxun* [Dream Memories of Taoan: Dream Quest for West Lake] [Shanghai: Guji chubanshe, 2001],

p. 3). The translations that follow are based on the text as found in this latter work. Zhang Dai likened his own chaotic age both to a "large touchstone fallen from Heaven" that revealed the "true face" of mortal man, and to a "grand year-end clearing of all outstanding accounts", for which see his *Kuaiyuan daogu* [Recollecting the Past in the Garden of Joy] (Hangzhou: Zhejiang guji chubanshe, 1986), p. 58.

3. "Author's Preface", *Taoan mengyi: Xihu mengxun*, p. 3. The "yellow millet" and the "anthill" referred to here allude to two Tang dynasty tales, the "Zhenzhong ji" [World Within the Pillow] by Shen Jiji and Li Gongzuo's "Nanke taishou zhuan" [Biography of the Governor of the Southern Branch] respectively, for which see Wang Pijiang, ed., *Tangren xiaoshuo* (Shanghai: Guji chubanshe, 1978), pp. 37–39 & 85–90. Both tales tell of men who, having experienced all the joys and splendours of life in a dream, realise the futility of it all once they awaken. For an alternative translation (and discussion) of this preface, see Stephen Owen, *Remembrances: The Experience of the Past in Classical Chinese Literature* (Cambridge, Mass.: Harvard University Press, 1986), pp. 131–41. For a complete (except this preface) French translation of Zhang Dai's *Dream Memories of Taoan*, see Brigitte Teboul-Wang, trans., *Souvenirs rêvés de Tao'an* (Gallimard, 1995). As the preface is undated, no firm date can be ascribed the work. As it is listed in Zhang Dai's "Inscription for My Own Tomb" which (on the basis of internal evidence) must have been written around 1665, this date provides a *terminus ad quem* for the completion of the work; the mention in the preface itself of "the past fifty years" would imply a date of around 1647. The first (incomplete) printed version of the book only appeared in 1775.

4. "Author's Preface", *Taoan mengyi: Xihu mengxun*, pp. 3–4.

5. In the "Gardens within the Town Walls" section of his "Yuezhong yuanting ji" [Record of the Gardens and Pavilions of Shanyin], Zhang Dai's friend Qi Biaojia provides the following note about this garden: "The Temple to the City Guardian stands on the right slope of Supine Dragon Hill, this being the site of Penglai Belvedere of old. Descending the hill, one comes across a single pine standing straight and tall, its ancient branches spread out in disorderly confusion. Here Master Zhang Mouzhi built a pavilion that he named Mushroom Skin and a tower which he named Beyond the Roseate Clouds. Gazing to the south, the mountains of Yue stand bright and elegant, and steep in the extreme. To the right of the pavilion is found Whistling Belvedere, sited here in order to afford a view of the roseate evening clouds, a sight that seems to transport one beyond the very edges of Heaven itself and is certainly not to be compared with the pleasures of merely living in seclusion on a single hill or fishing in a single stream. The Master wrote his own

account of the garden in which he enumerated its twelve internal scenes, its seven external scenes and its six minor scenes. His nephew Zhang Dai wrote a quatrain on each of these scenes in order to preserve their splendour." (*Qi Biaojia ji* [Beijing: Zhonghua shuju, 1960], p. 183)

6. In the "Gardens within the Town Walls" section of his "Yuezhong yuanting ji" [Record of the Gardens and Pavilions of Shanyin], Qi Biaojia provides the following note on this garden: "Late in his life, Master Zhang Rulin built his residence on the slopes of Dragon Hill, opening up a garden to the left. There, Fragrance of the Sea-Perch Pavilion overlooked Master Wang's Pond. Gazing downwards from its windows one could gather to oneself in their entirety all the various splendours of Dragon Hill. The Hall of the Flower of Longevity, the Study of the Clouds of Dawn, the Belvedere of the Intoxicating Sip all stood amidst the encircling water and rocks, within the lustre of the flowers and the trees." (*Qi Biaojia ji,* p. 183)

7. A reference to the painter Ni Zan (1301–74), one of the "Four Great Masters" of the Yuan dynasty.

8. The "Gardens within the Town Walls" section of Qi Biaojia's "Yuezhong yuanting ji" [Record of the Gardens and Pavilions of Shanyin] contains the following note about this site: "Beyond his residence, Zhang Yuanbian had a three-columned tower that served as his lecture hall. His great-grandson Zhang Dai had the place renovated and built his 'Yunlin's Secret Belvedere' behind it. Zhang Dai is a man addicted to antiquity and is a skilled poet and essayist. He has assembled a large collection of rare books and babbles of various kinds, all of which are quite exquisite. In truth, only Lazy Ni Zan's 'Belvedere of Pure Intimacy' provides a worthy comparison." (*Qi Biaojia ji*, p. 189)

9. Zhang Dai here gives Zheng Zizhao, but I accept Xia Xianchun's suggestion that this should be a reference to Sheng Mou (*zi* Zizhao; fl. 1310–60).

10. Again, in his "Yuezhong yuanting ji" [Record of the Gardens and Pavilions of Shanyin], Qi Biaojia provides a short account of this garden, included on this occasion within the "Gardens South of the Town" section of this work: "About a *li* beyond South Gate one comes across Orchid Pond, where the water and the sky seem coloured a self-same jade-green. If visitors care to board a small skiff and to cross the pond they will find themselves at the Garden of the Mirror of Heaven. This garden's excellence lies in the water it contains but is not confined solely to this. Here, distant mountains enter to take their allotted seats and fantastic rocks form the gate. There are halls and pavilions, terraces and ponds, and an entirely new vista presents itself at every turn, each and every one of which allows access to the afflatus of the hills and valleys

as the assembled marvels crowd one's senses. Often, visitors lose their way within the garden. Later, Master Zhang Wuxue built a new South Tower that proved quite surpassing. Of all the various gardens of Shanyin, this must be regarded as the crowning glory" (*Qi Biaojia ji*, p. 196). Zhang Wuxue was the son of Zhang Rumou, a younger brother of Zhang Dai's grandfather Zhang Rulin.

11. Du Shenyan (d. *ca.* 705), the early Tang poet and grandfather of Du Fu (712–70). For this poem (entitled: "Penglai sandian shi yan feng chi yong Zhongnan shan yingzhi"), see *Quan Tang shi* [Complete Poems of the Tang Dynasty] (Beijing: Zhonghua shuju, 1960), Vol. 3, pp. 731–32.

12. In the "Gardens South of the Town" section of his "Yuezhong yuanting ji" [Record of the Gardens and Pavilions of Shanyin], Qi Biaojia provides the following note on this garden: "Land of Accumulated Fragrance: Master Zhang Yaofang established a garden on the central embankment, naming its hall Savouring the Mountains. Here the thousand cliffs and myriad valleys pull open the folds of their gowns and sit facing each other, giving vent to their various opinions. With the Tang poet He Zhizhang's Half Bay and Fang Gang's Solitary Isle shedding lustre on either side, this is Mirror Lake's most splendid site." (*Qi Biaojia ji*, p. 197)

13. In the "Gardens within the Town Walls" section of his "Yuezhong yuanting ji" [Record of the Gardens and Pavilions of Shanyin], Qi Biaojia provides the following note: "This garden is found behind Master Zhang Wuxue's mansion, that is, on the southern foothills of Dragon Hill. Here stone cliffs stand sheer, below which water has been gathered to form a small pond. Flying plank and zigzag bridges provide circuitous passage across the pond, and pavilions and terraces have been built, all appearing like a bouquet of flowers on layered embroidery. I think that even in its own day, Golden Valley could not have stood comparison with this garden." (*Qi Biaojia ji*, p. 184)

14. In the biography of Yu Hong contained in the *Liang shu* [History of the Liang Dynasty] we are told that Yu Hong would often tell people that: "Any commandery that I take charge of can soon be said to suffer from the Four Exhaustions; the rivers are exhausted of their fish and turtles, the hills of their roebuck and deer, the fields of their rice and grain, and the villages of their populace. The hero born in this age is like finest dust that settles upon the yielding grass, like the white colt glimpsed as it bolts past the crack in the wall. The joys and pleasures, wealth and honour afforded man — how long do they last?" See *Liang shu* (Beijing: Zhonghua shuju, 1973), Vol. 2, p. 422.

15. A quotation from Ma Rong's (79–166) "Changdi fu" [Rhapsody on the Long Flute], for which see David R. Knechtges, trans., *Wen Xuan or*

Selections of Refined Literature, Vol. 3 (Princeton, N.J.: Princeton University Press, 1996), p. 261.

16. A reference to the "Biography of Tao Qian": "[Tao Qian] ordered that the public fields be planted out entirely in glutinous rice, saying: 'This will produce enough to keep me well and truly drunk.' When his wife and sons insisted that he also plant rice of the non-glutinous variety, he relented and had one *qing* and fifty *mu* planted in non-glutinous rice and another fifty *mu* planted in glutinous rice." See "Tao Qian", *Jin shu* [History of the Jin] (Beijing: Zhonghua shuju, 1974), Vol. 8, p. 2461.

WILLIAM DOLBY

A Twirl of Two Swords, East and West

The two poets were near-contemporaries, one in China, then under rule by Mongol khans, and the other from Wales, and they each wrote a longish poem exuberating about their sword. Some fog remains, but enough clarity for us to make the comparisons that seem cried out for. There's a strong similarity about some aspects of the two poems, and also strong differences, some of them most intriguing.

Shi Hui 施惠, courtesy-name Junmei 君美/均美, from Hangzhou, lived in the area in front of the City God Temple on Mount Wu 吳山 in Hangzhou, and, for his living, ran a merchandise depot, thus being a trader of fixed location.[1] Zhong Sicheng 鍾嗣成 (ca. 1269–after 1360), the prime contemporary biographer of the poets and playwrights of that period, says that his surname was also found as Shen 沈, a strange comment from a personal acquaintance, if indeed it was Sicheng's comment, and not that of some later editor.

A handsome fellow, with large eyes and magnificent whiskers, Shi Hui was fond of telling jokes and funny stories. Zhong Sicheng, in company with playwright Zhao Liangbi 趙良弼 (ca. 1279–1328), qu-aria poet Chen Wuwang 陳無妄 (?–1329) and a certain Yan Junchang 顔君常, once visited him at his home. Whenever Shi received guests, he would always talk a lot of lofty theory, but when the time came for poetry and wine, would devote himself whole-heartedly to the composition of ci-lyrics and qu-arias. He was a man of very wide interests, and produced a collection of his writings, as well as a work called *Ancient and modern jokes* (*Gu-jin qi-hua* 古今砌話), and another called *Common talk on separation and joining-on* (*Bie-xu chang-tan* 別續常談).

Other much more famous works have been attributed to him in Ming dynasty writings, but somewhat questionably. One of these is the long, witty Southern Plays drama *Secluded boudoir* (*You-gui ji* 幽閨記). Another is China's most famous, or second or third most famous, novel, the rumbustious *Watery badlands* (*Shui-hu zhuan* 水滸傳), a saga of rampaging bandits. In the latter theory, he is dubiously identified with Shi Zi'an 施子安 (ca. 1290–ca. 1365) of Dongdu 東都 (Luoyang in present Henan province), courtesy-name Nai'an 耐庵, cognomen Nai'an Jushi 耐庵居士, a man who held a mandarin post in Qiantang towards the end of the Yuan dynasty (1280–1368), but, not getting on with the regional authorities, abandoned his post, and went home and shut himself away writing books. The attribution of the novel to Shi Zi'an, commonly referred to as Shi Nai'an 施耐庵, is itself also doubtful.

More dependably, *Great Harmony pronunciation-correction tables* (*Tai-he zheng-yin pu* 太和正音譜) by Zhu Quan 朱權 (1378–1448) says that Shi Hui was author of the second act of the non-extant Variety Plays drama *Ptarmigan-feather coat* (*Su-shuang qiu* 鷫鸘裘).[2] The non-dramatic aria-set on a sword, translated below, has only a Ming dynasty attribution to him.

According to Zhong Sicheng's classification, he died before 1330 or so, and might, one reasonably imagines, have been born around 1280 or 1270, or earlier.

The aria-set just mentioned above, whoever the author, is a striking example of the category of poetic composition that the Chinese term Singing-of-things (*yong-wu* 詠物). Its frequent humour, and general air of swashbuckle, certainly fits what we know and may surmise of the character of Shi Hui, and what Chinese scholars of olden times assumed to be his other works.

My Sword

attributed to Shi Hui (ca. 1275–ca. 1325)

When it leaves its scabbard, it's as cold as those northern Ox and
    Dipper constellation stars,
      When it's in my hand, it assists the "winds and clouds" of
        mighty political accomplishments;
When it's stuck in at my waist, impudent traitors are quelled,
When it issues from my sleeve, demons and spirits are subdued:
    It sets a moral standard for righteousness and honesty.
On its fragrant sandalwood hilt, a tiger's jaws swallow a pair of
    pieces of jade;
      On its sharkskin sheath, the dragon scales are densely piled
        with pearl on pearl.
When I hang up its three feet length, it's a waterspout on my wall,
    When it rings in the middle of night, it's a driving rain-douche
      at the end of my bed.

Gold coiling flowers strewn here and there, its buckles hang,
Emerald intricately exquisitely carved jade-stones, its adornments
    are bound round it:
    Men have always vied in admiration of its celebrated beauty.
Lord's shabby shrewd retainer Feng Huan tapped it for a tune to
    his "Fish song" in his forlorn and empty lodgings,
      Future dynasty-founder Liu Bang cut the python in two with
      it on his long journey;
When I meet with noble-minded worthies,
I present it to them by the hilt;
    When I encounter bandits, it straightway eliminates them.
It's of truth more utterly special than the ancient sword Mo Ye,
    Even the ancient sword Gan Jiang couldn't for certain match
    it.
It once met up with the sternly upright knight Zhu Yun, who
    argued against the court slanderers,
It was clever enough to evade the bold martial fellow warlord
    Xiang Yu, as he sighed against the Blue Depths, Heaven,

It lived in fear of having to go around with the assassin Zhuan
    Zhu, as he avenged a private vendetta.
Of unique value,
Unmatched in the world,
    For scores of years it's been my family's heirloom.
It scares men's wits,
    It dazzles men's eyes,
And in company with ten thousand books and one bottle of wine
    It's roamed the wild land all over.

Laughing, I constantly bear it in my hand, dancing before the wine
    jugs,
    Drunk I pawn it, mostly redeeming it after I've sobered,
But just because I've not yet succeeded in being enfiefed as a lord,
    I've long left it overdue there.
Some day when I'm fashioning state laws and running military
    operations,
    It will drive off the southern barbarian vermin, and still the
        northern barbarian "slaves",
    So that it can settle the frontier lands for an age of "pure-time"
        great peace.

This intermingles lavish depiction of the weapon with much
mention of the purposes to which the sword can and should be
put.

The opening five lines of the first stanza proclaim the sword's
potential for great and good deeds. The next four, in contrast,
convey its physical beauty and fierce vitality, the mention of such
words as "tiger", "shark", "dragon", "waterspout" and "driving
rain" reinforcing the notion of it as a vigorous living being.

The second stanza begins with three lines presenting the
sword's beauty as more passively exquisite. Then, though, in lines
13–21, it's given mighty stature by claims that it was used by giant
figures of ancient Chinese history, and not used by others whose
association would have been less favourable! Then lines 22–28,
opening with two resounding two-syllable lines, praise its

matchless value for the poet himself, and say how much it has been his good companion.

Continuing in the personal vein, the final stanza declares the poet's faith that in the future he will use the sword to accomplish his noble ambitions, specifying with pious patriotism that they are not purely selfish, but for the peace and security of the whole empire! No small piety!

On the other side of the world, Dafydd ap Gwilym (ca. 1320–ca. 1380) is the outstanding poet of the rich Welsh-language tradition of poetry and song. Born probably in Brogynin within Llanbadarn parish, just north-east of Aberystwyth, he seems, from his poetry, to have been a romantic or womanising, and frequently itinerant, blade, doing the rounds of taverns and mansions in central and north-western Wales and Cheshire. Full of humour and panache, he often laughs at himself and his failures and tribulations, and depicts his frequent and troubled pursuit of fair ladies, in particular of Morfudd and Dyddgu. With his fine sword, no mere jealous and irascible husband is going to stand in his way!

The Sword

by Dafydd ap Gwilym (ca. 1320–ca. 1380)[3]

Full long you are, you grey form —
    Thank God! — you sword along my thigh.
Your blade, bold fair lord, allows
    No shame to me its companion.
I keep you on my right:
    May God preserve your keeper!
My pretty trinket you are,
    I'm your master, but you're my might.

The husband of my darling doesn't love my life,
    And stout his hindrance, the craftsman of craftiness!
The base notorious taciturn one,
    Plentiful of evil, with his foolish frown, like an ox.

Sometimes he stays quiet — a mood I like! —
    And sometimes he threatens me.

But while I possess you, you silent lord of violence,
    For all his threatening, my mighty weapon,
There's a cold curse over his bed,
    And your master's not hot with fleeing,
Neither on horse — irreverent thought! —
    Nor on foot, despite yon man,
Unless for two angry words from that abomination, the Jealous
    One,
    I'm occasioned punishment for your battling.

Enemy-repelling war-bite!
    You Cyrseus — Otfel's sword — you shearer of a man's lips!
A most elegant hand-stave you are!
    You're a flint, blemish-free.
A good tiding to the crows of battle, of combat's to-and-fro
    turmoil —
    Let the men of Deira retreat from you, you hard double-edge!
You beak of a belt of lightning-fire,
    In your lath-scabbard house I keep you.
Furrowing keen you are against my foe,
    A bright exquisite sharp-grooved sword!

A keen powerful weapon, here's my oath of gold,
    By which I give you my hand and freedom's-grant:
Should there be in a castle grove
    Some night-hawk to waylay us,
        As a little boy's flourish of his "baby-yard" fire-stick,
Run, oh steel, like an orbit of fire!
    And don't hide — you "shield of Cuhelyn" —
        In my hand, should that man come.

Stout wheel-whirl, bright assertion
    Of war you are, you seemly metal;
'Tis you preserve me from harmful men,
    Most righteous sword, grandson of Oliver's Hauteclaire.

I shall wander outlawed on long holiday
   Beneath the trees, me with my shy lady,
And shall not let myself be churlishly plundered,
   Should any man make ill-willed demand.
But part of the family placates me:
   Abundant my tracks by my golden lady's houses!
No fugitive am I! — I'm Ovid:
   "A loving heart is of lofty pride."

Another Singing-of-things poem, but, again, so much more than just of things.

Both poets heighten the resonance of their poetry by alluding to famous or powerful men and things. Neither poet is humble in his comparisons to his sword and himself.

The Ox and Dipper constellations were important in Chinese tradition and mythology. Feng Huan (fl. ca. 280 BC), turned up in tatty straw sandals to become a client of the powerful warlord Lord of Meng-chang. At first given poor food and bleak accommodation, he sat alone, and flexed his sword, singing protest songs to the twang of it. He later did Meng-chang signal service, securing him widespread popularity by feasting numerous of Meng-ch'ang's debtors and burning their loan-deeds.[4]

Liu Bang 劉邦, as Emperor Gao-zu 高祖 (r. 206 BC–195 BC), became founder of the Han dynasty (206 BC–AD 220). While still a rough countryman, he walked drunk through a marsh at night, and, with his sword, killed a big snake blocking his path. Later, at the spot where the snake had been, people found an old woman weeping, and she told them it was because her son, the son of the god White Emperor, who'd changed into a snake and had been "blocking the way", had been slain by the son of the god Red Emperor. This was seen as a sign that Liu Bang was going to change the dynasty, to his own, the Han. Liu subsequently fought the charismatic warlord Xiang Yu, China's greatest political nearly-was, for the mastery of the whole of China, in one of the most dramatic and momentous contests of Chinese history, Liu winning the day, and setting up the first enduring centralised Chinese empire, which lasted for over four hundred years. No mean sword-cut his!

The story of Gan Jiang and Mo Ye is the outstanding Chinese sword tale, at the very root of the Eastern sword-making tradition. It being so central to any discussion of Chinese swords, and to further convey the aura behind Shi Hui's allusion, I quote the source in whole:

Human Self-sacrifice for Making Two Wondrous Swords

by Zhao Ye (fl. ca. AD 40)[5]

Gan Jiang[6] was a Wu[7] man, and had the same master as Ou Yezi,[8] both of them being skilled at making swords. Yue[9] sent envoys to court to present three swords to the King of Wu, and, on receiving the swords, King Helü[10] of Wu viewed them as treasures, and so had sword-makers of his make two swords, one of the sword-makers being Gan Jiang, and the other Mo Ye,[11] Gan Jiang's wife.

To make the swords, Gan Jiang gathered the finest iron from the Five Mountains,[12] and the finest bronze in the Six Joinings,[13] the whole world; he watched for the right moment in Heaven and observed the appropriate time on Earth, when all the gods came and watched, and the vital energies from Heaven came down.

But the bronze and iron were so fine that they wouldn't melt and flow, and, Gan Jiang not knowing the reason for it, Mo Ye spoke up.

"You've come to the notice of the king because of your excellence in making swords," she said, "so if, when you're making swords, you still can't complete them after three months, surely there's some special meaning behind it?"

"I don't know what the reason for it is," said Gan Jiang.

"In such magicking of supernatural things," said Mo Ye, "a human is needed for their completion. In the present case of your making the swords, is it possible for you to complete them without having the human component?"

"In the past, when my master was smelting," said Gan Jiang, "if such metals as bronze or iron wouldn't melt, it would take a husband and wife's both going into the smelting-oven before the objects could be completed. In these present later times, when people go to the mountains to undertake smelting, they don hemp-cloth mourning clothes, and the fragrant rushes of mourning, before venturing to cast metal in the mountains. Is that where the reason lies for no transformation taking place, now that we're trying to make the swords?"

"If your master was aware that one must smelt one's body to complete objects," said Mo Ye, "where's the difficulty for us?"

So then Gan Jiang's wife cut her hair off, and clipped her nails, and threw herself into the oven. He had three hundred virgin boys and virgin girls work the bellows and pack in the charcoal, and the bronze and iron melted, and he completed the swords with them, the male one being called Gan Jiang, the female one Mo Ye, and the male one having tortoise patterns[14] on it, and the female one having flowing-water designs.[15] Gan Jiang hid the male sword, and took out the female one and presented it to the king, King Helü prizing it most greatly.

This story emanates from the historical pre-eminence in sword-smithing of the region of the Zhou dynasty (1122 BC–256 BC) countries Wu and Yue, the present-day provinces of Jiangsu and Zhejiang, in mid-easterly China. An excellence was established there that almost certainly had a strong influence on the esteem for sword metallurgy and on the sword reverence over the water in Japan.

Zhu Yun 朱雲 (fl. ca. 20 BC), the "sternly upright knight" of Shi Hui's second stanza, as a youth was a "knight-errant" ever-ready to fight in just causes, but later suddenly changed his ways and studied books, becoming a mandarin who was bold in giving direct warning counsel to the emperor. Because of this, he was regarded as a hero by later ages.

More briefly, since some of the European references are better known to an English readership, let's turn to Dafydd's allusions. It's not known for sure who Cuhelyn was. There was a Cuhelyn Fardd, a poet and elder contemporary of Dafydd's, but more likely it was some more ancient hero alluded to here, and the "shield of Cuhelyn" is mentioned in awe in earlier Welsh poetry. Conceivably, he was the same person as the Irish hero Cuchulinn.[16] Otfel must have been another hero, perhaps of Charlemagne's time.[17] Oliver, with his sword Hauteclaire, was one of Charlemagne's Twelve Paladins in the Chanson de Roland, who fought against his later great friend Roland in a mighty battle. Ovid (43 BC–AD 17 or 18), who describes a woman's hair as "like silken threads in a vivid Chinese screen",[18] was author of much erotic poetry, such as his *Amores*, *The Art of Love*, and *Cures for Love*, and of the *Metamorphoses*. He was indeed the supreme published European authority on Love, his name resounding through ancient and later European literature. He strongly advocated adultery of the "Courtly Love" kind among the well-to-do. As well as citing someone who is on the same wavelength as himself, Dafydd is evoking a giant name with enormous associations and enduring, massive cultural influence.

As with Shi Hui's original Chinese poem, Dafydd's prosody, in the original Welsh, is intricate, its language rich, and its mood is often happily braggart, although Dafydd's protestations of fearlessness might suggest a certain fundamental and comic admixture of trepidation as, putting his faith in his sword, he heads for his illicit assignation, with the morose-natured husband lurking. In the context of the "Courtly Love" that prevailed in his times, his mission was not as ignoble as modern times might judge it. Quite the contrary: he was doing what high fashion and high-ranking ladies, in the manner of Eleanor of Aquitaine and the troubadors, demanded of a young man worth his salt.

Were the two poets able to meet, as do the international men of literature in Liang Qichao's drama *New Rome*, they would surely laugh with pleasure at the spiritual coincidences and contrasts, the wit, and the shared flamboyant oomph, of their poems.

Notes

1. See Zhong Sicheng 鍾嗣成, *Lu-gui bu* 錄鬼簿, in *Zhongguo gudian xiqu lunzhu jicheng* 中國古典戲曲論著集成, Peking: Zhongguo Xiju Chubanshe, (1959) 1982, vol. 2, p. 123; Fu Xihua 傅惜華, *Yuandai zaju quanmu* 元代雜劇全目, Peking: Zuojia Chubanshe, 1956, p. 228; and Sui

   Shusen 隋樹森, *Quan Yuan sanqu* 全元散曲, Peking: Zhonghua Shuju, 1964, p. 537.

2. Zhu Quan 朱權, *Tai-he zheng-yin pu* 太和正音譜, *Zhongguo gudian xiqu lunzhu jicheng*, Peking: Zhongguo Xiju Chubanshe, (1959) 1982, vol. 3, p. 40.

3. Translated from Parry, Thomas, (gol.), *Gwaith Dafydd ap Gwilym*, Caerdydd: Gwasg Prifysgol Cymru, 1963, pp. 377–379.

4. For a full account of this, see Dolby W. and J. Scott, *War lords*, Edinburgh: Southside, 1974, pp. 78–81.

5. From *Wu Yue chun-qiu* 吳越春秋, "He-lü nei-zhuan" 闔閭內傳. See Yuan Ke 袁珂, *Shen-hua xuanze baiti* 神話選擇百題, Shanghai: Shanghai Guji Chubanshe, 1980, pp. 270–272.

6. Gan Jiang 干將.

7. Wu 吳.

8. Ou Yezi 歐冶子.

9. Yue 越.

10. He-lü 闔閭.

11. Mo Ye 莫邪.

12. Wu-shan 五山.

13. Liu-he 六合.

14. *guiwen* 龜文, i.e. squarish ones.

15. *manli* 漫理.

16. See Parry, op. cit, p. 547, note 39.

17. Ibid. p. 546, note 24.

18. See Green, Peter, (transl.), *Ovid: The erotic poems*, Harmondsworth: Penguin Books, 1982, p. 107.

David and Jean, Peking, 1951.

VIETA DYER

The Money-lender and the Pit

A Crime Story for David

I first met David and Jean in Beijing in 1950. David was completely besotted with the Chinese language and I remember him peering at me from among piles of books. But Jean and I had lots of free time and we used to explore the city, visiting the markets and temples. I knew my Beijing well and at that time it had so many fascinating sights to offer. It is always fun to show friends what you know and it was delightful to show my Beijing to Jean, especially as she was such an enthusiastic and pleasant companion. Yes, I have very happy memories of the two of us roaming the Beijing streets and visiting those special, out of the way places.

So, David, Jean and I became friends in 1950 and we are still friends now. Fifty-two years is a nice, long stretch of time!

As David was up to his ears in the Chinese language, I thought a Yuan dynasty "crime story" might amuse him on his birthday.

This story comes from the *Piao Tongshi* (朴通事), a thirteenth-century textbook of colloquial Chinese. It was written for Korean traders. It has 106 sections and here is one of them:

一箇放債財主。小名喚李大舍。開著一座解儅庫。但是直錢物件來儅時。便奪了那物。卻打死那人。正房背後掘開一箇老大深淺地坑。颺在那裏頭。有一日賣布絹的過去。那大舍叫將屋裏去。把那布絹來都奪了。也打殺撇在坑裏。又一日一箇婦人。將豆子來大的明真珠一百顆來儅。又奪了。也打殺撇在那坑裏。用板蓋在上頭。頻頻的這般做歹勾當。他有兩箇渾家。小媳婦與大妻商量説。我男兒做這般迷天大罪的事。假如明日事發起來時。帶累一家人都死也怎的好。大妻見那般説。對他男兒説勸。常言道。若作非理必受其殃。你做這般不合理的勾當。若官司知道時。把咱們不償命那甚麼。你再來休做。説罷。老李聽了惱燥起來。便要打殺那媳婦。那婦人便走了。走到官司告了。官人們引著幾箇皂隸。將棍繩到那家裏。把老李拿著背綁了。家後坑裏。都搜出三四十箇血瀝瀝的尸首和那珠子布絹。將老李打了一百七。木樁上剮了。一箇官人就便娶了那媳婦。那媳婦道。妻賢夫省事官清民自安。

191.1–195.11

The Money-lender and the Pit

A wealthy money-lender called Li Dashe ran a pawnshop. But what happened was that when someone brought valuables to pawn, Li Dashe appropriated the valuables and then killed the person. He dug an extremely large and deep pit behind the main house to throw the bodies in.

One day, a man who was selling cotton and silk cloth was passing by; Dashe called him into the house, appropriated the cotton and silk and, in the same manner as before, killed the man and threw his body into the pit. And on another day, a woman brought one hundred lustrous pearls to pawn, each about as big as a bean. Li Dashe again appropriated the pearls, killed the woman, and threw her body into the pit. He covered the pit with boards. And he did this evil deed repeatedly.

The man had two wives. The concubine discussed the matter with the wife and said: "Our husband is doing the most terrible things. If he was to be found out, it would involve the whole family in his trouble, and we'd all be put to death too." When the wife heard this she talked with her husband and tried to persuade him [to mend his ways]. "As the common saying goes: 'If one does wrong, one will inevitably suffer due retribution.' You are doing such terrible things; if the officials get to know about it, what else could they do but put us all to death? You must never do such things again." Old Li, when he heard what she had to say, flew into a rage and wanted to kill her. The wife ran away and went to the officials to make an accusation [against her husband]. The officials, together with several police runners, went to Li Dashe's home with clubs and ropes. They captured Old Li and tied him up with his hands behind his back. In the pit behind the house, they found between thirty and forty blood-soaked corpses; they also found the pearls, and the cotton and silk cloth. They gave Old Li one hundred and seven strokes, and then after the flogging they tied him to a stake and sliced his flesh off piece by piece.[1]

An official married the wife. Said the wife: "When a wife is virtuous, the husband has fewer problems. When the official is honest, the people are contented and [live] in peace."

Note

1. The Chinese commentary (195.7–8) adds that the criminal was tied to a large pillar in the execution ground and his flesh was cut off piece by piece and fed to the dogs. Eventually only the bones remained.

MARK ELVIN

Littérateurs and Voyeurs

Shanghai Men of Letters of the 1930s, as Portrayed in Ping Jinya's Novel *Tides in the Human Sea*

Introductory Remarks

This offering of mine on the occasion of David's eightieth birthday forms part of a more extended paper dealing with some fragments of literature, a paper entitled 'The Weeping Dog, or Survival in Shanghai between the Two World Wars'.[1] The fragments are from the second volume of a novel on Shanghai that was a best-seller sixty years ago, *Tides in the Human Sea*, by the lawyer Ping Jinya, writing under the pen-name of 'Spider in the Web'.[2]

Fragments translated. Commented on. Of what use is such literature to the historian?

Several answers suggest themselves. The most obvious is that it is the nearest we can quickly get, for past times, to the *experience* of living in the vanished society with which we are concerned.[3] It undoes, to some extent, the process of selection that underlies our construction of a historical analysis and historical narrative. It reminds us of how remote these products of our normal techniques of documentation and demonstration tend to be from the immediacy of life itself.

Of course, a pattern of understanding has already imposed itself on a work of literature, as it crystallizes in its author's mind, and we know from our own experience, if we are honest with ourselves, that most of life, as lived, is actually of an uncertain intelligibility. Each work can also seduce us with its particularity, with its own sensibility and perspectives. We worry whether it is

or is not representative. But best-selling literature presumably
does represent something that was of significance in its heyday.
More especially, in this particular case, since humour's social
function is the implicit instantaneous testing of the circuits of
communication between different individuals,[4] and much of *Tides*
is humorous, it must often have been touching a substrate of
perception and values common to both the author and his
readers.

Another approach comes from asking what contemporary
literature, especially the novel, is for? Socially, and psycho-
logically, *for*. The answer is so banal that it is usually forgotten.
People read novels to deepen their understanding of how life is
being lived, and to provide them with material for reflection on
how it should or should not be lived.[5] A text as a text is dead. It
comes to life again only as each new reader brings it into relationship with his or her own social and emotional circumstances, and,
directly or indirectly, their economic and political underpinnings.

As historians, with a certain acquired skill in soul-travelling,
we can try to access this process, looking over the shoulders as it
were of the readers of past times.

A third approach, once a work of literature has become
established, is to see it as a 'place of memory' in the sense made
familiar by Pierre Nora.[6] As a well from which readers repeatedly
draw images that refresh their conception of their local or national
identity. This seems to have happened to *Tides*. Immensely
successful when published in 1935, it fell into oblivion during the
period of ideologically dedicated Communist rule, only to
reappear in 1991 when old Shanghai had become the object of a
self-indulgent nostalgia.[7] But in this second incarnation it would
seem to be a different book from what it was in its first. Originally,
it was an expression of the crisis of absurdity that gripped China
between the wars,[8] but today it is a source for people to understand the delicious wickedness of the colourful past, and even to
"give new ideas to those in trade and tourism as to how to exploit
to the full the traditional characteristics peculiar to Shanghai."[9]
Heritage glitz and squalor.

What follows explores only a single theme from the handful dealt with in my longer essay: that of the world of men of letters. It expresses nonetheless Jinya's basic view of Shanghai life: the bizarre interweaving of a cruel and nearly irresistible social system with the freakish contingencies of individuals' lives, a casual daily brutality crisscrossed with camaraderie and kindness, and a grotesque deformation of traditional Chinese values in a way that was not Western, even if triggered by the impact of the West, but having its own nature. Both the longer essay and this extract illustrate and discuss his sense of humour, *passim*: a difficult and recurring examination of how far our own view of the world resembles his. Or doesn't.

I am particularly indebted to my colleague, Professor Liu Ts'un-yan, who lived in Shanghai during the 1930s, for the clarification of a number of obscure points in the text. Additional comments supplied by him are tagged in the notes with 'LTY'.[10]

Men of Letters

Cirrus,[11] a young man just up from the country, naive but intelligent, and his more experienced friend, Bullatus,[12] run into a coterie of local literary celebrities. These hacks symbolize the degradation of a once-great literary tradition. They earn their living by creating and destroying the reputations of the beauties of the floating world, and their admirers, with their columns in the local flysheets. When 'Spider' Ping Jinya set out, in the words of an old acquaintance recalling him half a century later, "to ridicule society and apply acupuncture to the customs of his times" in *Tides*, he was in fact in hiding to escape a lawsuit from a local woman poet, Blue City Lü (Lü Bicheng), whom he had lampooned in this way as "Scarlet Suburbs Li" (Li Hongjiao).[13] So he is to some extent speaking of himself, an insider obliged by circumstance to become for a time an outsider.

There is a gulf between the lofty pretence of the littérateurs and the sordid, sometimes silly, reality in which they live, a gulf symbolized by their sartorial eccentricity.

They were dressed in a variety of ways. Some were half-Chinese, half-Western. Others neither Chinese nor Western. One had a complete Western outfit under a lined silk gown on the outside. Another wore a light green and beige gown edged all round with a wide, soy-sauce-coloured satin lace. Outside this he had a Western-style sleeveless waistcoat. Another again, with exceptionally small feet, wore a pair of soy-sauce-coloured satin shoes in the style of the northern barbarians, with cotton-thread socks. His trousers, with their flared bottoms, were also lined with a broad band of lace. If one looked only at the lower half of his body one would have thought him a cheap trollop from Fuzhou Road, but on his upper half he had on a lined gown and mandarin jacket in a style that was conventional enough.

Bullatus pointed to this last-mentioned.

"That's Prædictulum Yu.[14] They call him the 'Little Female Demon'. As you can see, he's four-fifths feminine, with just the remaining fifth masculine."

The only emotion that Cirrus felt was one of surprise.

Another young man had on a light-blue cotton gown, outside of which he wore an unlined gown of heavy wool, with a pair of grey plimsolls. The laces were missing, and he had dropped the shoes down beside a rattan couch where they looked like two ears wide open, leaving his feet exposed to view. His silk socks had no soles, and the bottom of one of his trouser-legs was bound around with a hemp cord, the other being left untied. He supported a cup of tea in one hand while with the other he picked at the space between his toes.

"That," said Bullatus, "is the renowned literary lion Pluviolus Wen."[15]

"And those two?" enquired Cirrus.

"Probably both novelists," Bullatus answered. "Littérateurs. People unbridled by convention. Nothing to be surprised at."

"Alas!" Cirrus could overhear Mr Prædictulum Yu sighing. "I cannot meet with the ancients who preceded me, nor those who will come after! The man of worth can but sustain his seven-foot person[16] in a dignified fashion, cherish his unappreciated talent, and take as his models Jia Yi, when as Prefect of Changsha he wept tears of pain, or Minister Qu Yuan who threw himself into the Mi river and perished. Alack! How can it not be but an agony?!"

Someone nearby laughed and remarked: "Thank your family for your dignified seven-foot frame, Prædictulum. If you measure it with a metre rule [*sic*] you won't reach seven feet. And, if you are set on dying, there's no need to leap into the river. The Mandarin Duck Pool right here [in the New World entertainment centre] is enough to finish you off; but before you die or not, once you're in the pond and bawling to be rescued, don't forget to holler 'Alack! What an agony!'"

"No wonder he grumbles!" someone else put in. "He's got a myriad chapters in his breast, consummate skill in his person, but not one friend who appreciates him. Really an exceptional case for pity!"

As they were conversing, a gust of air blew the unpleasant odour from between Pluviolus's toes to Prædictulum, who, concerned lest anyone fail to savour the unusual smell, made a point of feigning surprise:

"What a fusty whiff! Whose cigarette end has burned their clothing?"

When the others heard this, none of them could refrain from opening their nostrils and sniffing. Having sniffed, they roundly cursed Prædictulum as a mischief-maker, besides saying to Pluviolus: "Worthy Master Wen, the aroma of your renowned scholarship might with advantage be emitted a little less!"

"He always behaves like this," said Prædictulum. "He's not inflicting a bad smell on you. He's not *just* picking at the space betweeen his toes. Picking at the space between his toes is his expression of his particularity as an unconventional intellectual. Take some of it away with you, retransmit it to the public, and I'll guarantee they'll welcome it, and aver you have brought them some of the colouring of a celebrated savant. If you don't believe me, think back to the day Ineptus Zhang[17] was being sent off to Japan. When he mounted the rostrum to give his address he scattered volley after volley of snotty snivel over his listeners, which was an exceptional honour for them. When they went back home they kept it in their handkerchiefs to show all and sundry as a souvenir. Everyone called it 'paste from a great man on the eve of his departure'."

During this time, Pluviolus had stopped picking at the space between his toes, in all likelihood because he begrudged bestowing on them the fragrant powder of a renowned scholar. (II, 8–10)

The physicality of intellectual processes is an old theme in Chinese humour. (Recall how Tang the Roamer in *The Destinies of the Flowers in the Mirror* farts out those of his writings not worth printing.) The sarcasm here suggests that the lack of refinement in the new breed of literati is not only on the surface but also in the soul. Spider savages their attempts at originality:

"Why," someone asked of Pluviolus, "is one leg of your trousers tied up and the other left loose? What's the use of that?"

Pluviolus gave a laugh.

"Many people leave their trouser-legs unbound, and many tie them up. I am unique in tying one up and not the other. My nature is a singular one. I have no wish to imitate others. I rise in lonely eminence." (II, 10)

This draws the comment from Prædictulum that he hopes everyone has grasped the fact that what makes a scholar famous is having one trouser-leg tied up and the other not. Talk then turns to Pluviolus's laceless shoes. It seems he has removed the laces on purpose, "so I can get in and out of them freely," as well as to be different. He has further smeared his shoes, brand-new, with coalash so that no one can tell if they are really black or really white, "so causing people to be in uncertainty, and preserving my spirit of jade-like authenticity." Prædictulum engages in a catty play on words:

"It would be hard to take *you* as a model. Let me ask all present: if *you* were to put on Pluviolus's honourable shoes and priceless socks, could *you* stir a step outside your main door? If you can't go out the main door (*chu da men*) you can't be reckoned to be a famous scholar. That Pluviolus can wear such things without a trace of embarrassment is *his* particularity as a famous scholar." (II, 11)

Pluviolus sighs, and quotes both the *Mencius* and — inaccurately — Qu Yuan's self-description in 'The Fisherman' in *The Songs of the South*: "Where now is the unsullied Sage? The Sage who acts in timely fashion? All the world is turbid, and I alone am pure!"[18] He explains in reply to a question that his book *Listening to the Rain* is "not to be compared to your hastily scrawled works," and has needed eight to ten years to complete. "For more than three months past I have written only two sentences with which I am satisfied." Some pages later, however, we learn he writes books on commission in a month or two.

There follows a discussion of pen-names:

"For more than a month now," said Pluviolus, "I've been pondering over a *nom-de-plume*, but without solving the problem. The difficulty of finding one is harder than ascending the blue vault of Heaven. All the pseudonyms that give one a good feeling have been grabbed by other people."

"For your last work," said Prædictulum, "you used something like 'Master Sheep-Can't-Safely-Graze' (*Yang-bu-shi sheng*),[19] which is not in the least conventional. You can hardly mean to tell us that *this* has also been pinched by someone else?"

"There was no literary source for that name," said Pluviolus, "so I only used it once. I'd now like to play around with a name featuring 'mountain dweller' (*shanren*) in it.[20] Mountain dwellers are all the rage on the market. Sobriquets — 'Master of such-and-such a studio' or 'Proprietor of this-that-or-the-other pavilion' — are *passé*. It has to be one with the 'mountain dweller' flavour. What mountain would sound good, do you think? And is agreeable to hear when read out loud?"

"Are there any mountains in your home region?" asked Prædictulum.

"Can't say," said Pluviolus. "I come from Taizhou, but we moved to Suzhou when I was young. Can you imagine — both 'Tiantai Mountain Dweller'[21] and 'Seven Sons Mountains Farmer'[22] have been grabbed by the said two people! I wouldn't want to get involved in a lawsuit with those two! [He forgets they are both long dead.] More detestable still, my maternal grandmother's family is from Changshu and I've had 'Mountain Monk of Wumu' pinched from me.[23] There's nothing I can do.... I've thought of this. I've thought of that. If only I could find another mountain, then I'd be able to contrive something."

"Are there any mountains in Shanghai that would be suitable?" said Prædictulum.

"There are no mountains in Shanghai," replied Pluviolus.

"You're only playing with the notion of 'mountain dweller'," returned Prædictulum, "and none of these writers in actual fact lived on the top of a mountain, did they? It was simply what Suzhou people call 'living off make-believe'. So you might as well go straight ahead and use a scenic feature right in front of you, by the bank of the Mandarin Duck Pool down there. Be a 'Fake Mountain Dweller' (*Jia shanren*)!"

"Three characters is too short for me," objected Pluviolus.

"The fake mountain's had cement poured over it," said Prædictulum. "If you feel an aversion to a short *nom-de-plume*, call yourself 'Cement Mountain Dweller' (*Shuimenting shanren*)."

"Five characters is distastefully long," said Pluviolus.

"That's really difficult, then," said Prædictulum. "There's nothing for it but battling with others for a mountain-top. Perhaps you could share a mountain stronghold? Instead of 'Seven Sons Mountains Farmer' you could be 'Seven Sons Mountains Fisherman', or 'Monk'. ..." (II, 11–12)

This sterile brainstorming is brought to an end by Vagans Wang[24] who tells them that when his wife was pestering him for a fancy alternative name he found it easiest to *steal* her one. Faced with incredulity from Prædictulum as to how this could have been done, Vagans explains:

"I've a talent for thieving, as I'll show you. It's also good for a laugh. There is a young lady called Selflove Yang in the Yang Mansion opposite where we live. She is fond of submitting articles to the flysheet newspapers. One day she pasted a strip of paper on her door that read:

Dwelling of the Mistress of Lightly Pencilled-In Moth Eyebrows.

When my wife saw this she burst into tears and berated me: 'Why couldn't you bust your guts and do your damnedest to think of something for *me*? *They* thought of something as soon as they tried.' It's more than I can bear to be so put down by her.

"I racked my brains and came up with a way of stealing it. It so happens that the line:

With lightly pencilled-in moth eyebrows she faces the Most Revered

comes from a Tang poem [by Zhang Hu]. So I wrote out in large characters

Abode of the Most Revered

and pasted it up on *our* door. [The term 'Most Revered' of course refers to the Emperor.] Before two days had passed, Lady Scholar Selflove Yang had become embarrassed and removed her own slip of paper. Once this had happened I myself wrote a strip in just the same manner that she had, and pasted it up. She made no trouble for us. I was exceptionally satisfied at having stolen this fancy appellation. It also makes a pretty story."

Prædictulum and Pluviolus both laughed when they heard this.

"Elder brother Vagans," Pluviolus asked, "does your respected wife really take pleasure in playing with those trifles that come from the tip of a writing-brush?"

"She doesn't know many characters," answered the other. "One could call her action copying what she sees in others."

"If that's the case," said Prædictulum, "what purpose was served by your thieving a name for her?"

"She has it written on her bag, and inscribed on her foot-basin," said Vagans. "There's no use of much importance for it."

"Careful then, elder brother! Careful!" said Prædictulum. "It could be that, having in her love-making ridden on top of the steed Red Hare, she's already embroidered it on his rump!"[25]

Vagans flushed red with embarrassment.

"You," he returned, "never have anything pleasant to say." (II, 13–14)

As Cirrus sits listening to this "extravagant talk and imposing discussion," he cannot repress his laughter. Bullatus rebukes him:

> "These are the literary lions of Shanghai. Every page of the flysheet newspapers is filled every day with their masterpieces. Even the foot-trimmers for men in the bath-houses for bathing in shared water (*huntang*), the vendors of stove-boiled water, the petty cobblers, and the poverty-stricken seamstresses, every last one of them reads their masterpieces with attention. No matter whether it's the review *Improved Saturday* or the *New Nineteen Feelings from the Female Body*, every section is perused and fixed firmly in the readers' minds.[26] You could call these people the troubadours of our times. You must not look down on them." (II, 15)

The predatory nature of journalists is shown by the behaviour of Twiceborn Yan[27] who writes a column headlined 'Histories of the Flowers', or, as he describes it, 'News from the world of pleasure'. (II, 18) While being entertained by the singing-girl Coral Blossom in the company of Cirrus, Bullatus, and others, he boasts that his paper has an exceptionally good intelligence system. Coral Blossom has to some extent brought trouble on herself by untruthfully denying that she is about to marry an elderly silk-cocoon merchant from Huzhou, called Mao. Twiceborn twists the knife in her heart by regaling the others with the true story in her presence:

> "Mao was as if bewitched when he saw her, but fearful she'd dislike him for being so old. So last month he shaved his whiskers clean off, then summoned her to come and see him. Don't you find that hilarious?! To ask a good-time girl in a house of pleasure to be one's secondary wife (*yi taitai*) and think it worth the pains of shearing off in a twinkling the whiskers one has nurtured for twelve years! Respected Mr Mao is the only one who has ever been willing to do such a thing. I am waiting for the very day they conclude this fine match, when I'll make the most robust fun of them in the paper with this episode."
>
> "Young gentleman," pleaded Coral Blossom with urgent concern, "please spare our feelings." (II, 23)

The media have already picked up the habit of damaging people's lives.

Cirrus and Bullatus, with another friend called Inritus Ma,[28] later set off to visit Pluviolus in his home, which is in an alley above a stables operated by a firm hiring out horse-drawn carriages. Having gone upstairs they find the door to the room half-open:

Inside they heard the sound of steps on the staircase. A woman's face emerged to take a look at them, then withdrew to take a small child by the hand, after which she nervously came out of the room door. Inritus recognized her as Pluviolus's wife.

"Is elder brother Pluviolus at home?" he asked.

"Inside," said the woman.

The three of them pushed at the door and went in. They spotted Pluviolus sitting on the edge of the bed and scribbling non-stop.

"Apologies for not coming to greet you," he called out in a muffled voice. "Everyone is welcome."

His brush continued to move as he spoke.

Inritus advanced and wiped a bench clean, inviting Bullatus and Cirrus to be seated on it, and sat himself down on the edge of the bed next to Pluviolus. The latter was obliged to stop writing, as he chatted with him.

Cirrus surveyed the interior of the room: apart from the bed, a table, and the bench there were only a few cooking pans, some bowls, and a wood-burning stove. Nothing more. Overall, it was an apartment built over a lane, and divided into two rooms. The door to the inner one was locked. A strip of paper on the door read *Residence of Chen from Weiyang*, in all probability another family. Across a small, airtight, window were stretched a number of cords with three pairs of bottomless socks hanging from them, and a couple of cloths of some sort or other.

The table-top held a variety of things: a pile of battered old Western and Chinese books; complete sets of Western and Chinese writing implements; and, in their midst, a small, make-believe, mountain glued together from lumps of coal and iron filings. On either side, in flower-pots as wide around as teacups, were planted three stalks of dried-up asparagus fern. In a glass bowl barely the size of an electric light bulb were two half-dead goldfish. A tinplate box was chock-full with false-topaz seals. A flower, in a small vase missing its mouth, appeared to be alive. Blackish-grey mosquito-netting was draped over purplish-grey coverlets. Four dents from buttocks were impressed on the cushions, exactly resembling the faces of kitchen-gods, being round and plump and only short of noses and eyes. At the head of the bed hung a girlie calendar, and to either side of it a pair of matching scrolls, inscribed by Pluviolus himself, as if to the rhythm of some old tune. The first of these read:

Mosquito-nets are the mosquitoes' world

while the second said:

And coverlets the homeland of the lice.

When Cirrus spotted these he could not prevent himself from sniggering.

His laughter induced a discomfited reaction from Pluviolus, who tossed his head and recited:

A room that is bare as a hanging stone-chime,
A house short of— even — one picul of rice,
Bespeak the Confucian's impoverished lot,
And life in the home of the far-renowned scholar.

When Inritus set eyes on the paired scrolls he also felt impelled to laugh.

"Contrary to what you may be thinking," said Pluviolus, "that couplet is a product of the Realist School. Not only are there a lot of stinking lice on the bed, but even more mosquitoes. The reason is the stables underneath, mosquitoes being a specialty product of theirs. Every evening we hear a rumbling like thunder as the carriages come to bring welcome guests to my halls."

Inritus wanted to push the window open to take a look at these stables, but did not dare do anything precipitate on account of the tattered socks and nappies that were hanging across it. (II, 36)

When Inritus asks if another family lives in the second room, Pluviolus answers:

"You could say so. It's the secret love-nest of a good-time girl from the Blue Lotus Pavilion teahouse [frequented by good-time girls] on Fuzhou Road."

"Having such a savoury neighbour is unexpected," observed Inritus, unable to prevent himself from being shocked.

Pluviolus uttered a cold laugh: "What you don't realize, elder brother, is that the name of my apartment — *Apartment Where One Listens To The Rain* — derives from this. From *this*. Can you not see, elder brother, that there are two holes in the wall? I use the smaller one when looking just by myself. The larger one is for my wife and me when we are peeping through together.

With scenes of amorous joy to view,
The night rain is worth listening to.

They pitch up and down all over the room, and engage in countless topsy-turvy tricks. That's why I have given my apartment the name it now bears."

Cirrus and Bullatus could not help tittering.

"There's another stanza I'm rather proud of," added Pluviolus. "Let me recite it to you. It runs:

At night-time in the little room
    Listening to the storms of sex
Needs flowers of chrysanthemum
    Next day purchased from the chemist."

"What's the meaning of the last two lines?" asked Inritus.

"When you have been watching the male phœnix inverted and the female bell-bird bottom-side up," replied Pluviolus, "when you've heard the clouds breaking apart and the raindrops spattering, it's hard for an inflammation not to rise and make one's eyeballs turn red. It is essential to go to the pharmacy and buy sixty cash-worth of mulberry-leaf sweet chrysanthemum for drinking and an eye-wash."

All three visitors burst into wild unstoppable laughter as he said this. (II, 37)

Bullatus then flips through the manuscript of some poems that Pluviolus has asked him to appraise. They have titles like 'Feelings on listening to theatricals from beside the *marrons glacés* stall', which causes Bullatus to smile. He observes, "Your masterworks take an equal delight in the refined and the vulgar." When he sees a manuscript volume bearing the title *As Yet Unfinished Drafts By The Dweller On The Iron-Pearl Mountain*, he enquires where Iron-Pearl Mountain is. Pluviolus enlightens him: "That's the new *nom-de-plume* I put on it yesterday evening. Iron-Pearl Mountain is right in front of you." And he points to the glued coal-lumps and filings on the table-top:

> "That, there. I've designated it 'Iron-Pearl Mountain'. This *nom-de-plume* is refined, captivating, and elegant, and with a clear resonance. It suits me well."
>
> "Henceforth," said Inritus [referring obliquely to the *Songs*[29]], "you may live atop a mountain and await the time for your advancement [*yanghui*]."
>
> "The reason I have gone out but little recently," said Pluviolus, "and written behind a closed door, is that it has afforded me much pleasure. You can see that I have planted bamboos [the asparagus ferns, which as *wenzhu* are 'bamboos' of a sort] and rear fish in order to cheer myself up. It's a shame that the goldfish bowl is a bit too small, not fit to be compared to the bridge across the river Hao [where the ancient philosophers Zhuangzi and Hui Shi long ago discussed the happiness of fish], and that the three asparagus ferns have withered all too easily — something over which [the Song-dynasty poet] Su Dongpo would have sighed in regret."
>
> "Your mountain studio is fresh and remote," observed Bullatus. "Peaceful your dwelling upon the crags. In verity, deeply suited to a man of refinement. The sole drawback is that, inevitably, the stables down below exert a noxious effect upon the scenery."
>
> "Even the stables have their advantageous aspects," replied Pluviolus. "In the second and third months of the year, I open the window to take a look. Down there it is, in truth,
>
> *Bridles of gold and neighing steeds on the fragrant grass below,*
>
> and, when our perfumed neighbour upstairs here has gone to sleep, it is also

Jade-storeyed Heaven, where man swoons drunk, and apricot blossoms blow."

As he spoke these lines,[30] the other three again started laughing. Inritus then handed some draft advertisements to Pluviolus to revise ... which the latter perused, shaking his head, while with his right hand he rubbed together pill-sized pellets of muck and sweat along his thigh, flicking them with two fingernails at the visitors opposite. Cirrus was inattentive enough to be hit by a couple of these, one on the lips and the other on his temple.

Bullatus, alarmed as a bird threatened with a crossbow, tugged Cirrus with the intention that the two of them should escape.

"We'll go together," said Inritus.

Pluviolus, however, wanted to read them a section on 'The One-Eyed Bonze'[31] from a tale of his on knight-errantry. Bullatus, who by now could endure no more, said:

"One-eyed bonzes have been much in evidence. Don't read it to us. We have to say farewell."

So saying, he pulled at Inritus, and all three of them went down the stairs holding their noses, and out of the stable alley, till they reached the fresh air, and their spirits revived.

"Just now you said of his section on 'The One-Eyed Bonze' that they have been much in evidence. You're not implying he's plagiarized it are you?" asked Inritus of Bullatus.

"I wouldn't dare accuse him of plagiarizing it," replied Bullatus. "I am merely conscious that this theme may be interpreted differently. All you have to do is to go to all those little cabins the Municipal Council has put up along the main streets and take a look. You'll see I don't know how many one-eyed bonzes!"

When it dawned on Inritus what this referred to [*membra virilia* in the municipal *pissoirs*], he couldn't stop laughing.

"I would rather go and look at the one-eyed bonzes in the little cabins," commented Cirrus, "than read what he's written about them." (II, 37–8)

The littérateur is thus a voyeur. But a voyeur who interferes with what he is looking at. Even ordinary people now live, at least in part, through the medium of the stories created for them by the media; and these concocted stories, spun from a mixture of fact, invention, and interpretation, can have an impact for good or for ill on the lives of the 'real' people co-opted, whether they like it or not, to take roles in them. Yet, as voyeurs, writers are parasites dependent on the emotions of others. They vaunt their authenticity while secretly obsessed with exploiting current fashions.

People are always testing each other out, quite frequently through the medium of humour. Laughter is more often the symptom of mockery, or teasing, than of honest merriment. It also serves, as only humour can, as a tacit reminder of the reality that everyone knows lies underneath the surface pretences. It is hard work, though, always keeping one's wits about one. And the literary crowd are the cruellest, subtlest, mockers of all.

And the glories of Chinese culture? They are now little more than a desperate embellishment that serves to cover a degraded tradition and a degrading urban modernity. To bestow a certain pretentious dignity on the undignified. The essence of the city is fakery. Ersatz.

And, last of all, perhaps worst, city life robs people of contact with nature, yet the hunger for nature remains pathetically intense. At best it finds a modicum of relief in such objects of affection as captive goldfish, wilting ferns, and a table-top 'mountain' glued together from coal and iron filings.

Concluding Remark

"We all know that art is not the truth," said Picasso. "Art is a lie that causes us to grasp the truth, or at least as much of the truth as we have been given the power to comprehend."[32] *Tides in the Human Sea* is such art. Illuminating falsehoods that light up the human darkness of the sober archives.

Notes

1. This extract from my hitherto unpublished paper is reprinted here by kind permission of the editor, Catherine Yeh. [We have preserved the author's convention of only using double quotes in the main text to indicate direct speech or a literal citation from an identified source. Eds.]

2. 'Wangzhu-sheng', *Renhai chao* (Shanghai: Zhongyang shudian, 1935), 5 vols., hereafter *Tides*. For more bibliographical details, see M. Elvin, *Changing Stories in the Chinese World* (Stanford: Stanford University Press, 1997), pp. 258–59.

3. Some excellent books have appeared recently on life in Shanghai. Examples are A. Roux, *Le Shanghai ouvrier des années trente: Coolies, Gangsters et Syndicalistes* (Paris: L'Harmattan, 1993); B. Goodman, *Native Place, City, and Nation: Regional Networks and Identities in Shanghai, 1853–1937* (Berkeley: University of California Press, 1995); and C. Henriot and A. Roux, *Shanghai années 30: Plaisirs et violences* (Paris: Autrement, 1998), to name only a handful. I mean no disrespect to these fine works when I say that what I think of as the distinctive 'voice' of the city only comes through them at a few moments, and they are among the best writing we have on the topic.

4. See M. Elvin, 'The Spectrum of Accessibility: Types of Humour in *The Destinies of the Flowers in the Mirror*', in R. T. Ames, Chan Sin-wai, and Mau-sang Ng, eds., *Interpreting Culture Through Translation: A Festschrift for D. C. Lau* (Hong Kong: The Chinese University Press, 1991), pp. 101–103 and 115–16.

5. Oliver Cohen, 'Litterature, mode d'emploi', *Le Monde*, 19.iii.99.

6. Pierre Nora, ed., *Les lieux de mémoire*, 3 vols. First published, 1984, 1986, and 1992, Paris: Gallimard (Quarto), 1997. See especially vol. 3, 'Singularités', for Antoine Compagnon's essay on Proust.

7. In the second collection of the *Shanghai-tan yu Shanghai ren congshu* [Series on the Shanghai Bund and Shanghai People] (Shanghai: Shanghai guji chubanshe, 1991), 2 vols.

8. Elvin, *Changing Stories*, chapter 3.

9. 1991 edition, publisher's blurb, p. 2.

10. Other resources include the *Shanghai cidian* [Shanghai dictionary] (Shanghai: Fudan daxue chubanshe, 1989), which is a basic reference for lexicographical and many other references, a gift for which I wish to thank Professor Hsiung Ping-chen of the Academia Sinica. The glossary provided in Hu Shi's edition of the *Haishang hua* [The Flowers of Shanghai] (Shanghai: Oriental Book Company [Yadong tushuguan], 1926), 4 vols., I, *Lieyan*, pp. 5–23, has also proved exceptionally helpful. So to a lesser extent has the *Tuhua ji'nan* [Guide to local speech] (2nd

edn., Shanghai: Cimu-tang, 1908), with a French translation entitled 'Boussole du langage mandarin, traduite et romanisée en dialecte de Chang-hai', kindly given to me by Dr Igor de Rachewiltz. Catherine V. Yeh, 'Reinventing ritual: Late Qing handbooks for proper customer behavior in Shanghai courtesan houses', *Late Imperial China* 19.2 (Dec. 1998), has a useful glossary.

11. Yiyun, 'raiment of clouds'. 'Cirrus', besides of course being a cloud, also denotes the fringe of a garment, or curly hair. Read Yiyún it can be glossed as 'wearing clouds'.

12. Biru, 'like a jade amulet'. 'Bullatus' means both 'wearing an amulet' and 'bombastic'. He is quick with verbal repartee, so this fits.

13. *Tides*, 1991 edition, *yinyan*, p. 1.

14. Xiaozhao, 'Little Omen'.

15. Shaoyu, 'Young Rain'.

16. A traditional classical phrase. The pre-Qin 'foot' was around 23 centimetres (roughly 9 western inches). See Qiu Guangming, *Zhongguo lidai du-liang-heng kao* [Researches on measures of length, capacity, and weight in successive Chinese dynasties] (Beijing: Kexue, 1992), p. 11. Seven such 'feet' were thus about 5 feet and 3 inches in our terms.

17. Zhang Chizi, 'Simpleton'.

18. J. Legge, trans., *Mencius* V.B.1; D. Hawkes, *The Songs of the South* (Oxford: Clarendon Press, 1959), p. 90, and Ma Maoyuan, *Chu Ci xuanzhu* [*The Compositions of Chu*, with selected notes] (Hong Kong: Xinyue, 1962), p. 222.

19. The *yang-bu-shi cao* or *zhizhu hua* is a kind of rhododendron reputed to make sheep stagger.

20. Usually of course rendered 'recluse' or 'hermit', but this prevents the translation of the ensuing games with words.

21. He Shi, the Ming poet and painter.

22. Unidentified, but these mountains are in Jiangsu.

23. This probably refers to Huang Zongyang, a monk of the late Qing and early Republic; less plausibly, to Yu Yi, the Qing connoisseur. (LTY) The second is given in the *Zhongguo renming da cidian* [Large encyclopaedia of Chinese names] (Hong Kong: Taixing, 1931), fulu, yimingbiao, p. 20.

24. Wang Sanke, or 'Gadabout'.

25. Prædictulum is insinuating that she is having an affair, like the maid of General Dong Zhuo, who owned the famous horse, and perished as a consequence of this infidelity. "Red Hare" is also a term for the *membrum virile*.

26. The first of these, *Gailiangliu*, may refer to the weekly *Saturday* (*Libailiu*). (LTY) The second may refer to the phrase 'the eighteen

feelings out of a female body' (LTY), but goes one better. [This must surely be Trinket's favourite ditty 'The Eighteen Touches', in Louis Cha's novel *The Deer and the Cauldron*, vol. 3, p. 236 et passim. Eds.]

27. Fusheng.
28. Kongji, 'Vain Hopes'.
29. B. Karlgren, *The Book of Odes* (Stockholm: Museum of Far Eastern Antiquities, 1950), number 293: Zhousong, 'Zhuo'.
30. From Wei Zhuang, an official and poet who lived mostly in Sichuan in the late Tang and early Five Dynasties.
31. A Buddhist monk. Monks of course had tonsured heads.
32. Cited by Philippe Dagen in *Le Monde*, 15.v.98.

BRIAN HOLTON

Frae the Nine Sangs

A Wee Pendicle ti "Suddron Sangs" bi Dauvit Hawkes

Ane
Michtie Monad, Eastren Lord

a seilie day, ay, the hour a luckie ane
mensefu we come, see, ti ser the Lord Abune
claymores in haun, ay, aa jade-heftit
gemstanes jinglin, see, wi sardane an wi beriall
wi jowelt rugs, ay, an wechts o jade
sae beir awa, see, the flouerie offrands
mappiemou mait, ay, an mats o mascorn
pour the cannel yill, see, the pepperie brose
lift the drumstick, ay, an touk the bodhran
hoolie the urlar, see, an slaw the sang
clarsach an chanter, ay, a sonsie skirl
hie-heidit the Cailleach, see, brankit sae brawlie
wi ferlie oams, ay, the haas are fou
the Five Souns monieplied, see, mellit thegither
the Lord taks pleasance o't, ay, crouse-like an cantie

Twa
Lord inben the Cluds

doukit wi spykarie, ay, locks wuishen sweet
claes o monie colours, see, braw wi the gingie-flouer
souple bends the Cailleach, ay, the Speirit's upon her
leamin in the lowe o't, see, mair yit ti come
sirs, he's ti rest, ay, i the Hous o Lang Life
like the sun and the mune, see, burnin sae bricht
dragon yokit, ay, wi mantill imperiall
nou the Speirit's on the stravaig, see, reingin aa roun
the Cailleach's fair a ferlie, ay, nou come doun
on a suddentie the Speirit flees, see, inben the cluds
he owreleuks the Nor-East, ay, an faur ayont it
the Fower Seas he traivels, see, an whae wad stent him?
think lang on the lord, ay, an mak great mane
be byornar hertsair, see, doilt wi dule

Thrie
Leddy o the Xiang

the Leddy disna muve, ay, she's switherin
eh, whae is't waitin, see, awa on the annay?
weill-faured an lousome, ay, buskit sae brawlie
smoothlie A skiff, see, in cannel-wuid coble
Yuan an Xiang Watters, ay, smaa be yir waves
lang Watter o Yangzi, see, saft may ye rin
A weary for the Leddy, ay, still she hesna come
wheeplin on her pipe, see, wha does she think on?
fleein dragon yokit, ay, norlin A gang
roun-about ma road, see, ti the Loch o Dongting
bindwood palins, ay, bund wi curl-doddie
graith o the seggans, see, pensell o the soucie
leuking owre ti Chenyang, ay, on the ither shore
owre the Muckle Watter, see, lat aefauldness be kent

lat aefauldness be kent, ay, tho it hesna happent yit
sweir is ma sister, see, makin mane for me
A think lang on the Leddy, ay, tho laich be ma place
airs o cannel-wuid, see, helmstock o the mascorn
kirnin at ice, ay, freithin't inti snaa
pou the bindwuid, see, out the watter
pouk the lillie, ay, doun frae the treetap
hairts no ane, see, a warsle for the match-wyfe
hairt-likin no deep, ay, licht'll be the twynin
river rack, see, pirlin an papplin
fleein dragon, ay, flichterin an flaffin
forgaitherin no leal-hairtit, see, lang'll be the canker o't
ye keepitna the tryst, ay, said ye'd nae by-time
i the dawin A skelp, see, owre watterside mosses
i the gloamin A rest, ay, on the Norlan Annay
birds reist, see, on ma riggin-heid
watter rins, ay, aa roun ma hous
A'll birl ma ring o jade, see, intil the Lang Watter
A'll fling ma enseignies, ay, in the Douce Burn
On Perfumit Annay, see, gaitherin the gingie-flouer
A'll haun it aa doun, ay, ti you yins at comes efter
this tid canna weill, see, be twice taen
A'm gaun raikin a whylie, ay, ti play on in pleisure

Fower
Guidwyfe o the Xiang

dochter o a god, ay, on the norlan annay
hyne-awa leukin, see, maks uis hairt-sair
wind o hairst, ay, souchin, souchin
faain leafs, see, on Dongting wave
on white seggans steppin, ay, A leuk outbye
trystit wi her, see, ahint hingins at een
hou's the birds forgaitherin, ay, awa i the rashes?
hou's the fishin nets, see, up i the treetaps?

angelica on Yuan Watter, ay, mascorn on the Li
for thinkin lang on Ma Leddy, see, A daurna tell
drowie, drumlie, ay, leukin farawa
watchin the rinnin, see, o watter onendin
hou's hert an hind, ay, inben the close?
hou's the burn dragons, see, up on the haughs?
i the dawin A ride, see, owre watterside mosses
i the gloamin A rest, ay, on the Westlin Carse
A hear ma luve, see, she's cryin on me
hurlin in ma cairtie, ay, we'll wheech awa thegither
we'll bigg a hous, see, in ablow the watter
theik the riggin, see, wi leafs o the lillie
waas o the seggan, ay, an purpie-wulk chaumers
tak perfumit peppers, see, ti mak the haas
cabers o the cannel, ay, an spykarie bauks
lintels o magnolia, see, bouer o angelica
weavit bindwuid, ay, ti mak the hingins
owretrees o riven mappie-mou, see, for the easins
white jade, ay, for the haa
skail stane-gress, see, for its sweet smell
theikit wi angelica, ay, chaumer o the lotus
wappit, see, wi cammavine
hunners o flouers, ay, fillin the haa
sweet oams skailin, see, in througang an yett
thrang on Mount Mislippen, ay, meeting thegither
comin o the speirits, see, monie as the clouds
A'll birl ma ring o jade, see, intil the Muckle Watter
A'll fling ma cuttie serk, ay, in the Douce Burn
On Peacefu Haughs, see, A'll pouk the gingie-flouer
an sen it, ay, ti Her Hyneawa
time canna weill, see, be taen mair as yince
A'll raik on a whylie, ay, ti play on in pleisure

A Chuckie Stane for Hawkes

"It is a given of modern translation theory, however, that the literary translator does not merely relay a message: she herself must also be a creator. Making creative decisions means also being prepared to face criticism for these decisions. But it is better, in my mind, to be criticised for excessive or misjudged creativity than to be criticised for translating the words but losing the poetry."[1]

Nine Sangs

In these Scots versions of the *Jiu Ge* poems, I have followed Hawkes' versions in *The Songs of the South*,[2] but fairly loosely. In the case of the first three *Sangs* I have rather relied for much detail on Geoffrey R. Waters' analysis and commentary in his *Three Elegies of Ch'u*,[3] but in all cases, I have made my own decisions in order to make a more perfect accommodation with the form I have chosen. I have not attempted to match the syllable count of the original, with its irregular lines of 5 or 6 syllables or more, but I have tried to restrict myself to 4-, 5-, or 6-beat lines, retaining the verbal caesura 兮 (now pronounced *xī*). However, I found that the continued repetition of a single sound through 15 lines was excessively heavy, and so have alternated between *see* and *ay*.

The interpretation of the originals is made difficult by the fact that much of the vocabulary in this work is contentious and obscure: I have taken that as a licence to build my own poem around my own interpretation of the texts as understood by both Hawkes and Waters, and the Chinese commentators I have consulted,[4] reserving the right to amend or discard any sense that did not help me towards making a living poem. Thus the Cailleach — who in modern Scottish Pagan imagery is the crone of winter displaced by the Nine Maidens of Spring, and who may equally be a simple wise woman or a wicked witch (in the Gaelic *cailleach* has the primary sense of "old woman") — serves for me as an image of the shamaness who may (or may not) be represented in the text by *líng* 靈. A confusion seems to exist over whether *líng* represents the spirit which animates the shamaness or the shamaness herself, and this gives me enough latitude, I feel, to render the term in whichever sense gives me more metrical precision and/or a more interesting sound structure.

Similarly, the real uncertainty about the precise denotational sense of many, if not most, of the botanical names allows a great deal of freedom to choose for rhythm, or for alliteration, or for a particular nuance of sound. James Legge pointed out in 1871 that "Confucius says (Analects XVII.ix) that from the *Songs* we become … acquainted with the names of birds, beasts and plants. We do learn names … but the birds, beasts and plants denoted by them, remain in many cases to be yet ascertained."[5] This is very much the case with *Chu Ci*.

As for Waters' thesis that these poems have what he terms a paraphrastic reading, whereby they are read as political allegory, I have not read the texts in this way; he may very well be right, and he does make a convincing case for the traditional allegorical readings, but my preference is for the splendour and colour of the metaphrastic reading, which takes the texts as having a religious function. It is not my place here to argue how in fact these poems were read by the author's (or authors') contemporaries, for we have little or nothing to go on, particularly if the poems do in fact date back to Qu Yuan himself; I aim instead to produce a variation on Hawkes' versions, much in the way that Brahms would write a variation on a theme of Bach's.

I have tried to choose terms which can combine to give the Scots text a density similar to that of the original text, which, for the modern Chinese reader, is dense with unfamiliar or barely recognisable vocabulary. To this end I have ransacked the dictionaries for obscure and obsolete terms (especially for plants and flowers), and have not been shy to adapt or borrow terms to suit my purpose. Like Hugh McDiarmid before me, I will happily range through dictionaries and thesauri in search of rare and delightful words.

The term *urlar*, for instance, I have borrowed from Scottish Gaelic in which tongue it is the term for the "ground" of the variations which make up the pibroch (i.e. *Ceol Mór*: the classical music of the Great Highland Bagpipe): the *urlar*, though not necessarily solemn or stately, is often so, and is the slowest section of the pibroch's theme and variations. I make no apology from borrowing *bodhrán* from the Irish, though I omit the accent — I like the sound of it, it fits well with the sound of the line, and it avoids the repetition of "drum" and "drumstick" (it's pronounced *bow-'ron* in Irish, though usually *'boh-ran* in Scotland). Besides, the bodhran has been so much a part of Scottish music for the last thirty-odd years that I suppose it must be naturalised by now.[6]

A Note on Scots

In the introduction to the invaluable *Concise Scots Dictionary*[7] Scots is defined as "the language of Lowland Scotland", and a brief history is given, from its Old English ancestor, through Scandinavianised Northern English to, in the fourteenth century, what had become "the dominant spoken tongue for all ranks of Scots east and south of the Highland line …" The story then continues through the appearance of prose and poetry in the fourteenth century and the statutes of the Scottish parliament in the fifteenth, until "… Older Scots became the principal literary and record language of the Scottish nation …" At that time, as the editor points out, there were two distinct national languages in use in the two separate nations of the British Isles: Tudor English, and Older Scots. "Though these were politically or socially separate languages, linguistically they were distinct but quite closely related dialects, much as is the case with the Scandinavian languages today."

Though for much of the time since — and especially in the late eighteenth and nineteenth centuries — it was widely held that Scots was a dying language, Scots has proved remarkably persistent, and is still widely used today. Further, the Scottish literary renaissance of the early twentieth century and the explosion of new writing in Scots over the last twenty-five years would seem to suggest that R. L. Stevenson's "elegant and malleable tongue" has a lot of life in it yet.

I choose to use Scots because it is one of my mother tongues, and a flexible and powerful literary language. I do not write mediaeval Scots or Older Scots, nor am I attempting some antiqued pastiche of the great writers of the past, but I do aim to use a living modern idiom, which can be enriched with borrowings and coinages, like any other living tongue. I do not and would not suggest Scots is "better" than English, and while I accept that language choice in a multi-lingual environment like Scotland is an act which can have profound political implications, I have no political axe to grind. I merely hope to show that this is a tool which is fit for the job in hand.

A Personal Note

As far as I know, I am the only Chinese–Scots translator working today.[8] How I came to be doing this, and what connection it has with David Hawkes, is what I want to tell here.

About five or six years after graduating from Edinburgh University, I was wrestling with my first attempt at translation. As an undergraduate I had been delighted by *Shuihu Zhuan*, and terribly disappointed by existing English versions (as I remain to this day), so I tried to do it better. It didn't work. I couldn't get the English right: my draft was lifeless, stiff, unnatural, and quite as dreadfully uninspiring as any of the other versions.

One day in the spring of 1981 I was explaining this to my first wife, Monika Dunlop, when she interrupted and said, "You've spent the past few years reading all you can find in Scots — why don't you try it in Scots?"

I was initially dubious. I had recently heard that Jacques Dars had published a French version of *Shuihu Zhuan* which, I was told, had made use of terms from Gascon and other French dialects, but it was to be a year or two before I finally saw this wonderful translation.[9] Later that week, I made my first attempt to translate into Scots, and it was a revelation: the first paragraphs of the prologue were drafted in no time at all. I was amazed: I had never written anything in Scots in my life — like the majority of Scots speakers, I was educated in English, and, like most Scots, schooled to express myself in writing in English and English alone. I was amazed at how the Scots was supple enough to bend to the easy colloquial grace of the original narrative, and rich enough to provide, via the language of Scots law and of Scottish officialdom, a medium for the formal prose of the Imperial Court. I was equally amazed by the fact that I could do it: I had begun my first translation.

After what seems now like a few days, but must have been more like weeks, I had translated the first half of the prologue, and though I knew I liked what I had done, I needed the approval of wiser and more experienced heads, so I sent copies to my teachers in Edinburgh University, William Dolby and John Scott. Bill not only gave me some excellent advice, but also liked the draft so much he sent it down to Buccleuch Place to Glen Murray, then editor of the Scottish literary quarterly *Cencrastus,* who in turn immediately cleared space in his next issue, and not only did he publish the piece as it stood, he also wanted to serialise the next few chapters. And this happened so quickly that what first appeared in print[10] is actually my second, barely-revised draft (the first draft was hand-written, the second produced on a typewriter).

After several issues,[11] Glen Murray stepped down as editor, and his successor decided to discontinue *Men o the Mossflow.* So after a couple of years trying my hand at different Chinese texts, extending my range in Scots,[12] I turned back to *Mossflow,* and found a friendly welcome from the editors of the *Edinburgh Review,* principally Peter Kravitz and Murdo MacDonald. Their encouragement greatly heartened me in a period where, no matter how wide I cast my net, I could find no other support for the *Mossflow* project, either from publishers or from organisations such as the Scottish Arts Council. *Mossflow,* from beginning to end, has been done as a labour of love. When I began it I was unemployed, and it was continued at evenings and weekends, squeezed into the corners of a life often busy with several jobs at once. Only rarely have I been able to devote myself to it uninterrupted, as I did during vacations, while teaching at Edinburgh University in 1990–92.[13]

In the mid-1980s I wrote to David Hawkes to send him copies

of *Mossflow*, and once I was able to decipher his famously difficult handwriting, began a correspondence that continued on an occasional basis for several years. His reaction to my work was more than I could have hoped for: having worked in near-total isolation for several years, I had little experience of the generosity of scholars, and was happily surprised by his enthusiastic support for my work in Scots.

At the time of writing, though we have corresponded and even spoken on the telephone, I have not yet met David Hawkes, but he has been a constant inspiration to me since my undergraduate days, when John Scott introduced us to his *Little Primer of Tu Fu*, and the first volume of the then newly-produced Penguin Classics edition of *The Story of the Stone*.

On a personal level, Hawkes' warmth, his humanity, and his kindness to a young translator often kept me going when I was tempted to throw it all in. And on a professional level, his published work has provided me with a standard to aim for, an example of excellence (as he has done, I'm sure, for all of us). I owe a great deal to him, as much for his example as for his personal encouragement: he has shown us the way forward, and as literary translators, all our work must be measured by how close we come to approximating the work of Hawkes.

I am proud and delighted to lay this wee chuckie stane of mine on the cairn we translators of Chinese are building together: it is a cairn whose foundations lie in the work of giants like James Legge, Arthur Waley, and David Hawkes.

Hong Kong, May–June 2002

Notes

1. Jones, Francis R., *Bringing Mak into the Mainstream: Textual and Cultural Issues in Translating Dizdar's Kameni Spavac* at http://www.ifbosna.org.ba:91/publikacije/bosnae/11-01/16.htm#6.
2. Hawkes, D., tr., *The Songs of the South* (Harmondsworth: Penguin, 1985).
3. Waters, G. R., *Three Elegies of Ch'u* (Madison: Wisconsin UP, 1985).

4. Of which the most helpful has been 湯炳正, 李大明, 李誠, 熊良智 eds. (1996) 楚辭今注, 上海：上海古籍出版社, closely followed by 胡念 ed. (1984) 楚辭選注及考証, 長沙：岳麓出版社.

5. Legge, J., tr., *The Chinese Classics, Vol. IV, The She-King, or Book of Poetry* (Hong Kong: Lane Crawford, 1871), pp. 2–3.

6. For the life of me, I couldn't think of any Scots words for different types of drums apart from the tenor, bass and snare drums used by pipe bands, and music is an area where the *Scots Thesaurus* (Macleod, I. et al., eds., [Aberdeen: Aberdeen UP, 1990]) is unhelpfully silent: other such areas are clothing, jewellery, dance, transport, holding and touching, etc. However, within its limitations the *Scots Thesaurus* is a very useful tool.

7. Robinson, M., ed., *Concise Scots Dictionary* (Aberdeen: Aberdeen UP, 1985), p. ix.

8. Though the great Aberdeenshire translator James Legge did publish a few (rather dreadful) Scots versions in Legge, J., tr., *The She-King: or the Book of Ancient Poetry, Translated in English Verse* (London: Trubner, 1876). For a history of translation into Scots, see Corbett, J., *Written in the Language of the Scottish Nation* (Cleveden: Multilingual Matters, 1999).

9. Dars, Jacques, tr., *Au bord de l'eau* (Paris: Gallimard, Bibliothèque de la Pléiade, 1978).

10. *Men o the Mossflow* cap. 1 pt. 1 (*Cencrastus* 7, 1981).

11. Which included *Men o the Mossflow* cap. 1 pt. 2 (*Cencrastus* 8, 1982) and *Men o the Mossflow* cap. 2 (*Cencrastus* 16, 1984).

12. See, for example, Lu Xun, "Yin Wee Thing" (Yijian Xiao Shi) (*Cencrastus* 13, 1983), and Shen Jiji, 'The Cod" (Zhen-zhong Ji) (*Lallans* 18, 1982).

13. Resulting in *Men o the Mossflow* cap. 5 (*Edinburgh Review*, 1993).

To dear David Hawkes
on the happy occasion of his
Eightieth Birthday on July 6, 2003

An Erudition that
Unites East and West:
An Art that is
Enjoyed on Five Continents

Jin Di and Yuruo

霍克斯學長　八十大壽

學貫中西
文傳五洲

金隄
玉若　敬賀

二〇〇三年

TONY HYDER

The Legend of Zhongtiao Mountain by Li Jianwu

The Wangwu and Longmen ranges span the southern part of Shanxi Province, reclining majestically like a pride of dozy lions. Within the mountains the Yellow River flows in a torrent, scattering sand and pebbles with an angry roar — but now, apparently, it tires and with a long-drawn sigh turns east following the lie of the hills. In the still of the night, so the story goes, the River Earl, who has his home beneath the stream, used to squat on a rock by the bank and sob until daybreak, venting the pent-up misery of his long confinement among the crags, deprived of the sight of sunlight; his silver beard would brush the ground and where it caught crevices would appear from which springs gushed ten feet into the air. At such moments tigers and wolves hunting for food pricked up their ears in alarm and, tails between legs, ran for their rocky lairs to await with bated breath whatever fate might have in store; murky eddies described wild laughter with their cavorting and sudden, terrible tornadoes whipped up the fractious sand and threw it to the banks; then pebbles on the overhangs began to shudder, some falling obliquely, softly into the forest, perplexed by their strange journey, but others tumbling giddily into the river with a plop. All in all, a gloomy picture. The folk living in the shadow of the mountains reckon the Yellow River has finally found peace in this desolate spot, for the River Earl's anguished cries have not been heard there now for many years.

On the river's northern bank, besieged by interlocking cliffs, live contented, honest people; tilling, trading, saving and sleeping

are their normal daily tasks; sun and moon provide their only
guide to work and rest; Emperor Guan and Squire Yue are their
heroes; and they conserve the glories bequeathed over millennia
by the emperors of yore as matter for appraisal in the course of
conversation. So peace and well-being have flowed in their veins
from ancestral times. As to those vast mountains and rivers
constantly invading their sleep with the wailing of the wind, self-
pity is not something ordinary people have any patience with —
fate behaves that way.

If you look down from one of the highest ranges you can just
make out clusters of small white grave-like mounds — valuable
things, these: ponds for the production of cooking salt. Occasionally people would boast to their fellow provincials: "One thing
we're not short of is white salt," but now the communal ponds
have been taken into the joint management of local government
and foreigners. Not far to the north-east lies one of China's four
great villages, Lu Village — or Yuncheng — a bustling market
town. Immediately to the south-west of the salt ponds, between
Longmen and Wangwu, sits, solemnly and silently, a lofty peak:
Zhongtiao Mountain. Its height and inaccessibility kept local
people away, except for a few woodcutters who teamed up there
to play the game of life.

Once, an adventurous woodcutter, a youngish fellow, lost
touch with his companions and was making his way over these
perilous heights alone. When dark stole in through the dense
woodland, enveloping the mountains on every side, there was
nothing for it but to grasp the axe firmly and pass the night
squatting in a deep cavern. When his friends assembled beneath
the mountains early next morning and realised one of them was
missing, they all glanced swiftly at the menacing clouds over the
mountains and, with a sense of gloomy foreboding, maintained a
sombre silence. Hen harriers circled in the sky above while the
wind in the leaves made a plaintive sound. Far away and faint, on
a mist-enshrouded mountain path, they could make out the young
woodman lurching downwards as if pursued by some invisible
monster. Abandoning their shoulder poles they moved in a tide to

greet him. Pale, tense and perspiring the youth propelled himself into their midst like a crow in full flight; where he had left his axe and basket was anyone's guess. His hair streamed wildly from his head and his clothes blew in tatters about him; he gasped, waved in warning, cried out in distress and fell dead to the ground.

"Gold head, silver body, iron tail …" were the young man's conundrum-like dying words. None of the woodmen could make any sense of this, so they all thought he had been referring to some strange and savage beast.

Of course all the woodcutters quit the profession and kept well away from this eerie spot. Often, after dinner, they would mention the story and mumble the riddle, whereupon the recollection of their much-loved young companion would send huge tears running down their cheeks; neither were their audiences any wiser, apart from those who hazarded a tiger or a wild ox. When, one by one, the woodcutters eventually departed in peace in search of their brave young companion, the riddle and its tale accompanied them to their graves and no-one ever mentioned it again.

Quite out of the blue, many years later, a traveller found the entrance to a cave beneath the cliffs of Zhongtiao Mountain and it got about that the cavern exuded an indefinable aura of mystery, was well off the beaten track and had two great doors of burnished stone that shone like jade — tight shut and yet to be seen ajar. A flat slab of rock protruded above the cave shielding it from the rain like eaves; nearby a brook burbled softly by before the doors, the grit on its shallow bed glinting like the gemstones we call "cat's eyes". And beside the brook there stood erectly an ageless ancient pine, its needled branches spreading out across the sky and checked at the mid-slopes like drifting clouds. Its ripening seeds dripped into the greenery below, like smiles transmitting from the babe in arms to the grown woman in her lover's embrace; and spiders wove webs well out of the way, in clefts in the rock and on the tips of the pines, privy apparently to the cavern's mysterious secret. Moreover on the doors, clearly and deeply etched in large letters, were the words "Stone Portals".

However, since no-one had ever seen them open or a resident emerge, it was thought the doors were simply imitations. Later on when some enterprising individuals planned to cart off the two hefty lumps of stone, the impossibility of the task gradually made itself clear, for anyone escaping serious illness when setting out met with misfortune on the way. It was not long before the Stone Portals gained recognition as the mysterious cave abode of an immortal.

When the Guangxu Emperor was fleeing south from the Capital to the province of Shaanxi, the day he passed through Lu Village was one ordinary folk would never be able to forget, for they actually got to gaze at that most venerable of countenances. At dusk that day a farmer named Zhang Shifang, an honest fellow known for his courage, was returning from town to the village where he lived. He was in an exuberant mood and, just like a happy, plump black duck, was waddling along the road and singing, somewhat out of character, the sort of bawdy songs he usually found distasteful. Sometimes he would glance at the tangled undergrowth beside the path as if the plants — dandelions, foxtails and such — were paying court to his charisma. At other times he would gaze up into the blue at the passing clouds onto which the sunset seemed to project cheeks, apple-red and smiling in envy of his good fortune. "The emperor was so genially pale and thin, the dowager so graciously sleek and portly. He's a good man and no mistake: he accepted the dates I offered and when he was getting out of his carriage he patted me on my left shoulder …" Sinking deep into daydream he felt his left arm flutter gently as if it were trying to detach itself from his body and fly high into the distance. It occurred to him that he should forgive his old woman her blunder, for all she had done was smash a couple of eggs. So, without a care in the world, he went jauntily on his way below Zhongtiao Mountain.

Rapidly, the shadow of the peaks enveloped him in a greyish gloom and a gentle breeze blew from the gullies, teasing his new cotton gown. The ranks of dates proudly lining the path shed small, green, unripe fruits: halfway up the mid-slopes the leaves of the poplars howled like ghosts, forcing the wild dates around them to shudder and to sway. A few squirrels, suspended rakishly from the outcrops, uttered weary, drawn-out sighs. All of a sudden his happy musing was brought to an end and he began to tremble uncontrollably. In a flash he called to mind all those volatile, headstrong ghouls he had heard of as a boy as well as lots of frightening stories — and the tales of the woodcutter who had met his end on Zhongtiao Mountain and of the impenetrable Stone Portals especially seemed to float before him. He was afraid to sing and his eyes he kept strictly to the front.

Over the mountaintops a jovial moon appeared and beamed.

From within the trees came a clear note, rising slowly to a crescendo as in a concert performance. Gradually but quite unmistakably he became aware that he was hearing someone call his name in measured tones, the echo reverberating endlessly from one side of the mountain to the other. "Zhang Shifang! Zhang Shifang!" Trying to compose himself he looked around but there was no-one to be seen. A stream made a steady trickling sound and silvery wrinkles were reflected from its ripples; now and then a pine seed would drop onto his hat and roll off again into the grass below. Up in the sky a squadron of wild geese flew by, line after line, each responding to the other's call; the fallen leaves ceased their rustling as if it had been whispered to them that life was short. All these things filled him with a strange foreboding. Suddenly a pebble fell in front of him. When he looked up all he could make out was a large stone slab jutting out above his head like the eaves of a house and masking the starlight. How he came to be here he had no idea.

The fearsome grotto was there beside him.

He was about to take to his heels when he heard a more insistent cry: "Zhang Shifang — trim the snuff from this wick!" Still he could see no-one.

Slowly the stone doors parted, just enough to allow a person through. Barely visible in this dark place was a table and on it there was an old-fashioned nickel-silver lamp, flickering drowsily, its wick splayed like a cabbage flower and swamped by the oil.

The clear, sonorous voice continued as before: "Zhang Shifang! Quick, trim off the snuff!"

The farmer was on the verge of passing out when he was suddenly reminded of those supernatural beings Emperor Guan and Squire Yue, and thoughts of good overcoming evil began to cross his mind. What is more, he experienced a pleasant sensation of impatience — it seemed right to go in and have a try. "I can make a quick job of cleaning the wick. After all, what difference does it make? Life and death are in the gift of fate. Let's have a go, then; trim the snuff ..." And so he finally came to a decision.

He tip-toed gingerly through the stone doors and groped his way towards the table like a frog, quaking in terror as he went. Too frightened to look about he rapidly removed the black tracery of the snuff. The feeble lamplight spluttered into life like a shooting star, dispelling the surrounding gloom. Much to his astonishment there was neither sign nor smell of man or spirit. However, something did catch his attention and what an amazing thing it was. There glinting brightly beside the lamp lay a silver bar; and weighted beneath it was a flat slip of paper on which were written the words: "For trimming the wick, a service kindly rendered, fifty silver taels are herewith tendered."

There stirred within him an indescribable feeling of sweet surprise that he had never encountered, even in his dreams — of course we all go a bit crazy when there is money in prospect. And, no doubt about it, fifty taels of sterling silver is a sizeable sum. He slipped it quickly into his breast pocket and, in a state of euphoria, considered lingering there, even staying on for good. Everything about this gloomy cave seemed attractive. In the end, though, he came to his senses and made it outside in two or three strides. Sure enough, as soon as his last limb was through, he heard a clunk as the doors closed tightly again. Thenceforward, never, ever did the mysterious Stone Portals reopen.

Naturally, when he got home, he kept this incredible story to himself, fabricating other incidents to replace it; he lied about the silver bar, for instance, claiming it was a reward from the Guangxu Emperor. Only on his deathbed did he relate the entire matter to the members of his family. "… On the ground beside the table," he said, "lay a rusting axe … and the remains of a mulberry-wand firewood basket …" (Regrettably, he made no mention of the young woodcutter's dying cry: "Gold head, silver body, iron tail …") "In there," continued the fortunate farmer, "it really seemed to reek of gold and silver."

At his bedside, with tears rolling down her cheeks, his devoted wife murmured consolingly: "There! Gently now, don't talk too much … That very night it was, I fancied I heard the River Earl wailing again, over there in the hills."

We have had a revolution now and Zhongtiao Mountain has become a barren mound, reposing peacefully to the south-west of the salt ponds. Foreigners have journeyed there and concluded, after a thorough survey, that the mountain is very rich in ore. This is of no interest to those honest folk and busy bureaucrats: they live out their uneventful lives oblivious. But for the Yellow River's indignant roar (all day, all night), nature's world stays as calm and silent as the folk that inhabit its domain.

December 1924, in the *Chenbao Supplement.*

Translator's Note

Li Jianwu (1906–1982), who went on to be a major dramatist, critic, translator and scholar of French literature, was only eighteen and in his last year at the school attached to Peking Normal University when this story was written. By that time he had already established a reputation for himself as a player of female rôles in the new, west-inspired spoken drama developing on the campuses, and had three published plays to his name. He had attracted the attention of Wang Tongzhao, modern novelist and editor at that time of the *Chenbao's* Literary Supplement (which had carried one of the plays), but this was Jianwu's first work of fiction to appear in print.

The story is set in the region of the Li family's home village. Jianwu's father was an important military figure in and after the 1911 Revolution and used the local mountains as a refuge for his troops during campaigns against Yuan Shikai and Yan Xishan. Surprisingly, given the story's vivid descriptive passages, Jianwu spent only the first few years of his childhood there, having been evacuated to the countryside of Shaanxi and Hebei for safety. He eventually rejoined his family in Peking, not long before his father's imprisonment (1918) and assassination (the following year). In 1924 Jianwu was living with his mother, in much reduced circumstances, in a hostel close to the slums of Nanxiawa.

Commenting on the story in 1935 Lu Xun (whom Jianwu had invited to lecture at his school in January 1924) said: "[Li Jianwu's] 'The Legend of Zhongtiao Mountain' is simply dazzling and even today, ten years afterwards, one can still detect the body and the soul beneath its raiment of eloquence." Lu Xun included the work in the second short story volume of *Zhongguo xinwenxue daxi*, on whose text this translation is based. Reference has also been made to the (similar) version found in Zhang Daming ed., *Li Jianwu chuangzuo pinglun xuanji* (Beijing: Renmin wenxue chubanshe, 1984).

The assistance of Yin C. Liu and Ian McMorran is gratefully acknowledged. For a convincing solution to the riddle the search continues!

MABEL LEE

Dream Waves

A Prose Poem by Gao Xingjian

On the brink of waking, in dream I saw myself lying on the waves of the sea. Arms outstretched, facing the sky, eyes closed, you were floating on a sea resplendent with sunlight. Your body was rocking, and your hands and feet were moving a little to keep balance. It was very pleasant. It seemed that by just opening your eyes, you would see the wisps of white clouds in the blue sky. It was as if you could already see them, but couldn't be bothered making the effort to open your eyes. You could feel the warmth of the sun on your eyelids as the sea swept over your cheeks, and you opened your mouth to spew out salt water and to breathe in air. When the waves below bore you up, it was even more pleasant. Because afterwards you would gently drop between the crests of the waves, still floating, your body rocking and heavy with sleep. You were light, floating, while the seawater was heavy, but it gently caressed you. It was an awareness of leisurely freedom submerged in the subconscious dreaming of sleep and it was when, after learning to swim, you discovered that by lying flat on your back you could float on the sea. As soon as you overcame your fear of the sea, you obtained the freedom of controlling yourself on the sea, and obtained pleasure for your body and mind, and loving the sea became a blessing, a wonderful enjoyment.

I also saw in dream the daughter of the sea emerging from the sea. She seemed to have just come out of the bath and her long wet hair clung to her shoulders. She was so serene, yet seemed

somewhat sad. But, then she no longer seemed to be the daughter
of the sea and the body-hugging dress she was wearing was not
wet. Her face was flushed a bright red but her body was icy cold.
She looked like a girl you once secretly loved but when you tried
to make sure, she no longer completely resembled her. There was
nothing of you in her eyes, only sadness. That was how the
daughter of the sea emerged from the sea, that is, if she really was
the daughter of the sea, and if there really was a daughter of the
sea, this was how she emerged in the hazy dream of your sleep.

I also saw in dream the eastern seacoast of the Atlantic Ocean,
where black waves reached the skies and even on fine days the
wind was very strong. Actually, it was not dream at all, but
recollection. Although it was hazy, it was after I was awake, so
even if I had opened my eyes wider, the image would have been
the same. Maybe this was because it had been stored securely in
my memory. Maybe it was because a poet I had loved dearly was
on the eastern seacoast of the Atlantic Ocean as he lay on his
deathbed.

I will always remember the Viareggio seacoast in Italy, less
than a hundred paces from the Grand Royal Lodge where we were
staying at the time. The waves of that big bowl, the Mediterranean,
were somehow very wild. I always feel that I have failed to
adequately show my friendship, that I should have written
something for this seaside city, but have never managed to write
anything. Maybe this is why those waves are forever surging up
before my eyes, towering up, and pushing right up to me.

We had been invited by the Italian Writers' Union to attend the
grand prize-giving ceremony of the Viareggio Literary Awards.
Afterwards we strolled on the street along the sea-front back to the
hotel and again we heard the crashing of the waves. I then went
on my own down to the beach to enjoy the beauty of the
Mediterranean at night. The colourful beach umbrellas above the
swimming pool had all been closed and looked like so many small
trees in the darkness of the night, and the sound of the sea
drowned out the din of the amplified band playing outside a bar
on the street. In my memory, the Mediterranean waves have

always been associated with the relief on the bronze medallion presented to each of us by our Italian friends. It was the side view of a naked man, sitting, his spine prominent on his lean back, but nothing of the face visible. This provocative work is the image of a person deep in thought. He is perhaps engrossed in looking at the mighty sea. As searchlights swept the water, a pair of lovers headed out into the sea. They are lovers of the sea, they really understand the beauty of the sea. This was not a dream.

It was only once that I saw the sea very clearly in dream. This was in the courtyard of the *hutong* where I lived, far away from the seacoast. The ink-black sea did not have a hint of a wave and I stood for a long time in the very middle of it. The quiet seawater cut off everything all around. My feet stood on a piece of solid sand. There was no moon, there were no stars, no waves, and there was no sound, just a vast silence, so silent that it made me feel lonely, yet calm. I wanted to go into the water and swim into the distance, but wherever I went the sea quietly receded and my bare feet stood on solid sand, wet, moist, warm, covered with seaweed. I had a great desire to go into the water to immerse myself, to swim in the warm water, even float on it for a while. But wherever I went, the sea would quietly recede, soundlessly. I began to wonder whether I was in the sea. Yet I could clearly see myself actually standing in the sea. The sea should not be like this, it should be in motion, noisy, surging, tempestuous, even engulfing everything. It should give us more than just calm. But the murky-black sea was so clear that one could see the seaweed. It was more like a marsh. My despair increased my loneliness. The loneliness of the dream world was transparent like the sea, like the tangled mass of green seaweed in the clear water. And moreover, that tangled mass of seaweed seemed to be a tangle of worries. Even the worries themselves were so very quiet, so utterly soundless. There was not a single bubble bursting in the marsh. And there was no mud! No matter where you went you trod on solid sand. The ink-black sea and the silent seawater always surrounded you quietly, like that circle of transparent intangible worries. You just could not get out of that vast territory.

When eventually you got out of the dream of sleep, when you were completely awake, that state of consciousness from the dream remained before you, with clear contours, like the reflection of a bright mirror. And you could always see it, it was always just as clear, you could not erase it from your memory. So, you couldn't help wondering about its meaning, pondering it at length, thinking and staring at this clear reflection, that expanse of calm, so calm that it was disturbing, so disturbing that it was transparent.

The meaning of this dream, I think, lies in this disturbing calm. It is a state of mind. But while it is disturbing, it is permeated with faith in the self. Moreover, this faith in the self, it should be said, is a persistent exploration of the self.

I also think that, during writing, this is a germinating impulse, something in the process of gestation that is hard to express clearly right away: this dream world is a reflection of the mental world when it is not fully conscious. However, even this indistinct mental world can be expressed. When encountering problems in artistic creation, this faith in the self is required. Only through skilfully overcoming those gloomy difficulties can one achieve the total enjoyment of lying on the sea in the sun, eyes closed, and drifting with the waves that comes with being passionately absorbed, physically and mentally, in one's work.

September 1981, in Beijing
translated 12 July 2002, in Sydney

Source: *Huacheng*, 3 (1983).

ANDRÉ LÉVY

Haoran zhi qi
浩然之氣

May I say that I met David Hawkes thrice? Enough to turn a long-standing admirer into a friend? The first time, as far as I remember, was some two score years ago when David delivered a brilliant talk at the Sorbonne, in French, on the symbolism in Hongloumeng [The Story of the Stone]. *I was then, I believe, a graduate student. David was a fully fledged scholar. In fact I just saw and heard him, feeling quite a distance in age and knowledge. It was only on the second occasion that we really met. I even had the privilege, on that second occasion, of being invited to his house. It was a time of crisis in Oxford about which I felt bewildered, the time when he had decided to retire, while I was just starting in earnest to get into the profession. The third time we were both in retirement. I no longer felt a sizeable age gap. In a way David had become younger than I ever was. How? Because he had it. What? Well, he had the gusto I would associate with that elusive Mencian concept of* haoran zhi qi. *Is this something one is born with and needs to nourish, for it to be full-blown later in life? That seems likely, but I dare not say I know anything more about it. Anyhow it seems easier to grasp its meaning than to translate it.*

So far I have only come across one occurrence of haoran zhi qi *in Pu Songling's collection of stories,* Liaozhai zhiyi. *Posing as the Chronicler of the Strange,* Yishishi, *Pu judges that the hero of his tale possessed it. This is what enabled him to stand fast, unmoved by spooks or foxes. For Pu the notion comes close to that of fortitude,* force d'âme *or* force de caractère, fermeté.

There is indeed more to it in Mencius, who forged the term, unusually more yogical than logical in this first part of his second book, second section. A glance at the ways in which the expression has variously been translated may be enough for our purpose, without my launching into a discussion that would be beyond my competence. Let me throw in an incomplete list, in rough chronological order: Pauthier (1845): "L'esprit vital qui coule et circule partout". *Legge (1875):* "Flowing passion nature". *Séraphin Couvreur (somewhere around 1898):* "Sensibilité largement répandue". *Dobson (1963):* "Greater physical vigour". *D.C. Lau (1970):* "Flood-like ch'i". *Wing-tsit Chan in his* Source Book *(1969, p. 784) offers* "Strong, moving power". *François Jullien quotes Rousseau's* "sensibilité surabondante" *as the best way of translating this surely untranslatable expression, in his* Dialogue sur la morale *(1995, p. 171). Does this throw Mencius in with the utopian romantic crowd? Is this perhaps the key to Jean Lévi's incredible loathing for Mencius in his recent* Confucius *(2002)?* "Mencius opère la dénaturation la plus complète de la doctrine de son modèle, en s'en proclamant le fils spirituel... plus bêlant [literally, bleating] qu'Elie Wiesel lors d'une commémoration du martyre juif" *(p. 247–8). Of course he is talking of Mencius without his* haoran zhi qi. *Let us conclude with Anne Cheng, who proposes in her* Histoire de la pensée chinoise *(1997),* "énergie débordante" *(p. 162).*

We may as well stop at that: in any case, it does describe fairly well what I felt when David began telling me about his interest in Welsh, as we climbed the (thankfully) not too steep Norwegian mountains.

To make something short unnecessarily longish, may I append my tentative translation of the famous section from Mencius, done more than twelve years ago? And at the risk of making bad things worse, may I add my draft of a French version of Pu Songling's story?

ॐ

Mencius
Book II, "Gongsun Chou", Part 1, Chapter 2

"Maître," s'enquit Gongsun Chou, "au cas où vous occuperiez la charge de premier ministre et obtiendriez de pratiquer la Voie, il n'y aurait rien de surprenant à ce qu'il en résultât même l'hégémonie de Qi. Dans ce cas, ne vous sentiriez-vous pas remué?"

"Non," répliqua Mencius, "depuis que j'ai passé mes quarante ans plus rien ne m'affecte." [1]

"S'il en est ainsi, Maître, vous surpassez de cent coudées Meng Ben !"[2]

"Rien de plus facile. Maître Gao[3] y était parvenu avant moi."

"Y a-t-il un art d'y parvenir?"

"Oui. Beigong You[4] nourrissait sa bravoure de cette façon: il ne reculait d'une épaisseur de peau ni ne clignait de l'oeil; la moindre brimade de la part d'autrui lui était aussi insupportable que d'être fouetté en place publique; ce qu'il n'acceptait pas d'un manant en ample bure, il ne l'admettait pas non plus d'un prince à la tête d'un pays de dix mille chars. Le trucider n'aurait pas été à ses yeux plus grave que poignarder un pauvre hère. Il n'y avait pas seigneur à respecter, si grand soit-il, lorsqu'il s'agissait de rendre une insulte.

"Meng Shishe[5] disait nourrir son courage de la manière que voici: 'Je considère l'invaincu comme vaincu:[6] n'avancer qu'après avoir évalué les forces de l'ennemi, n'engager le contact qu'après avoir estimé la victoire probable, c'est prendre peur devant les trois corps d'armée ennemis. Comment serais-je sûr de vaincre? Il me suffit d'être sans peur.'

"Meng Shishe ressemblait à Zengzi, Beigong You à Zixia.[7] Je ne saurais dire lequel de ces deux maîtres de courage était le plus sage, mais c'est Meng Shishe qui s'en tenait à l'essentiel.

"Jadis Zengzi, s'adressant à Zixiang,[8] déclara: 'Tu aimes le courage? J'ai appris auprès de notre maître, Confucius, ce qu'est le plus grands des courages: "Si je reconnais mon tort en retournant en moi-même, comment rester sans crainte, même devant un pauvre hère en ample bure? Si je me trouve dans mon droit après examen de conscience, j'irai le faire valoir quand bien même il me faudrait affronter des milliers ou dizaines de milliers d'hommes.'"

"La force d'âme de Meng Shishe ne vaut à son tour le courage qu'évoque Zengzi en s'en tenant à l'essentiel."

"Puis-je me permettre de vous interroger sur votre impassibilité comparée à celle de maître Gao?"

"Selon maître Gao il ne faut chercher dans son esprit ou son coeur ce qu'on ne trouve dans les mots; ce qu'on ne peut tirer de son esprit, il ne faut le solliciter de la force du souffle.

"Qu'il ne faille chercher dans le souffle ce qu'on ne peut obtenir de l'esprit, je l'admets, mais non pas que l'on doive écarter de l'esprit ce qu'on ne trouve dans les mots. La volonté commande au souffle qui remplit notre corps. Là où va la volonté, le souffle suit. C'est pourquoi l'on dit: 'Maintenir sa volonté et ne pas faire violence à son souffle.'"

"Puisque vous avez dit que le souffle suit, là où va la volonté, que signifie 'maintenir sa volonté sans faire violence à son souffle'?"

"Unifiée, la volonté anime le souffle, lequel, unifié, anime aussi la volonté. Or, que l'on tombe ou court, c'est par un effet du souffle, mais il réagit sur l'esprit."

"Puis-je me permettre de vous demander en quoi réside votre supériorité, Maître?"

"Je comprends ce qu'on dit et je suis expert à nourrir le souffle de la vigueur."

"Puis-je me permettre de vous demander ce que vous entendez par 'souffle de la vigueur'[9]?"

"C'est difficile à dire. En tant que souffle, c'est la chose la plus vaste et la plus résistante qui soit; nourri de droiture, sans être lésé, il remplit tout l'espace entre le ciel et la terre. C'est le souffle qui s'accorde à la Voie et la justice. Sans lui, tout languit. C'est le produit d'actions morales accumulées, qui ne saurait être capté par des actes isolés. Il s'étiole s'il y a des choses qui déplaisent à la conscience dans notre conduite. C'est pourquoi j'ai affirmé que maître Gao n'a jamais rien compris à la justice parce qu'il l'extériorise. Il nous faut la servir, mais sans la rectifier, il nous faut jamais l'oublier, mais sans en forcer la croissance. Ne ressemblons pas à cet homme de Song qui se désolait du manque de croissance de ses pousses: après avoir tiré dessus, il était rentré en titubant de fatigue et avait annoncé à ses proches: 'Je suis crevé! Ouf, j'ai fini d'aider les pousses à grandir.' Quand son fils courut aller voir, elles étaient desséchées. Rares sont ceux qui ne prétendent aider les pousses à croître en ce monde. Ceux qui les laissent à elles-mêmes en estimant que c'est inutile, ne les sarclent pas non plus. Quant à tirer dessus pour les aider à croître, c'est non seulement inutile mais encore nuisible."

"Que vouliez-vous dire par 'comprendre ce qu'on dit'?"

"Des paroles partiales me font comprendre ce qui l'aveugle, des affirmations excessives les pièges qui s'y cachent, des mots dépravés ce qui l'écarte du droit chemin, des échappatoires m'indiquent ce qui met son esprit à bout d'arguments. Les mots qui naissent du cœur et de l'esprit peuvent nuire au gouvernement; s'ils s'y expriment, ils nuisent aux affaires. Si le Saint Homme[10] réapparaissait, il ne manquerait pas d'approuver ce que je dis."

"Zai Wo[11] et Zigong[12] savaient bien discourir. Ran Niu,[13] Minzi[14] et Yan Yuan[15] aimaient parler d'actes vertueux. Confucius, qui excellait dans les deux, disait néanmoins qu'il ne savait manier la rhétorique. Serait-ce, Maître, que vous êtes déjà un 'saint'?"

"Comment? Que dis-tu là! Jadis, lorsque Zigong demanda à Confucius s'il était saint, celui-ci répliqua: 'De sainteté, je ne suis point capable; j'étudie sans me lasser et enseigne sans m'en fatiguer.'[16] Zigong répliqua: 'Etudier sans se lasser est preuve de sagesse; enseigner sans s'en fatiguer est effet de la bonté. Bon et sage, Maître, vous êtes donc un saint.'

"Ce titre de saint, Maître Kong lui-même le récusait. Que dis-tu là!"

"J'avais entendu dire autrefois que Zixia, Ziyou[17] et Zizhang[18] avaient tous comme un membre du Saint Homme, tandis que Ran Niu, Minzi et Yan Yuan les avaient au complet mais à un faible degré. Puis-je me permettre de vous demander où vous vous placer."

"Laissons cela pour le moment!"

"Que pensez-vous de Boyi[19] et Yi Yin[20]?"

"Nous ne suivons pas la même voie. Refuser de servir qui n'était son seigneur, refuser de conduire ceux qui n'étaient de son peuple; accepter des charges si le pays était en bon ordre, se retirer en cas de désordre, telle était l'attitude de Boyi. Quant à Yi Yin, tout prince qu'il servait était le sien, comme tout peuple qu'il gouvernait; ordre ou désordre, il acceptait toute charge qu'on lui offrait. Pour Confucius on occupe un poste qui peut l'être, comme on s'en retire quand il convient, on y dure s'il est permis d'y durer, on abrège s'il faut l'abréger. Tous étaient de saints personnages du temps jadis dont je ne suis point capable suivre les traces. Mais ce que je voudrais, c'est suivre l'exemple de Confucius."

"Mettez-vous Boyi et Yi Yin sur le même plan que Confucius?"

"Non. Depuis que les hommes vivent sur terre, il n'y a pas eu d'autres Confucius."

"Mais ont-ils quelque chose en commun?"

"Oui. Auraient-ils obtenu un territoire égal à un carré de cent *li* de côté pour y régner, tous auraient été capables d'amener à leur cour les grands vassaux et posséder le monde. S'il leur avait fallu commettre une seule injustice, tuer un seul innocent pour l'obtenir, ils ne l'auraient pas fait, aucun d'eux. C'est cela qu'ils ont en commun."

"Puis-je vous demander en quoi ils différaient?"

"Zai Wo, Zigong, You Ruo[21] avaient assez d'intelligence pour reconnaître le Saint Homme, sans se laisser aller à de basses flatteries. 'A mon avis notre maître est de loin plus sage que les antiques empereurs Yao et Shun,' disait Zai Wo.

"'Aux rites qu'il pratique on reconnaît son gouvernement,' disait Zigong, 'sa vertu, à la musique qu'il fait entendre. Dans cent générations, on l'élèvera plus haut que tous les rois, nul ne saurait en disconvenir. Depuis que les hommes vivent sur terre, il n'y eu aucun autre Confucius.'

"Quant à Youruo, il disait: 'Comment cela serait-il vrai seulement chez les peuples? La licorne parmi les bêtes qui courent, le phénix parmi les oiseaux qui volent, le mont Tai[22] parmi les montagnes et collines, les fleuves et les mers parmi les cours d'eau, tout cela sont des cas analogues. Il en est de même du Saint parmi les hommes. Sortant de la même espèce, il a été élu au-dessus de la foule. Depuis que naissent les hommes, nul n'a été aussi grand que Confucius.'"

Pu Songling
Spectre et Renard n'en mènent pas large
Liaozhai zhiyi IV.156

Fils de feu Li Jinzhuo, qui fut sous-préfet à Suining, Monsieur Li Zhuming était un homme de caractère, hardi et sans peur. Il était devenu le beau-frère cadet du regretté Wang Jiliang de Xincheng.

La résidence de ce dernier comprenait un grand nombre de tours et pavillons où l'on voyait souvent circuler d'étranges créatures. Monsieur y venait régulièrement passer la nuit les mois les plus chauds pour profiter de la fraîcheur du soir à l'étage. On lui avait parlé des maléfices qui s'y produisaient, mais il n'avait fait qu'en rire et s'était obstiné à ordonner d'y placer son lit. Le maître de maison s'était incliné et avait donné des instructions pour qu'un des domestiques lui tienne compagnie pendant son sommeil, mais il s'y était opposé: "J'aime bien dormir seul. D'ailleurs je n'ai jamais su ce qu'était la peur."

Le maître de maison fit enflammer du benjoin dans le brûle-parfum, lui demanda dans quel sens faire son lit, puis les chandelles éteintes, referma les vantaux et s'en fut.

Monsieur reste un bon moment étendu, la tête sur l'oreiller, à regarder sous le clair de la lune la théière posée sur le guéridon. Elle se penchait, tournait mais sans jamais tomber, ni s'arrêter de bouger. Monsieur finit par pousser un grognement d'exaspération. La théière s'arrêta net dans un bruit sonore de tintement.

Puis ce fut comme si l'on avait tiré les bâtonnets d'encens du brûle parfum pour les balancer dans le vide en formant des arabesques lumineuses en tous sens. Monsieur se dresse et tance l'insolent : "Quel genre de diablotin a l'impudence …" Il descend tout nu du lit dans l'intention de l'attraper, cherche ses sandales sous le lit, n'en trouve qu'une, renonce à chercher l'autre, mais au moment où il allait pieds nus passer la main là où s'agitaient les bâtonnets, toutes retombent se ficher dans le brûle-parfum et le calme revient.

Tandis qu'il tâtonnait, penché, dans tous les recoins, lui saute à la figure quelque chose qui avait tout à fait l'air d'être sa sandale. Il cherche, en vain. Il ouvre les vantaux, descend les escaliers, appelle de ses gens pour apporter du feu et rallumer la chandelle. Rien. Il retourne à son lit se rendormir.

Au petit matin il fait fouiller la pièce par plusieurs personnes qui retournent le lit, secouent les nattes. Rien. Où avait bien pu passer la sandale? Le maître de maison lui en donne une autre paire. Le lendemain, levant par hasard la tête, il aperçoit une chaussure coincée entre les chevrons du plafond. D'un bond, il l'attrape, la descend. C'était la sandale manquante de son invité!

Monsieur, qui était de Yidu, avait emménagé dans la résidence d'un certain Sun de Zichuan. C'était une vaste demeure, entièrement vide, dont il n'occupait que la moitié. La cour du sud avoisinait un pavillon élevé dont elle n'était séparé que par un muret. De temps à autres les vantaux du pavillon s'ouvraient et se fermaient tout seuls, ce qui le laissait indifférent.

Monsieur parlait avec ses gens dans la cour quand s'ouvrit une porte du bâtiment voisin. Un nain parut et s'assit face au nord. D'une taille de moins de trois pieds, il était en robe verte et chaussettes blanches. Tous le regardaient en le montrant du doigt, mais il ne bougeait pas. "C'est un renard," décréta Monsieur en s'armant précipitamment d'un arc et de flèches. Il s'apprêtait à tirer. Le nain l'aperçut et disparut avec un ricanement sonore de spectre. On ne le voyait plus. Monsieur empoigna un couteau et grimpa dans la pavillon. Il eut beau fouiller partout en jurant, il revint sans l'avoir trouvé.

Dès lors les manifestations insolites cessèrent. Monsieur y habita plusieurs années en paix et sans autres ennuis.

Son fils aîné Yousan, un parent par alliance, en a été témoins, ce sont des choses qu'il a vu de ses yeux.

Le chroniqueur de l'étrange:

Je suis né trop tard pour avoir eu la possibilité de présenter canne et chaussures à Monsieur. Mais ce que j'ai appris, je le tiens des anciens. Ce qu'ils en disent ne laissent pas de doute sur sa fermeté et son courage.

Ces deux incidents invitent en tout cas à la constatation suivante: spectres ou renards ne peuvent rien contre ceux en qui demeure la force de caractère [*haoran zhong cun*].

Notes

1. *Sishi budongxin*: cf. *Les Entretiens* de Confucius, II, 4: "… à quarante ans je n'avais plus de doutes …"
2. Meng Ben: un brave mentionné dans divers ouvrages anciens comme étant de Wei selon certains, de Qi selon d'autres.
3. Gaozi: s'agit-il du même maître Gao que l'adversaire idéologique de Mencius, 6.A.1? Dobson n'en doute pas. Yang Bojun propose de l'identifier à un disciple ou ancien disciple de Mo Di, mort une dizaine d'années avant la naissance de Mencius. Comme le calculait Liang Qichao (1873–1929), Mencius aurait pu avoir connu ce Gaozi à la fin de sa vie. A ses disciples qui l'engageaient à s'en écarter, Mo Di aurait répondu: "Gaozi sait fort bien argumenter et comme il parle de bonté et justice, il ne m'est pas opposé"; la remarque convient assez bien au Gaozi mis en scène dans le *Mencius*.
4. Beigong You: on ne sait rien de ce personnage, si ce n'est qu'il est identifié à un maître Beigong du *Huainanzi* et déclaré de Qi par le glossateur Gao You (*floruit* vers 200 après notre ère).
5. Meng Shishe: on ne sait rien de ce personnage; selon Zhao Qi *Shi* n'est qu'un préfixe; pour Yan Ruoju (1636–1704) le mot fait partie du patronyme Mengshi; Zhai Hao (1736–1788) maintient que Shishe serait le prénom.
6. *Shi busheng you sheng ye*: l'énoncé se prête à des intreprétations divergentes; ainsi, Couvreur et Lau vont dans le sens de Pauthier ("Je regarde d'un même oeil la défaite que la victoire"); Dobson: "I look upon victory and defeat indifferently"; Yang Bojun comprend: "Je traite l'ennemi invincible comme celui qui peut l'être (vaincu)."
7. Zixia: appellation de Bu Shang, un disciple de Confucius.
8. Zixiang: ce serait un disciple de Zengzi, selon Zhao Qi.
9. *Haoran zhi qi*.
10. *Shengren*: c'est à dire Confucius.

11. Zai Wo: Zai Yu, disciple de Confucius.

12. Zigong: Duanmu Ci, disciple de Confucius.

13. Ran Niu: Ran Geng, disciple de Confucius.

14. Minzi: Min Juan, disciple de Confucius.

15. Yan Yuan: Yan Hui, disciple de Confucius.

16. Ce n'est pas une citation textuelle des *Entretiens* tels qu'ils nous sont parvenus, mais elle correspond substantiellement à VII,34, dans ma traduction, *Les Entretiens de Confucius*, Paris: GF-Flammarion 1994, p. 63: "S'il s'agit de la sainteté et du sens suprême de l'humanité, comment oserais-je y prétendre!"

17. Ziyou: Yan Yan, disciple de Confucius.

18. Zizhang: Zhuansun Shi, disciple de Confucius.

19. Boyi: avec son frère cadet Shuqi, modèle de dévouement et loyauté; ils finirent par abandonner la seigneurie paternelle que l'un des frères entendait céder à l'autre; ils préférèrent mourir de faim plutôt que manger le millet de la dynastie nouvelle des Zhou, bien qu'ayant dénoncé la tyrannie du dernier Shang-Yin, au XIIe siècle avant notre ère.

20. Yi Yin: le ministre quasi-légendaire du fondateur de la dynastie des Shang, Tang le Victorieux.

21. Youruo: un disciple de Confucius.

22. Taishan: le mont le plus sacré de Chine, celui de l'est, au Shandong.

JOHN SCOTT

A Xinhai Memento

大漢四川軍政府都督示

1. 布告大漢國民　政府已經改革
2. 現在四川全省　同時實行獨立
3. 省城設新政府　政策取決公議
4. 事事主持和平　力求甯人息事
5. 外國人及教堂　本省行政官吏
6. 滿洲駐防人民　一律照常待遇
7. 省外同志民團　已達圓滿目的
8. 急宜釋兵歸農　大家力圖新治
9. 從前損失喪亡　優子撫恤賑濟
10. 舊日弊政苛捐　急籌減除廢棄
11. 至於社會秩序　務求安靜如昔
12. 凡我士農工商　一切各安生業
13. 所頒條件禁令　大眾均須注意
14. 從此共享治平　同盡國民天職

黃帝紀元四千六百九年十月日

Some twenty years ago I obtained a wood-block printed proclamation poster of the 1911 revolutionary forces. The circumstances of the acquisition I shall later outline. First a short description of the proclamation. Printed on coarse paper, it measures one hundred and thirty centimetres long and fifty-six centimetres wide. For purposes of preservation I had it mounted on cardboard and framed.

The text is preceded by the following caption:

Da Han Si-chuan Jun-zheng-fu Du-du Shi
Proclamation by the Commander of the Military Government of Sichuan in Great Han

There is a red tick written over the character *Shi*, presumably denoting the approval of the promulgation of the proclamation. The actual text of the proclamation consists of fourteen six-character couplet lines. In the transcription of the Chinese characters (the original was too difficult to reproduce photo-graphically), I have numbered each couplet line to facilitate easy reference. What follows is a pinyin romanisation and English translation of each line:

1. *BU-GAO DA-HAN GUO-MIN*
    ZHENG-FU YI-JING GAI-GE
    (WE) PROCLAIM TO THE PEOPLE OF THE GREAT HAN NATION THAT THE GOVERNMENT HAS BEEN REFORMED.

    Here I feel the terms *DA-HAN* and *GAI-GE* are significant. The former loudly trumpets the patriotic fervour of the revolutionaries, whilst in contrast, *GAI-GE* is a somewhat mild term to describe their armed overthrow of the Qing government.

2. *XIAN-ZAI SI-CHUAN QUAN-SHENG*
    TONG-SHI SHI-XING DU-LI
    NOW THE WHOLE PROVINCE OF SICHUAN
    HAS AT THE SAME TIME SET IN MOTION ITS INDEPENDENCE.

    Obviously this does not mean that Sichuan has proclaimed its independence, but simply that it has rid itself of the old order and that now the local administration of the republican forces is operating independently.

3. *SHENG-CHENG SHE XIN ZHENG-FU*
    ZHENG-CE QU-JUE GONG-YI
    WE HAVE SET UP A NEW GOVERNMENT IN THE PROVINCIAL
    CAPITAL
    WHERE POLICY IS DETERMINED BY PUBLIC DISCUSSION.

    This all sounds just a touch too democratic to be true and I
    cannot help wondering what the good Military Commander
    meant by *GONG-YI*.

4. *SHI-SHI ZHU-CHI HE-PING*
    LI-QIU NING-REN XI-SHI
    IN ALL OUR DEALINGS WE WILL MAINTAIN PEACE
    AND STRIVE FOR RECONCILIATION.

    Here the Military Commander seems to be assuring the
    population of the revolutionary faction's aim to establish long
    term peaceful civilian rule as opposed to harsh military
    control.

5. *WAI-GUO-REN JI JIAO-TANG*
    BEN-SHENG XING-ZHENG GUAN-LI
    FOREIGNERS AND THEIR CHURCHES,
    AS WELL AS ADMINISTRATIVE OFFICIALS THROUGHOUT THE
    PROVINCE,

    I assume *XING-ZHENG GUAN-LI* to refer to the officials and
    civil servants of the Imperial administration.

6. *MAN-ZHOU ZHU-FANG REN-MIN*
    YI-LÜ ZHAO-CHANG DAI-YU
    AND MEMBERS OF THE MANCHU GARRISON TROOPS,
    ALL THESE WILL BE TREATED UNIFORMLY AS BEFORE.

    A further assurance of the revolutionaries' good intentions —
    this time to foreigners and both the military and civil service of
    the old regime. For this reason I have translated *ZHAO-
    CHANG* not as "as usual" but "as before".

7. *SHENG-WAI TONG-ZHI MIN-TUAN*
   YI DA YUAN-MAN MU-DI
   THE MILITIA UNITS SHARING OUR OBJECTIVE OUTSIDE THIS
   PROVINCE
   HAVE NOW ACHIEVED THEIR COMMON AIM.

   I assume this slightly ambiguous line to mean the successful
   revolutionary action throughout the other provinces of China,
   rather than units coming from beyond Sichuan who supported
   the military activities of the revolutionaries in that province.

8. *JI YI SHI-BING GUI-NONG*
   DA-JIA LI-TU XIN ZHI
   SOLDIERS SHOULD BE SPEEDILY DEMOBBED
   AND EVERYONE DO HIS BEST FOR OUR NEW ORDER.

9. *CONG-QIAN SUN-SHI SANG-WANG*
   YOU-ZI FU-XU ZHEN-JI
   FOR THOSE WHO HAVE SUFFERED IN THE PREVIOUS
   HOSTILITIES
   THERE WILL BE RELIEF AND FOR THEIR DEPENDENTS
   PROVISION WILL BE MADE.

10. *JIU-RI BI-ZHENG KE-JUAN*
    JI-CHOU JIAN-CHU FEI-QI
    THE HARSH TAXES OF THE FORMER OPPRESSIVE REGIME
    WILL BE EITHER REDUCED OR ABOLISHED ALTOGETHER.

11. *ZHI-YU SHE-HUI ZHI-XU*
    WU-QIU AN-JING RU-XI
    AS REGARDS PUBLIC ORDER
    ALL MUST BE DONE TO KEEP THE PEACE AS IT WAS PRIOR TO
    COMMENCEMENT OF HOSTILITIES.

    Here I assume *RU-XI* refers to the time before the uprising and
    not to some far distant golden age of piping peace.

12. *FAN WO SHI-NONG GONG-SHANG*
YI-QIE GE-AN SHENG-YE
ALL OF US WHETHER OFFICIAL, FARMER, ARTISAN OR MERCHANT,
MUST GO ABOUT HIS LAWFUL BUSINESS CONTENT WITH HIS OWN OCCUPATION.

13. *SUO-BAN TIAO-JIAN JIN-LING*
DA-ZHONG JUN-XU ZHU-YI
ALL LAWS AND PROHIBITIONS PROCLAIMED BY US
MUST BE UNIFORMLY OBEYED BY THE PUBLIC.

14. *CONG-CI GONG-XIANG ZHI-PING*
TONG-JIN GUO-MIN TIAN-ZHI
FROM NOW ON, MUTUALLY ENJOYING PEACE AND GOOD ORDER,
WE SHOULD ALL DO ALL WE CAN TO CARRY OUT OUR HEAVEN-BESTOWED DUTY TO OUR NATION AND PEOPLE.

The juxtaposition of the two terms *GUO-MIN* (nation) and *TIAN-ZHI* as the very last words of the proclamation add particular authority to the Nationalist decree, by marrying the new terminology of the revolutionaries with the time-honoured traditional Confucian concept. The term *TIAN-ZHI* is first seen in the Second Wan Zhang section of the book of Mencius, where it has been traditionally described by the major commentators as duty or office bestowed on worthy men by heaven and not the prerogative of monarchs or rulers. In short the idea conveyed in this last line is that the emperor has lost his *TIAN-MING* 天命 or Heavenly Mandate, and the people are now blessed with heaven-sent rights and duties to rule in his place, even if (Winnie the) Pu Yi was not to abdicate until the following year. We have already seen in couplet twelve the use of traditional Confucian social stratification terminology to emphasize their commitment to upholding social order, but here it is used to give the stamp of legitimacy to the act of rebellion.

At the end of the text of the proclamation comes the date:

HUANG-DI JI-YUAN SI-QIAN LIU-BAI-JIU NIAN SHI-YUE-RI
FOUR THOUSAND SIX HUNDRED AND NINE YEARS FROM THE
ASCENT OF THE YELLOW EMPEROR TO THE THRONE, IN THE
TENTH MONTH.

The day has not been recorded, but in the space where it would have stood is an illegible scribble in red ink, presumably merely another sign of official approval for the document to be released for the public to read. According to tradition, the Yellow Emperor reigned from 2697 to 2597 B.C., outstripping those two other long-distance monarchs Queen Vic and the Emperor Hirohito. It is interesting to see that this system of dating was chosen by the Chinese Nationalists as they seized control in the months preceding the proclamation of the Republic in 1912. It underlines their pride at having rid the Chinese of the alien regime that had humiliatingly subjugated them ever since the collapse of the last truly indigenous dynasty in 1644. Whilst on the subject of nationalism, history presents us with a sinister parallel dating system in the case of Japan. During the extreme nationalistic period prior to their country's defeat in 1945, all Japanese children were made to learn by heart the names and dates of all the twenty-eight legendary emperors starting with the first one 神武 Jimmu 660–585 B.C. Indeed, the kiddies were taught never to question the veracity of the existence of any of these dream-time monarchs. Especially not Emperor Jimmu, the great progenitor of all preceding the diminutive Hirohito. Worse still, the nation was ordered to date all years in future from the ascension 紀元 *KIGEN* of Emperor Jimmu in 660 B.C., with the result that 1940 became the year 2600. Interestingly enough, although this cranky system was abolished in the Occupation period, it did not take long for the devious Japanese Nationalists to disguise the celebration of Jimmu's ascension day by renaming it 國立紀年日 (Kokuritsu Kinenbi) National Foundation Day, and proclaiming it a national holiday. Enough said.

The circumstances behind my acquisition of this document are as follows. Whilst employed as a lecturer in Chinese in the University of Edinburgh, I was contacted by a lady asking advice about what she thought was a Chinese Buddhist scroll. On seeing the document I quickly assured her that it had nothing to do with Buddhism or any other Oriental religion and was merely "a Chinese Revolutionary poster". I cunningly omitted to tell her which revolution. On learning this the good lady lost all interest in it and was more than happy to part with it. Having acquired the document by an act of underhand deception worthy of Cao Cao 曹操, I was unwilling to press my luck by asking how and when it had come into her possession, lest my eager curiosity should cause her to have second thoughts. To try and atone for my rather shabby stratagem I have at last decided by this small description and transcription to share my historical acquisition with better sinological folk than myself, chiefly with my old friend and much respected mentor David Hawkes, whose continued longevity will, I trust, outstrip that of both the Yellow Emperor and Emperor Jimmu. Interestingly enough I remember years ago how David showed me an equally fascinating pamphlet — a leaflet addressed to the citizens of Peking by the commander of the P.L.A. prior to the capital's capture in early 1949. David's document was (unlike mine) honestly acquired. That's the difference between a true scholar and gentleman, and fellows of my kind.

DENIS TWITCHETT

The Horse and the Tang State

Very early in Xianzong's reign, when Bo Juyi and Yuan Zhen were writing satirical verses attacking the political failures of the time, they each included among their satirical New Yuefu poems a piece entitled "The Road from Yinshan".

The road from Yinshan was the main route linking Chang'an and the central region of Guanzhong province with the Tang military outposts along the great northern bend of the Huanghe, and beyond that to the Yinshan mountains and the grasslands on their northern slopes. For those responsible for the empire's defences this route was not simply a vital link in the communication network of the northern border. It was a crucial trade route by which the late-eighth and ninth century Tang government imported horses for their military, which they procured at great cost from their Uighur allies of convenience.

Earlier in the dynasty, the Tang, as we shall see, had maintained a huge establishment of official stud farms and pastures, mostly in the area now covered by the modern provinces of Gansu and Qinghai. At their peak these official pastures held vast numbers of livestock, not only horses but cattle, donkeys and mules, sheep, and camels.

The outbreak of the An Lushan rebellion in 755, and its aftermath, changed all this drastically. By 764 the whole of modern Qinghai and almost all of modern Gansu province had fallen into the hands of the Tibetans, and the Tang government had not only lost almost all of their pasture lands, but the entire complex of horse-raising that the government had once sustained. Ineffective attempts were made to encourage the breeding of horses in other parts of China, even in Fujian, but the rural economy was nowhere organized to undertake large scale livestock breeding on the scale the state required, and the native horses from Sichuan and elsewhere in the south and west were too small to serve as cavalry mounts. The government was forced more and more to depend on sources of supply beyond her borders. The rich pasture lands of the north-west border and the Qinghai region were in the hands of the Tibetans, the Tang's principal adversaries, and control of these grasslands had been the cause of the constant wars and disputes between the two states. The north-eastern frontier peoples, the Qitan and Xi were an alternative source, but until 845 they had submitted to the suzerainty of the Uighurs, although they continued to send embassies to Chang'an, and large groups of tribesmen regularly came to Youzhou (modern Peking) where they engaged in horse trading. But these sources of supply could produce only a few drops in the ocean of the empire's needs.

The only realistic alternative source was the Uighur empire, now the dominant force in the Gobi and the steppe areas immediately north of the northern frontier zone. The Uighur had given material assistance to the Tang government during the An Lushan/Shi Siming rebellions, and were the main adversaries of Tibet in a multi-state struggle for control of the former Tang territories and populations in the north-west and in the Tarim and Dzungaria, a struggle which also involved alliances with the Nanzhao state and even the Arabs.

The warfare of this period was highly mobile, and largely involved cavalry forces on both sides. China's enemies were all pastoral peoples with more than adequate supplies of horses, and populations reared from childhood with natural skills as horsemen. China's defense needed to be able to match them in the field on their own terms. The threat of depriving the Tang state of an adequate supply of horses was as potent a form of blackmail as the threat of an oil embargo against the western powers by

OPEC in the early 1970s. It was not only a threat to the mobility of the armed forces, but potentially a threat against the mobility of a highly mobile society.

Like the western powers in the 1970s, the Tang state had little option but to play for time and pay the price the Uighurs demanded.

ॐ

The Road from Yinshan

Bo Juyi

On the Yinshan road,
Green pastures are lush, the water good.
But when the season comes for the Hu to send us horses
Along the road for a thousand *li*, not a blade of grass remains.

The pastures exhausted, the springs dried up, horses fall sick and
    grow feeble;
The brands Fei and Long mark only skin and bone.
For every horse we pay out fifty lengths of finest silk,
This silk is paid out and horses arrive with never a day's respite.
We keep beasts that prove useless, paying out what should not be
    paid,
And year after year six or seven of every ten of the horses die.

There is not enough silk thread, and the spinners suffer.
To make up their quota of pieces, they weave loosely and make
    short lengths;
Pieces a mere three *zhang* long, woven loose as spiders' webs
    from fibres of lotus root …
The Uighurs complain they have no use for it.
The Xian'an Princess is the Uighurs' Queen,
And from afar she constantly complains on her Qaghan's
    behalf.

The second year Yuanhe; new orders are sent down,

The price for the horses is to be paid in gold or silk from the
    Palace itself,
And an edict orders that the silk woven in Jianghuai to pay for the
    horses
May no longer be coarse-woven and in short lengths.
Their General Heluo wished our Emperor long life,
And respectfully accepted the gold, silver, and precious silks.

Who was to know that this would simply make the cunning slaves
    more greedy still!
The next year twice as many beasts arrived!
The better the silk,
The more the horses.
Barbarians of Yinshan,
Whatever can we do about you?

The Road from Yinshan
Yuan Zhen

Year after year we purchase horses by the Yinshan road;
The horses die — silk squandered for nothing.
Our Yuanhe Emperor, considerate to the weaving women,
Pays gold and silver from his privy treasury to pay the price
    instead.

I would like to say one word about this, at the risk of death,
Gladly risk life or death to requite his benevolent brilliance.
Waste of resources does not arise simply from buying horses;
Squandered silk and damage to the artisans can be caused by
    other sorts of robbery!

I have heard that
In normal times there were seven hundred thousand horses;
In Guanzhong you could hardly be free of the sound of their
    neighing.
The forty-eight state pastures could choose dams fit for dragons
And seasonal tribute was still paid to Court in well-made cloth.

But now of our frontier plains not a tenth remains,
All of our horses trample and crowd one another in the Feilong
 pastures.
A myriad trusses of hay and fodder must be supplied morning and
 evening,
Thousands of *zhong* of beans and grain constantly dragged to the
 feed-troughs.

Our standing armies, prefectures, more than a hundred garrisons
Annually offer up fine yellow silk, though their people are hard
 pressed, even through winter and spring.
Taxable households flee their homes, extra levies constantly have
 to be made;
Officials take other goods in lieu, unrelenting in their heedless greed.

New patterns are chosen and the weave changed so that wasted
 effort is redoubled,
They give up the old and tried, to follow new fashions which
 catch people's taste.
To weave one length of Yue crepe or raised damask,
Means more work than to weave ten of fine plain silk.

Families of magnates, the rich and noble overstep the normal
 rules,
Encouraging their clans and kinsmen to abandon refinement and
 restraint.
Their attendant horsemen and favourite slaves wear garments of
 finest linen,
Their huntsmen boys, falcons at the wrist, wear scabbards of cloud
 brocade.

When all his subjects serve their own advantage and aim to usurp
 power,
The Emperor, in deepest sincerity will grieve in vain.
If he spaciously lays down patterned tiles for the phoenix and
 pheasant ranks of his courtiers,
When can we hope the benevolent waves, the rain and dew that
 flow from him will ever be requited?

BURTON WATSON

Five Poems by the Song Poet–Official Lu You (1125–1210)

The first was written in 1173; the remainder date from the poet's late years, when he was living in rustic retirement on the outskirts of Shaoxing in Zhejiang.

Late Afternoon Shower
(five-character regulated verse)

Softly it glided over the banks of the pond;
dimly it shines on encircling walls.
Under its weight the dust no longer stirs;
the earth, suddenly dampened, emits a fragrant smell.
Its voice clatters among the catalpas and paulownias;
fresh, it lends a coolness to pillow and mat.
I turn my head and all at once it's gone —
now the setting sun hangs by a corner of the eaves.

Big Wind
(seven-character old style)

Fierce heat this year, beyond endurance,
gleaming sweat like rain, the thinnest robe a torture.
August Heaven, repenting harshness, makes it up in one downpour;
autumn winds take care to arrive right on time.
With a roar like angry waves they jar the earth's axle,
in the night break down the bamboos by my southern study.
At dawn the retiree gets up to a wondrous sight:
the whole window green with featherings of a phoenix tail!

First Month, Fifteenth Day
(five-character regulated verse)

First month, fifteenth day, out into the countryside as far as Gold Stone
Terrace.

Getting old, hate to see the seasons pass;
how could I forget my fondness for outings?
Snowy weather over, sky a light blue;
spring stirring, pale yellow on the willows.
Talk and laughter ease the burden of age and debility;
climbing up, peering down, we stay on till the evening sun.
No need yet to hurry for the ferry —
let me rest a while longer in my folding chair.

Writing about the New Cool Spell

(seven-character regulated verse)

Lying in bed, I look at bird tracks on the green moss;
in window and door, newborn coolness — what a delight!
Jumbled cicadas sing in the trees, hurrying the setting sun;
wind-blown leaves skitter over the stairs, presage of coming autumn.
Lingering illness — true, a mere sojourner in this world,
but in drunkenness I still cherish the heart and mind of a child.
From now on, the day permitting, I'll pursue my leisure time joys,
pick the last chrysanthemums by the hedge, search for streamside
    plums.

By Boat to Fan River

(seven-character regulated verse)

By boat to Fan River, stopped to rest in a house there and was served a meal.

Traveler's fare — what harm if the feast is fern shoots?
In evening sun I knock at the farmer's door.
Bleak ruffling in my short hair, the first of autumn's chill;
silent, still, deserted village, year on year poor harvests.
The boat slices into weed-grown banks, wild geese start up in
    alarm;
a flute sounds over the misty pond, calling cows to come home.
Difficult times, yet ideas for poems keep on coming.
Being a failure in life is not all bad.

WONG SIU-KIT

Rhyme-prose on the E-pang Palace by Du Mu (803–852)

The six states are no more,
The four seas are united,
The Shu mountains have been shorn of all trees,
And E-pang Palace stands before us.
Its weight presses down on more than
      three hundred miles of land,
It cuts off the sun and the heavens.
The buildings begin north of Mount Li and turn west,
Running on to the city of Xianyang.
Rivers Wei and Fan pour on,
Flow into the palace walls.
You walk fifty steps there is a turret,
Ten steps there is a tower.
The mid-level corridors among them meander,
The beaks on the roofs peck at the air.
Every edifice occupies a unique position,
Their hearts are intertwined, their horns in combat.
Ah the twirl,
The whirl.
Beehives and whirlpools,
All erect, you do not know
      how many thousand mansions there are.
A long bridge lies upon the water,
And you wonder why without clouds there should be a dragon.
A hanging passage-way crosses the sky,

And you ask why there should be a rainbow
    when there has been no rain.
Different heights, some higher, some lower, so confusing,
There is no telling where east or west is.
The warm music of the singers' platform
Is aglow with spring;
The cool, fluttering sleeves in the dancers' hall
Are desolate wind and rain.
Within the same day
And the confines of the same palace,
So various are the climates.

෧

Ladies, maids and damsels,
Sons and grandsons of royalty,
Bidding farewell to palaces in the six nations,
Are come by carriage to the state of Qin.
Singing in the morning, playing the lyre by night,
They make up the harem of Qin.
Twinkling stars
Are the mirrors of their toilette;
Black clouds pile on black clouds,
When they comb their coiffure at dawn;
The River Wei flows greasily
With discarded make-up;
Mist and fog everywhere
From the burning of orchid and pepper;
Deafening thunder
As palace carriages go past;
Rumbling that becomes more distant,
And you can't tell where they are gone.
Each face, each glimpse of complexion,
Spells the ultimate in grace and beauty.
Looking into the infinite distance, standing an eternity,
The one hope is to be favoured.

But some have not been seen in all thirty-six years.

∽

All that was collected by the states of Yan and Zhao,
Schemed to amass by Han and Wei,
Treasured by Qi and Chu,
Over how many years, how many ages,
Things that had been possessions of the people,
Are now accumulated into mountains.
What the six nations failed to protect
Now found their way here.
Cauldrons are now cooking pans,
The finest jade has become pebbles,
And slabs of gold are treated as common clay,
All strewn about everywhere,
And the men of Qin
Didn't know their worth.

∽

Alas,
How one man feels
Is no different from how a million men feel.
If the Qin Emperor loved luxury,
Ordinary mortals too cannot forget their home.
Why then should he deprive them of every penny,
And spend it like a cartload of sand?
Why must there be more pillars supporting the beams
Than there are farmers in the field?
Why more rafters
Than weaving-maids at the loom?
There are more sparkling nails
Than the grains of rice in the granary,
More tiles
Than threads of wool in your clothes,

More bars and thresholds
Than the number of cities in all Cathay,
More cacophonous notes from the strings and pipes
Than the murmured words of the market place.
Why this stopping of all mouths
While the anger is universal?
The arrogance and stubbornness of him
Whom no one loves increases by the day.
Then comes a shout from the frontier guards,
And Hangu Pass surrenders;
Then comes a fire raised by the men of Chu,
And lovely E-pang Palace is a burnt offering.

                                 ∽

Alas! The destroyer of the six nations is not the state of Qin, but the six nations themselves. The annihilator of Qin is not the world at large, but Qin herself. What a thought it is that had the six nations loved their people they would have been strong enough to resist Qin; and if Qin on her part had loved the people of the six nations, she could have retained the imperial throne for three generations, nay, for ten thousand generations, and no one could have demolished her. As the rulers of Qin were too busy to mourn their own destruction, posterity must mourn for them; but if in mourning the destruction of Qin posterity fails to learn the lesson, then posterity's posterity will have to mourn for posterity itself.

ANTHONY C. YU

Fourteen Lyrics by Wu Zao (1799–1863)

To the tune of
"Seductive Autumn Waves"
(***Qiubo mei***)

Inscribing a White Lotus Scroll
by Woman Scholar Wang Yuanlan

Cool west wind enters the lotuses' fall
And cuts off the white-reeded islet.
>Wordless, with scant make-up,
>They gently walk the waves
>Midst how much idle grief.

The sun passes by their shadows one by one.
Hasn't their sweet slumber deepened?
>Dusk is fast approaching.
>Where does the moon light up?
>One stretch of floating fragrance.

To the tune of
"Willow in the Wind"
(***Feng zhong liu***)

Drifting Floss

From where is the drifting floss
      Blown to the vacant courtyard,
      So clingy and bound up with sorrow?
Bidding the wind not to be sudden,
Begging the willows to tie them up,
I reckon this time
      I have retained one strand of Spring.

The roguish orioles
      Simply must dart through to break them,
      Leaving specks of them to drift and vanish.
How unlike spider webs
      Which, still wont to be chivalrous,
      At wall's end would wrap up fallen reds!

To the tune of
"Bitter Longing"
(***Ku xiangsi***)

Double gates are silent, for the deep yard's locked.
      I just rise from sleep
      And grief's already here.
I feel my hair loosened and pins half-fallen.
      At dawn I tire to comb and tie;
      At night I tire to comb and tie.

On the mats by gauze screens who could sleep through
      A bitter sick realm,
      Or bear a tight load?
How could twenty years pass like a dream?
      At first I grieved for myself.
      Now, too, I grieve for myself.

To the tune of
"Shouting Fire: A Song"
(*He huo ling*)

The bamboo mat cools as if newly washed;
The plantain screen has yet to snare a dream.
I'd sleep, but rise again to neaten my ice-white silk.
Beneath the blue-gauze windows let me
          Mutely pick incense to burn.

My woes I dread telling Heaven;
Most poems I scan when I'm ill.
Once more this night is like the night before:
          The same lamps aglow,
          The same clock dripping on and on,
          The same moment waking from wine
          As the moon climbs the flower-tips.

To the tune of
"Flight of Young Swallows"
(*Ru yan fei*)

Sadness

Don't think that sadness comes too soon!
Since birth it's been like your form, your shadow,
      Always entwining you —
An ancestral root found everywhere
      That none (read past and present) can sweep out.
When it spreads abroad,
      What divers longings will it become?
Grievous songs of heroes, lover's tears;
Still more, the aging outcasts and sickly poets.
      When you feel the pain,
      The tune will be the same.

Aiding sadness are such idle things:
At Heaven's edge
      The morning wind and fading moon,
      The setting sun and fragrant grass.
I'm, too, one despondent 'midst humankind,
      Such taste I've fully savored.
Besides, by morning or night
      How much more is added
      On the brows and eye-tips that's unbearable.
Facing the gauze windows
      I hold the brush to chant some more,
      To tap out one page
      Of sadness inscribed.

To the tune of
"The Beautiful Lady Yu"
(*Yu meiren*)

Twilight, darkened moon, autumn sounds astir
        Outside a smallish window:
I hear wind, I hear rain, but nothing's distinct
Except the soughs and sighs
        That fill the empty yard.

A cold lamp trimmed low, I'm tired to chant;
        This long night should be half gone.
The pond's Spring grasses are all a maze.
That makes me feel
        A dream tonight is worse than none!

To the tune of
"Nuptial Branches"
(*Lianli zhi*)

I fear not the flower branches' ire;
I fear not the flower branches' laugh;
I blame the Spring wind only
        That on this day each year
        Would blow such sadness here.
The blinds just lowered,
        I sat cross-legged for not even a while[1]
        When early bees would brawl with butterflies.

Since when has Heaven grown dear?
Since when has the moon been kind?
That beneath the eyes, above the brows,
        There's no love but only regret,
        I ask who would own such knowledge.
I reckon since birth
        I have ne'er wronged my pure talent.
        Could being smart have done me harm?

**To the tune of
"Charming Nian Nu"
(*Nian Nu jiao*)**

**Inscribing a Painting of
"Listening to the Rain on a Vacant Mountain"
by Junxiang**

Pearlike brows and moonlike face!
Think, in your former life:
       Were you a flower-strewing celestial maid?
In silent halls where Sanskrit chants desist
       There's someone deep in deepest space.
A single strand of cool mist —
All around the chilly green —
       A few sprinkles of pattering rain.
The lamp-trimming person tires,
And dreams of gods ripen in the hall of cranes.

A Yellow Court sketched just so,
A Golden Chestnut painted —[2]
       All befitting a carefree aim.
Sparse bamboos and orchids transmit colors and forms,
       Unlike windblown willows of a house.
Affinities of incense and fire,
Such rhetoric and such language,
       Sing the utmost of nature's friendship.
Take this for a laugh:
       What for jadewhite plums is Spring like?

To the tune of
"Groping for Little Fishes"
(*Mo yu'er*)

In a little while
This splendor will slowly age,
Though light overcast stays inklike as of old.
Each strand of willow with its starry floss
  Now shows by two-thirds the hues of Spring.
Fair is not for sure!
Here's light rain again,
  Its fine threads frolic to wet window-gauze.
Swallows coming will know,
Recalling how by walls plastered green,
  Near the red-brick pavilion,
  One hanging painted screen divides.

On roads to River South
  Do we know how apricot flowers fare?
Tomorrow's already the Cold Food Feast.[3]
Double phoenix shoes, flat-headed, though firm
  Are, I fear, too weak to tread the green.
I can't keep worrying,
  But, as I meet people before me
  Or stand with a swing behind me,
  As I "search, search and seek, seek,"[4]
  I'd grumble at the east wind —
  That idle busybody —
  For creasing half a pond of green.

To the tune of
"Prince Lanling"
(*Lanling wang*)

I dread Spring going.
With wine in hand I talk to Spring:
       On the road to Heaven's edge,
       As flowers fall and water flows,
       By whom could time be halted finally?
       Amidst willow strands of ten thousands
       Where is that cuckoo deeply hidden?
Spring is going home!
       With no strength to keep her,
       We must let Lord East Wind himself decide.

My grief darkens as if decocted:
       I've done counting the fading reds
       Or kneading the flying floss.
For several times I'd lift the screen to look
       At a place filled with fair grasses
       Half-traced by slanting light.
Butterflies arriving are still soaring;
       They know, I think, my poem's mood.

Gut-wrenching lines proliferate
       To deplore sojourner Time
       Who is truly faithless.
Rails crack for slapping, this waiting's in vain:
       Only few specks of fragrant vapor
       And two rows of misty trees.
       Twilight has just come
       When we face one more sprinkle of rain.

**To the tune of
"Branches in Union"
(*Lianli zhi*)**

Summer Begins

Try the new cicada-gauze gown
As a gentle breeze sweeps your face.
Droplets of fading reds
And mists of falling floss
     Will vex your mood and thought.
The drawn out make-up is done!
     Stick in once more the jade head-scratcher.
     Put on the cherries and the plums.

Agéd brew stains like pear-flowers;
Fava bean scent fills my fingers;
The time's past for swapping butterflies;
The feast for fêting Spring is done —
Nothing at all by boudoir windows.
Such a splendid time
     That in one instant is urged to leave!
     I fault the cuckoo for misdeeds.

To the tune of
"Song of Golden Threads"
(*Jinlü qu*)

Since I came from the Blue Lotus Realm,[5]
How many grievous verdicts I have overturned,
And to whom must I answer?
I'd scoop three thousand fathoms of the Milky Way
To wash off just once a girl's familiar form;
Packing up eyeshadows and leftover rouge,
I would not mimic Orchid Terrace's autumnal plaint[6]
But only boast of smashing through the Cosmic Pass.
> Let me draw a long sword
> That leans toward the sky.[7]

Many are the seas of pleasures in the realm of man!
They all have their bannered arbors and painted walls
Where the double chignons would bow low.
When wine and singing stop, they still must leave
For all things return to a choiceless end.
Ask where are the ruined ashes of yesterday.
Learn of non-negation, the truth of truths,[8]
For even gods are stumped by emptiness.
> This dusty world's affairs,
> Why should they surprise?

To the tune of
"Song of the Grotto Immortal"
(*Dongxian ge*)

For the Courtesan Qinglin of Wumen

Such a bony, slender frame,
Like that of a Jade City divinity's mate!
Smiling we met, quite forgetting how to speak.
You were always picking flowers,
Though your sleeves grew cold from leaning against bamboos;
In that empty valley
I thought I could see your dear, secret thoughts.[9]

While scented lamps cast our shadows low,
We gamed with wine, assessed our poems,
Only to sing at once those heartbreaking lines
        Of "Recalling River South."
Alike we are — "brushed-eyebrow talents" both —
But I'm so simple and wild
That I'd want to enjoy this beauty's pledge of heart.
Here's a hazy stretch
        Of mist and waves across Five Lakes of Spring:
        Let me buy a red boat, my love, to take you there.

To the tune of
"Flight of the Young Swallows"
(*Ru yan fei*)

Reading *Dream of the Red Chamber*

Of what use was the wish to patch up the sky
When one's soul could be consumed in red chamber's depths?
Kingfisher-wrapped and perfume-enclosed,
Foolish girl and silly boy, I fear, will never wake up —
Daily, bitterly, sowing their seeds of love.
      Which one of them, I ask,
      Is the true seed of love?
Stubborn Stone has sentience but a sylph has woe:
Their three lifetimes reap but spun-thread sorrow, waxen tears,
      With one stroke thus concludes
      The dream of Supreme Void.

Though murmurs fall futile on greenish moss,
      They cling and cling like
      The jade pin atop her head,
      The small phoenix on *wutong*-blossoms.
"Yellow earth", "gauze windows" — these, the words of doom,
Dissolve with pain a beauty's heart.
      Where could I mourn
      An old grave of buried fragrance?
Flowers fall, flowers bloom, but the person is gone;
      Weeping in the wind of Spring,
      I have tears to match the flowers' pain.
      Flowers stand mute
      But my tears flow.

Notes

1. Sat cross-legged: presumably in a posture of Buddhist meditation.
2. In this and the previous line, the poet is punning. Yellow Court (*huangting*) can mean literally a courtyard of such color and the title of an early Taoist scripture. Golden Chestnut (*jin lü*) refers simultaneously to the description of either cassia flowers or chrysanthemums and one name of the transformed Buddha.
3. Cold Food Feast: In a period from the 105th to the 107th day after the winter solstice, food is supposed to be eaten cold or uncooked in order to commemorate a virtuous official Jie Zitui of the Spring and Autumn (approx. 770–403 B.C.E.). Refusing to serve King Wen of Jin after he had been restored to power, Jie fled to the mountains. When the king tried to force him out by setting fires, Jie burned to death by hugging a tree.
4. "Search, search and seek, seek," is a quotation of a famous line opening a lyric by the celebrated woman poet of the Song, Li Qingzhao (1084?– c.1151).
5. The Buddha's eyes are said to resemble the shape of blue lotus leaves or Utpala. The region so named was also a favourite conceit of the Tang poet, Li Bo (701–762), who often referred to himself as the "banished immortal" from the Blue Lotus Realm.
6. Wu's line here makes two allusions to the shadowy figure of Song Yu (c. 290–223 B.C.E.). In the *Wen Xuan*, the anthology of literature compiled by Xiao Tong, Crown Prince of Liang in the sixth century, Song's literary activities were always preceded by a conversation with King Xiang of Chu on the Orchid Terrace. Secondly, the association of Song Yu with poetic lamentations of autumn is traceable to the "Nine Changes (*Jiu bian*)" section of *The Songs of the South*. See pp. 209–219 of David Hawkes' translation (Penguin, 1985).
7. An allusion to the *yitian jian* mentioned in Song Yu's "Great Utterances Rhymeprose (*Dayan fu*)" and in Li Bo's "Great Hunt Rhymeprose (*Dalie fu*)".
8. Non-negation or *wuwu* is a technical term for the state of ultimate purity in religious Taoism.
9. Lines 3–7 exploit several rhetorical borrowings from a famous poem, "The Beautiful Person (*Jiaren*)" by the Tang poet Du Fu (712–770). Du's poem tells of a beautiful woman "alone in an empty valley", living in desolation and poverty inflicted by war and abused by a heartless, lecherous husband. Adversity, however, serves only to foster her virtue. Although the poem has been regarded by a few critics as an account of a real woman encountered by Du Fu shortly after the An Lushan rebellion, by far the dominant interpretation has followed the venerable

practice of political allegory. The beautiful woman, therefore, is another instance of the loyal and talented scholar–official slighted by a negligent prince. Wu Zao's appropriation of Du Fu's imageries and rhetoric to compliment her courtesan lover is thus highly subversive.

Notes on Contributors

Steve BALOGH, of whom it has been said, "I'd trust him with my life, but not my car …", was born in 1946 in Oxford, England. Once, long ago, he was a keen student of animal behaviour, until one day he discovered "evolutionary psychology" and has ever since been running in the opposite direction! He went on to study Chinese at Edinburgh and London, and now translates from Chinese to English.

Cyril BIRCH was born in 1925 in Bolton, Lancashire, and studied Chinese at the School of Oriental and African Studies, London. From 1960 he taught at the University of California, Berkeley, and retired there as Agassiz Professor of Chinese and Comparative Literature in 1990. A prolific translator and scholar, he is perhaps best known for his two-volume *Anthology of Chinese Literature*, and his translation of Tang Xianzu's lyric drama *The Peony Pavilion*.

Duncan CAMPBELL studied in China in the mid-1970s, since when he has taught Chinese Language and Literature in New Zealand, at both the University of Auckland and Victoria University of Wellington. His research focuses on the literary and material culture of late Imperial China. He has very happy memories of days spent with David and Jean during their trip to New Zealand.

Red CHAN is finishing her doctoral degree at the Institute of Chinese Studies, Oxford University. Her thesis investigates the English translations of contemporary mainland Chinese fiction. She is also a freelance translator and interpreter.

CHOW Tse-tsung took his Ph.D. at the University of Michigan in 1955. Until his retirement, he was for many years Professor of Chinese Literature and History at the University of Wisconsin at Madison. His writings include *The May Fourth Movement, Wen-Lin: Studies in the Chinese Humanities*, and many articles on Chinese literature and culture in both Chinese and English.

Arthur COOPER was born in 1916 of Anglo-Irish parents and as a boy explored foreign languages and poetry, starting with Icelandic, later turning to Japanese and Chinese. He entered the Foreign Office in 1938, served in Hong Kong and Singapore 1939–42, and for several years in Australia under the British High Commission. After his retirement in 1968, he devoted himself to Chinese poetry and language, publishing a monograph on *The Creation of the Chinese Script* in 1978. He died in 1988.

William DOLBY became actively interested in Chinese in his teens, and studied it at London, Cambridge, and Hong Kong universities. He went on to teach Chinese Language and Civilisation in various universities East and West, also publishing a number of works on Chinese topics, including a history of Chinese drama, and translations of poetry, fiction, and philosophy. He met David some decades ago, and has been constantly inspired by his dedication to Chinese literature.

Vieta DYER was born Svetlana Rimsky-Korsakoff in Harbin, China, in 1931. She graduated from Catholic Fu Jen University, Peking, in 1952, and then left China for Australia. She taught the Chinese language in the Australian National University for fifty years until her retirement in 2002. Her main interests are the Dungans (the Chinese Muslims in Russia), and the thirteenth-century Chinese textbooks, *Lao Qida* and *Piaotongshi*.

Mark ELVIN took his B.A. and Ph.D. at Cambridge, and has worked at Cambridge, Glasgow, and Oxford universities, as well as the École Normale Supérieure. He is currently a Research Professor of Chinese History at the Australian National University. Although his main concerns have been economic and environmental history he has always had an additional interest in perceptions and representations, which are the subject of his *Changing Stories in the Chinese World* (1997) and of his contribution to the present book. His best-known books include *The*

Pattern of the Chinese Past (1973), and *Sediments of Time: Environment and Society in Chinese History* (1998), edited with Liu Ts'ui-jung. His new book, *The Retreat of the Elephants: An Environmental History of China*, will be published by Yale University Press in 2004. He has also written a trilogy for children. He is married to Dian Montgomerie.

FANG Zhaoling was born in 1914 in Wuxi, eldest daughter of the industrialist Fang Shouyi and his wife Wang Shuying. She studied at the University of Manchester (1937–9), and at the University of Oxford (1956–8), where David Hawkes was one of her supervisors. She has exhibited her paintings and calligraphy in galleries all around the world. Zhang Daqian was among her many teachers and mentors.

Jacques GERNET was born in Algiers in 1921. He studied at Algiers University (French Literature and Classical Studies), and at the University of Paris after the war (Chinese Studies). He was Professor of Chinese from 1957–74 at the University of Paris, and from 1975 until his retirement in 1992 he held the Chair of Social and Intellectual History of China at the Collège de France. His numerous writings include *La vie quotidienne en Chine à la veille de l'invasion mongole* (1959), *Le monde chinois* (1972), and *Chine et christianisme: la première confrontation* (1982). He is at present completing a full-length study of the philosophy of Wang Fuzhi (1609–1692).

Alain GINESTY was born in Paris in 1928, but has always been at heart a Mediterranean, with a passionate interest in both history and possible futures. An agronomist by training, he has spent his working life as a Chartered Surveyor. These apparent contradictions, and others, have been tempered by his lifelong interest in classical Chinese thought, which has taught him that the Way lies in the harmonisation of opposites.

John GITTINGS was based in Hong Kong and Shanghai as The Guardian's East Asia Editor from 1998–2003. He first visited China in 1971 and his books include *Real China* (1996) and *China Through the Sliding Door* (1999). He read Oriental Studies at Oxford under the enlightened guidance of David Hawkes from 1958–61.

Clare GOLSON was born in 1924 in Ngaruawahia, New Zealand, the eldest of five children, to Dat Chong Joe and Lucy Young. She moved to Wellington in 1930, and was educated at Wellington East Girls College, going on to train as a nurse at Wellington General Hospital. In 1962 she married Jack Golson in London, and returned with him to Canberra, Australia, a few months later.

James Robert HIGHTOWER was born in 1915. He earned a B.A. in Chemistry from the University of Colorado in 1936 and, after a sojourn in Heidelberg and Paris, gained an M.A. in Comparative Literature at Harvard University in 1939 and a Ph.D. in Far Eastern Languages in 1946. In between he studied in Peking, spent several months in a Japanese internment camp, and served in the Army. He was again in Peking, 1946–48, with his wife Florence ("Bunny") and children. He then taught Chinese Literature at Harvard, and as Visiting Professor in Hamburg and Oxford, retiring in 1980. His publications include *The Poetry of T'ao Chien, Topics in Chinese Literature*, and (with Yeh Chia-ying) *Studies in Chinese Poetry*. Widowed in 1981, he lives in the house he and Bunny bought in 1953, cooks for guests, and cultivates his garden.

Pieter HOLSTEIN was born in 1934 in the Netherlands. He is a graphic artist, retired teacher, and is married to Marianne de Graaf. They live in France. "I met David Hawkes and his wife Jean at the house of their daughter Rachel. At the time he lent a more than willing ear to my account of a (to Marianne and me) very exciting stay of 4 months at Xiamen University, Fujian, in 2000. Spending time with them again always turns out to be superbly interesting."

Brian HOLTON was born in Galashiels in the Scottish Borders, and educated at the universities of Edinburgh and Durham. He has taught Chinese Language and Literature at Edinburgh, Durham and Newcastle universities. He established the UK's first postgraduate Chinese<>English translating and interpreting programme at Newcastle University. He is currently teaching Translation at the Hong Kong Polytechnic University. His first published translation, in 1965, was of Latin poetry. He began publishing Chinese–Scots translations in 1981.

Colin HUEHNS combines research interests in Asian music, composition, and performance on bowed stringed instruments. He was awarded a Ph.D. for a thesis *Music in Northern Pakistan* by Cambridge

University in 1992, and has made a number of ethnomusicological fieldwork trips to China and Central Asia. As well as his *Six Settings of Poems by Qu Yuan*, his compositions include a chamber opera *The Soul of Ch'ien-nu Leaves Her Body* and choral, orchestral, chamber, and solo works. Originally starting out as a violinist, recently he spent several years living in the Xi'an Music Conservatoire and Hohhot College of Fine Arts learning to play the instruments of the Chinese *erhu* and Mongolian horsehead fiddle families, on which he gives occasional performances and broadcasts. He is currently a Lecturer at the Royal Academy of Music, London.

Daniel HUWS lives near Aberystwyth, Wales. He worked for thirty-one years in the Department of Manuscripts of the National Library of Wales and has written and still writes about Welsh manuscripts. *The Quarry*, his second book of poems, was published in 1999. He came to know David and Jean well after their move to Wales, having first met them through his brother-in-law, Jacques Pimpaneau, and through his mother, Edrica Huws, the artist, who had become a close friend of theirs in Oxford in the 1970s.

Tony HYDER was born in 1942. Fortunate to read for a degree in Chinese at Oxford from 1961–65 during David Hawkes' professorship, he was inspired (like so many students), then and thereafter, by David's passion for poetry and his dancing calligraphy. After a short period as a graduate student in London and Glasgow, he returned to Oxford in 1968 as Librarian of the Oriental Institute group of libraries which, in 1994, incorporated the new Institute for Chinese Studies Library. Since summer 2000 he has worked from home as a freelance translator and editor. His publications include *It's Only Spring and Thirteen Years: Two Early Plays by Li Jianwu* (1989), translated from the Chinese.

JAO Tsung-i was born in 1917, in Chao'an, Guangdong Province. A distinguished and versatile scholar, calligrapher, painter, poet and musician, he has taught at the University of Hong Kong, the University of Singapore, The Chinese University of Hong Kong, and at numerous other institutions of learning throughout the world. In 1977, Paul Demiéville wrote of him: "He knows everything. He is a living encyclopedia. His memory is a storehouse of the treasures of the Chinese tradition. And yet he is at the same time the freest and most open of men … an exemplary model of the most humane of civilisations."

Di JIN was Professor of English and Translation at the Foreign Languages Institute in Tianjin, China, until he retired in the late 1980s. He has been both a translator and translation theorist. His translations include *The Chinese Earth* (Stories by Shen Ts'ung-wen, in collaboration with Robert Payne) and James Joyce's *Ulysses*. His recent English works on translation include *Shamrock and Chopsticks* (2001), and *Literary Translation: Quest for Artistic Integrity* (2003).

Joseph S. M. LAU was born in Hong Kong. He received his B.A. in English from National Taiwan University in 1960, and his Ph.D. in Comparative Literature from Indiana University in 1966. In 1998 he took early retirement from the University of Wisconsin, Madison, and returned to Hong Kong to begin a second career at Lingnan University as Chair Professor of Translation. With John Minford he co-edited *Classical Chinese Literature: An Anthology of Translations (Vol. 1: From Antiquity to the Tang Dynasty)* (2000). His translations into Chinese include George Orwell's *Nineteen Eighty-Four*, Bernard Malamud's *The Assistant* and *The Magic Barrel,* Saul Bellow's *Herzog,* and Isaac Singer's *Gimbel the Fool and Other Stories.*

Mabel LEE was until January 2000 an academic at the University of Sydney. She has translated into English two novels by the 2000 Nobel Laureate Gao Xingjian, *Soul Mountain* and *One Man's Bible,* as well as three collections of poetry by Yang Lian, 1999 winner of the Italian Flaiano Prize for Poetry. "Two meetings with David Hawkes (Sydney and Canberra) left a deep and lasting impression: this great scholar and translator of Chinese literature emanates a beautiful aura."

André LÉVY was born in Tientsin in 1925. His interest in China was awakened when he was a primary school pupil in the French Concession of that city. He completed his Baccalauréat de Philosophie-Lettres in France during the troubled period of the German Occupation, and was obliged to escape to the maquis of the Auvergne, whence he re-emerged to begin his studies of Chinese and Hindi in Paris. From 1958, he worked in what was left of the École Française d'Extrême Orient, first in Hanoi, then in Kyoto and Hong Kong. He has published countless studies and translations of Chinese fiction. He was Professor of Chinese at the University of Bordeaux from 1969 until his retirement in 1994.

Dorothy Yin Cheng LIU was born in 1914 in Tientsin, China. She taught part-time at Nankai University, and arrived in London in 1949 to teach Chinese at the School of Oriental and African Studies, University of London. She came to know David in the mid-1950s whilst doing some teaching for the Department of Chinese at Oxford, and has been friends with David and Jean ever since. She is now retired and lives in Ealing.

LIU Ching-chih was born in Shanghai. During the period from 1966–2001, he served as translator at the British Broadcasting Corporation, then as an administrator and researcher at the University of Hong Kong, and latterly as Professor in the Department of Translation, Lingnan University. Since 1986, he has been President of both the Hong Kong Ethnomusicology Society, and the Hong Kong Translation Society. He is the author and editor of numerous books, articles and reviews on music, classical Chinese literature and translation.

Tao Tao LIU was born in 1941 in Tianjin, China, and came to England in 1949. She was supervised by David for her doctorate thesis on Yuefu poetry. Now she is Lecturer in Modern Chinese at the Institute for Chinese Studies, University of Oxford, and also Fellow in Oriental Studies, Wadham College, Oxford. She has done translations of Chinese literature into English. Her research interest is in Modern Chinese Literature, mainly the early Republican era.

LIU Ts'un-yan was born in 1917, in Peking. He is Professor Emeritus of Chinese at the Australian National University, and a Foundation Fellow of the Australian Academy of Humanities. He studied at Peking University, and was awarded a Ph.D. and D.Litt. by the University of London. He has written extensively on an enormously varied range of topics, from history and the history of religion, Chinese philosophy and Taoist Studies, to traditional Chinese fiction. He is also the author of a full-length novel, recently republished in China under the title *Dadu* (The Capital).

Michael LOEWE, as a University Lecturer at the School of Oriental and African Studies, London (1956–63), and at Cambridge (1963–90), has concentrated his research on the history of the early Chinese empires, particularly Han. He has called on epigraphical and material evidence to supplement the literary record and has published eight books on religious, intellectual and institutional aspects of the period, with attention both to the parts played therein by men and women and to the philological, bibliographical and archaeological problems that are concerned.

Göran MALMQVIST was born in 1924. He was Lecturer in Chinese at the School of Oriental and African Studies, London University, 1952–55; Cultural Attaché at the Swedish Embassy in Peking, 1956–58; Senior Lecturer in Chinese, Canberra University College, 1959–61; Professor in Chinese and Dean of the Faculty of Asian Studies, Australian National University, 1959–65; and Professor in Sinology, Stockholm University, 1965–90. His publications span the fields of Chinese dialectology, ancient and modern syntax, metrics and semantics; he has done numerous translations from Chinese literature — Ancient, Medieval, Modern and Contemporary. He is a member of the Swedish Academy.

Ian McMORRAN is presently Professor, Chair of Chinese Civilisation, at the University of Paris 7. He was previously University Lecturer in Classical Chinese (1965–90) and fellow of St. Anne's and St. Cross colleges, Oxford. "I originally read Chinese (1956–59) with David as my first tutor, before studying in Hong Kong, Japan and Taiwan as a Scarbrough research scholar. David also supervised my D.Phil. (obtained in 1968)." Principal publications are in Ming–Qing history and thought, particularly that of Wang Fuzhi, e.g. *The Passionate Realist: An Introduction to the Life and Political Thought of Wang Fuzhi 1619–1692* (1992).

Donald MITCHELL was born in 1925. Two composers have been central to his writings on music: Gustav Mahler and Benjamin Britten. He is perhaps best known for his three-volume study of Mahler: *The Early Years* (1958), *The Wunderhorn Years* (1975), and *Songs and Symphonies of Life and Death* (1985). He is Trustee Emeritus of the Britten–Pears Foundation, and was founder Professor of Music at the University of Sussex (1971–76).

PANG Bingjun was born and brought up in Tianjin. He graduated from Nankai University in 1953 and started a teaching career, in China at first, and then in several English-speaking countries after the mid-1980s. Since his retirement in 1997 he has been enjoying a contented, retired life in total silence and seclusion in a Melbournian suburb. He still dabbles in some translation from and into English and hopes to finish his memoirs before his memories pass into oblivion.

Jacques PIMPANEAU was a student of Professor David Hawkes in Oxford from 1963–65. Afterwards he taught at the Institut National des Langues et Civilisations Orientales (Langues 'O) in Paris up to his retirement in 1999. He also created the Kwok On Museum in Paris, the collections of which have now been donated to the Orient Foundation in Lisbon. But he prefers to be introduced as an amateur puppeteer.

John SCOTT's interest in Chinese language and culture began in 1952 whilst he was still at grammar school. He spent two years working in the Chinese bookshop opposite the British Museum — where the customers included many of the day's outstanding sinologues, including David Hawkes, who became his friend. He then went on to study Chinese at Cambridge. He taught at the School of Oriental and African Studies in London, and for twenty years at the University of Edinburgh. After spending ten years as Professor of English at Fukuoka Prefectural University in Japan, he retired in 2002 to live in Riga, Latvia.

Vikram SETH is the author of *The Golden Gate: A Novel in Verse* and two other novels, *A Suitable Boy* and *An Equal Music*. He has written several books of poetry, including translations from Li Bai, Du Fu and Wang Wei, published under the title *Three Chinese Poets*. While a graduate student at Stanford University in the 1980s, he lived for two years at Nanjing University, from where he carried out research in economics and demography in seven villages in Jiangsu; *From Heaven Lake* is his account of a hitchhiking journey home to Delhi via Sinkiang and Tibet. He taught himself what classical Chinese he knows almost entirely through David Hawkes' *A Little Primer of Du Fu*; and he has corresponded with his admired guru from time to time, though they have met face to face only once. Recently he has taken up calligraphy and seal-carving, and wishes he had learned to enjoy these pleasures earlier.

Margaret SOUTH was born in Bathurst, Australia, in 1926. She studied at the University of Sydney and the Australian National University, where her doctoral thesis was a study of the life and times of the Tang poet Li

He. Until her retirement in 1992, she taught at the University of Auckland, New Zealand. She first met David Hawkes in Oxford in the winter of 1965–66, when she went to pay her respects to him as an examiner of her thesis, and remembers a very pleasant afternoon at his home exchanging views about the thesis and news about her former teacher A. R. Davis, who, with David, had been a pupil of Arthur Waley.

Michael SULLIVAN studied Architecture at Cambridge and then went to China in the winter of 1939–40 to drive trucks for the International Red Cross. He later transferred to the Chinese Red Cross headquarters in Guiyang, where he worked on designs for a new hospital and met his future wife Khoan, a bacteriologist. They moved to Chengdu, where he worked in West China Union University and Ginling College till 1946, when they went to London. There he held the Chinese Government Scholarship at the School of Oriental and African Studies. David Hawkes had the same position at Oxford, but they did not get to know each other well till years later. After a teaching career that took him to Singapore and Stanford, he settled, with Khoan, in Oxford as Fellow by Special Election at St. Catherine's College. He has written a number of books on Chinese art.

Denis TWITCHETT entered the profession after wartime training in Japanese. He studied at the School of Oriental and African Studies and Cambridge where he took his doctorate, and then spent a year of graduate study in Tokyo. He taught Far Eastern History at London and Classical Chinese at Cambridge, before moving to Princeton University as Gordon Wu Professor of Chinese Studies from 1980 until his retirement in 1994. He has written on legal economic and social history, historiography and political history. He is chief editor of the *Cambridge History of China* (12 volumes to date), which has taken up too much of his time. "I knew David well in the 1960s and early 1970s, and occasionally taught history for him at Oxford before his retirement. I am full of admiration for his deep understanding of Chinese literature and culture and I rate him as the best living translator in our field, as well as one of the nicest people to have graced our profession. My congratulations and warmest greetings on your 80th birthday."

Burton WATSON was born in 1925 in New York. He studied Chinese at Columbia and Kyoto universities and received his doctorate from the former in 1956. He has taught at Columbia and Stanford and translated a number of works of Chinese and Japanese literature. Among these are *Records of the Grand Historian* (3 volumes), *The Complete Works of Chuang Tzu*, and selections from the poetry of Du Fu, Bai Juyi, Su Dongpo and Lu You. He got to know David in Kyoto in 1966.

Günter WOHLFART was born in 1943 in Frankfurt, and studied Philosophy, Psychoanalysis and German Literature at the universities of Frankfurt and Tübingen, completing his doctoral thesis on Kant's aesthetics. From 1987 until his retirement in 2003 he has taught philosophy at Wuppertal University, specialising in Comparative Philosophy and East Asian Studies. He is the author of several books on Taoism, and two recent studies of Zhuangzi.

Laurence WONG received his B.A. and M.Phil. from the University of Hong Kong and his Ph.D. from the University of Toronto. Currently he is Professor and Head of the Department of Translation at Lingnan University, Hong Kong. His publications include books of poetry, collections of critical essays, translations, and collections of essays in translation studies. His Ph.D. thesis is on English, French, German, and Italian translations of the *Hongloumeng* with special reference to David Hawkes' English version.

Siu-kit WONG, having been taught in his youth by Professor Jao Tsung-i and trained and inspired by Professor David Hawkes in his prime, thought he might develop into a scholar of some weight. This was not to be, but he has ended up devoting all his years of active service to the education of the young, an alternative course he has come to accept and enjoy.

Anthony C. YU, a native of Hong Kong, has taught Religion and Comparative Literature at the University of Chicago since 1968. Best known for his 4-volume translation of *The Journey to the West* (University of Chicago Press, 1977–83), he also published in 1997 with Princeton University Press *Rereading the Stone: Desire and the Making of Fiction in Dream of the Red Chamber*.

(4) THE LADY OF THE XIANG (XIANG FU-REN)
To
Andante (♩ = 84)
1
Flute
Clarinet
pp sempre
pp sempre
Harp
Baritone Soloist
Child of God, de-scending the northern bank, Turns on me her eyes that
mp
Violins
pp sempre
pp sempre
Violas
'Cello
pp sempre
Double Bass
pp sempre
PAN-A3 18 STAVE